Drew Studies in Liturgy Series
General Editors: Kenneth E. Rowe and Robin A. Leaver

The Matter and Manner of Praise

The Controversial Evolution of Hymnody in the Church of England 1760–1820

Thomas K McCart

Drew Studies in Liturgy Series, No. 5

The Scarecrow Press, Inc.
Lanham, Maryland & London
1998

SCARECROW PRESS, INC.

Published in the United States of America
by Scarecrow Press, Inc.
4720 Boston Way
Lanham, Maryland 20706

This book is a revised version of a Ph.D. dissertation, "The Matter and Manner of Praise: The Controversial Evolution of Hymnody in the Church of England, 1760–1840," presented in 1994 at Vanderbilt University.

British Library Cataloguing in Publication Information Available

Library of Congress Cataloging-in-Publication Data

McCart, Thomas K, 1948–
   The matter and manner of praise : the controversial evolution of hymnody in the Church of England, 1760–1820 / Thomas K McCart.
      p.   cm.—(Drew studies in liturgy ; no. 5)
   Includes bibliographical references (p.   ) and index.
   ISBN 0–8108–3450–2– (cloth)
   1. Church music—Church of England—18th century. 2. Church music—Church of England—19th century. 3. Hymns, English—History and criticism.   I. Title.   II. Series.
ML3166.M33   1998
782.27′0942′09033—dc21
                                                            97–39136
                                                            CIP
                                                            MN

Contents

Editor's Foreword

It is too often forgotten that hymns are liturgical, that they are the songs of the congregation at worship.

Hymns are studied as poetry, literature, expressions of theology, as well as reflections of cultural norms, barometers of social change, markers of linguistic modification, and indicators of semantic shifts. Much in hymnological studies is given over to discussions of the authors of the hymns, their periods of writing—especially the particular circumstances surrounding the origins of the hymns—together with the leading ideas of the texts and how these concepts are expressed. But what is not always considered are the liturgical functions of hymnody in worship.

Even when liturgical functions have been scrutinized to some degree in post-Tractarian studies of Anglican hymnody, they are marred by the assumption that liturgical hymnody was the exclusive product of the Oxford Movement. But, as Dr. McCart demonstrates here by his careful research, the transition from metrical psalmody to hymnody was affected not so much by the ideals of nineteenth-century Tractarians as by the practice of eighteenth-century Evangelicals, who were innovative with regard to the liturgical use of hymns. John Wesley, in his pioneering Anglican hymnal, *A Collection of Psalms and Hymns,* published in Charleston, South Carolina, in 1737, arranged the hymns and psalms for public worship on Sundays, Wednesdays, and Fridays.[1] Later, his brother Charles—always an Anglican and never a denominational Methodist—not only incorporated the language and thought-forms of the Prayer Book in his hymns, but also provided hymns on the festivals of the church year for Evangelical Anglicans to sing. These are found in his supplementary collections of hymns for the Nativity, Resurrection, Ascension, Pentecost (*Hymns of Petition and Thanksgiving*), and Trinity, issued in sequence between 1744 and 1746.[2]

The Wesleys were not the only ones promoting hymnody in the eighteenth-century Church of England. As is clearly shown in this study, both Evangelicals and non-Evangelicals were actively promoting hymnody during the last quarter of the eighteenth century and in the early decades of the nineteenth century. It is here that Dr. McCart's important study breaks new ground. First, he adds a further dimension to recent research that demonstrates that the Anglican church was not as moribund in the eighteenth century as earlier studies have commonly portrayed. Second, he establishes that the growing practice of singing hymns during this period was much more widespread than was previously thought, and by no means confined to Evangelicals. Third, he clarifies the nature and details of the significant ecclesiastical court case of 1819, clarifying the legality of hymns in Anglican worship, that in previous studies has been imperfectly or misleadingly assessed.

This book is a major contribution to the understanding of the development of an important and hitherto neglected period of Anglican hymnody, which also has significant ramifications for study of nineteenth-century hymnody in general.

Robin A. Leaver
Westminster Choir College of Rider University
and Drew University

Notes

1. See *Facsimile Copy of John Wesley's First Hymn Book* (Nashville: United Methodist Publishing House, 1988).
2. See Robin A. Leaver, "Charles Wesley and Anglicanism," *Charles Wesley: Poet and Theologian,* ed. S.T. Kimbrough Jr. (Nashville: Kingswood, 1992), 157–175.

Acknowledgments

In several respects, writing a book is very much an enterprise undertaken by an individual. In other respects, it is a collaborative endeavor. Acknowledgment of the many and varied contributions made by colleagues is never an easy task. Chance remarks that give rise to insights are virtually impossible to trace to their sources. Ultimately, responsibility for the use, or misuse, to which I have put their help is mine alone.

Nonetheless, many people have made significant contributions along the way. Professors Dale Johnson and Frank Gulley have given invaluable advice, direction, and guidance through their supervision of an earlier form of this work, which was successfully submitted for a Ph.D. degree to Vanderbilt University. Dr. William Hook, director of the Divinity Library, Vanderbilt, aided in the location of important materials through a computer search of eighteenth-century publications. The staffs of several libraries were welcoming and helpful far beyond any call of duty: the British Library, Lambeth Palace Library, the Borthwick Institute of Historical Research (York), the Evangelical Library (London), the Elias Library (Westminster College, Cambridge), and especially the staff of the Divinity Library, Vanderbilt. I am also grateful to the Very Reverend Robert Giannini and the Vestry of Christ Church Cathedral, Indianapolis, for providing several opportunities for extended periods of research in England. I would like to express my gratitude to several individuals who have helped by allowing me to share various stages of this work with them and who have offered valuable comments and advice along the way: the Reverend Canon Alan Luff, the Reverend Canon Donald Gray, Professor R. William Franklin, and Professor John Fitzmier. I am particularly indebted to the late Reverend Dr. Geoffrey Cuming for his willingness to share his immense knowledge of liturgical developments in England during the year I studied with him at Oxford.

In the course of preparing this book for publication, one essay based on this material has been published: "The Development of Hymnody in the Anglican Church" (*As We Gather to Pray: An Episcopal Guide to Worship,* New York: Church Hymnal Corporation, 1996). I thank the copyright holder, The Church Pension Fund, for its kind permission to include the contents of that essay in this work.

Finally, it is doubtful that this work would have ever been written had it not been for the life and ministry of the late Reverend Dr. Norman Mealy, professor of church music at the Church Divinity School of the Pacific, Berkeley, California, who instilled in me his great love of hymns and to whom this work is dedicated with deep affection.

—Thomas McCart

Introduction

The writing of church history has often imposed a far too rigid pattern on a particular period by aligning persons or groups within tightly defined denominational parties. As G. Kitson Clark has correctly observed, "such attempts should be viewed with suspicion, they are very often polemical in origin, and they are very often based on impressions which have not been confirmed by what ought to have been rather elaborate and laborious research."[1] The same could also be said of the writing of the history of church music, and perhaps in no single area of church music is this more true than in the study of hymns.[2]

For almost a century and a half, the story of the development of hymnody within the Church of England has been written from the vantage point of the enormous success of *Hymns Ancient and Modern* (1861).[3] As

---

1. G. Kitson Clark, *The Making of Victorian England* (London: Methuen, 1962), 281–282.

2. For purposes of this study a hymn is defined as a text of human composition that may or may not include scriptural allusions or quotations from scripture. A metrical psalm is a paraphrase of a "divine" prose psalm, or portion thereof, put into meter. Both are functional pieces, said or sung, insofar as they are designed to accompany the activity of worship. The distinction is, at times, difficult to draw. Distinguishing between a hymn or metrical psalm is further complicated by the fact that, in the period under consideration, the term *hymn* might be used when referring to a Prayer Book canticle and the term *psalm* could refer either to a prose psalm or a metrical psalm. A careful reading of the text has usually been sufficient to enable a correct identification. In those cases where doubt remains, it has been duly noted. When referring to the music accompanying either, the terms *hymn tune* or *psalm tune* will be used.

3. For a thorough analysis of this publication, see Susan Drain, *The Anglican Church in Nineteenth Century Britain: Hymns Ancient and Modern (1860–1875)* (Lewiston, N.Y.: E. Mellen, 1989).

a consequence, scholars in a number of disciplines have remained largely unaware of the controversies that surrounded the development of hymnody. Contemporaries, however, were keenly aware of the issues. Writing in 1821, one writer observed:

> The origin and progress of psalmody [i.e., congregational singing] in England is a subject which has attracted the attention and exercised the pens of several of our distinguished writers. Both the general principle of versifying portions of the Holy Scriptures, and the performances of those who have made attempts of this kind, have been brought under discussion; have been attacked and defended with no ordinary degree of interest.[4]

If the evolution of hymnody involved such widespread discussion and debate, why has it received so little attention from scholars? Church historians generally have ignored church music or have made reference to it in passing, usually (more often than not) in anecdotal form. Owen Chadwick, for example, devoted only four and one-half pages to church music in his monumental two-volume survey of the Victorian church, with no mention whatsoever of any controversy concerning it.[5] S. C. Carpenter, in his *Eighteenth Century Church and People,* made the passing observation that "Church people were dubious" about hymns, but due to the Evangelicals the "custom gradually became general."[6] Such an observation obscures the depth and degree of the feelings of the eighteenth-century church toward the increasing use of hymns in the liturgy and fails to recognize the diverse cast of characters involved in this development. Moreover, a number of scholars have perpetuated generalizations about the development of hymnody, making it difficult for a more precise picture to emerge. For example, Conrad Donakowski portrays the early Evangelicals as being of one mind concerning what could be sung in church, although, as will become clear, such was not the case.[7] In similar fashion, Geoffrey Rowell commented that "hymn-singing was all but unknown in the Church of England" in the 1840s.[8] L. E. Elliott-Binns attributed "the revival of Church

---

4. H. Cotton, "On Psalmody," *The Christian Remembrancer* 3 (June 1821):327.

5. Owen Chadwick, *The Victorian Church,* 2 vols. (London: A. and C. Black, 1966, 1970), 2:396–400.

6. S. C. Carpenter, *Eighteenth Century Church and People* (London: J. Murray, 1959), 228.

7. Conrad Donakowski, *A Muse for the Masses: Ritual and Music in an Age of Democratic Revolution, 1770–1870* (Chicago: University of Chicago Press, 1972), 282.

8. Geoffrey Rowell, *The Vision Glorious: Themes and Personalities of the Catholic Revival in Anglicanism* (Oxford: Oxford University Press, 1983), 105.

music in the ordinary parish church" to the Tractarians "most of all."[9] Likewise, Brian Wibberley held that "it was not until the Oxford Movement originated, that hymnody began to be fostered within the Establishment."[10] As will become apparent, these statements are not accurate. Some scholars have discerned the contributions that the study of hymnody can make to one's understanding of a number of subjects.[11] Nonetheless, their work has neither focused specifically on the controversies nor charted in depth the evolution of hymnody.

Hymnologists have written extensively about hymn texts and tunes and about the authors and composers of hymnody. Daniel Sedgwick was among the first, if not the first, to direct attention to hymnody, publishing in 1860 his *Comprehensive Index of Names of Original Authors and Translators of Psalms and Hymns*. Others followed Sedgwick's lead, most notably John Julian, whose *Dictionary of Hymnology* (which was first published in 1892) remains a standard reference work.[12] Only a handful of scholars, however, have focused their attention upon the history of the development of hymnody.

---

9. L. E. Elliott-Binns, *Religion in the Victorian Era,* [2nd ed.] (London: Lutterworth, 1964), 371. Andrew Wilson-Dickson also attributed the shift from metrical psalms to hymns to the work of the Tractarians. See his *The Story of Christian Music: From Gregorian Chant to Black Gospel, an Authoritative Illustrated Guide to All the Major Traditions of Music for Worship* (Oxford: Lion, 1992), 135.

10. Brian Wibberley, *Music and Religion: A Historical and Philosophical Survey* (London: Epworth, 1934), 131.

11. For example, Lionel Adey, *Class and Idol in the English Hymn* (Vancouver: University of British Columbia Press, 1988); Susan Tamke, "Hymns for Children: Cultural Imperialism in Victorian England," *Victorian Newsletter* 49 (1976):18–22; Stephen Wilson, "Religious and Social Attitudes in 'Hymns Ancient and Modern' (1889)," *Social Compass* 22 (1975):211–236; Mary Ann K. Davis, "Images of Death in Victorian Hymns," *Cithara* 24:2 (May 1985):40–48; Dale A. Johnson, "Is This the Lord's Song?: Pedagogy and Polemic in Modern English Hymns," *Historical Magazine of the Protestant Episcopal Church* 48:2 (June 1979):195–218; Susan Tamke, *Make a Joyful Noise unto the Lord: Hymns as a Reflection of Victorian Social Attitudes* (Athens: Ohio University Press, 1978); Roger Elbourne, *Music and Tradition in Early Industrial Lancashire, 1780–1840* (Woodbridge, Engl.: Brewer, 1980); Robin A. Leaver, "Theological Dimensions of Mission Hymnody: The Counterpoint of Cult and Culture," *Worship* 62:4 (July 1988):316–331.

12. John Julian, *A Dictionary of Hymnology: Setting Forth the Origin and History of Christian Hymns of All Ages and Nations,* revised edition, with new supplement (London: J. Murray, 1907). Another disciple of Sedgwick was William Thomas Brooke (1848–1917). A businessman, Brooke became a well-recognized hymnologist, contributing significantly to Julian's work.

Louis F. Benson was the first scholar to write a survey of the development of hymnody in England from the Reformation to the opening decade of the twentieth century.[13] Benson's work established the benchmark for all subsequent studies, and many of his conclusions have remained unchallenged. The broad scope of his study, however, did not allow him to explore in depth the character of the controversies that surrounded the introduction of hymns into the liturgical life of the Church of England. Benson did note that this development was controversial. In a significant but unexplored observation, Benson wrote:

> By means of these [i.e., endowed lectureships] the opportunity was found to preach an evangelical gospel within the Church of England; and also to introduce hymn singing into its services, without having to encounter the opposition inevitable in parish churches with long-established traditions in favor of psalm singing.[14]

By not exploring this "inevitable" opposition, Benson failed to heed his own observation: "In view of the extraordinary success ultimately attained, it is easy to form an exaggerated idea of the facility of their actual introduction into public worship."[15]

Similar observations regarding the controversial character of this departure from tradition are to be found in numerous works by church historians,[16] musicologists,[17] liturgical scholars,[18] and hymnologists.[19] In every case, however, the controversy itself remained unexplored.

This study seeks to bring to the fore many of the arguments that surrounded the introduction of hymns into the liturgical life of the Church of

---

13. Louis F. Benson, *The English Hymn: Its Development and Use in Worship* (G. H. Doran, 1915; reprint edition, Richmond, Va.: John Knox, 1962).

14. Benson, *English Hymn,* 329.

15. Benson, *English Hymn,* 122. Although Benson was referring specifically to the Independents, the same holds true for the Church of England.

16. Specific references will be cited throughout this study.

17. For example, Kenneth Long held that "it was the Oxford Movement that eventually broke down the prejudice against hymns" and brought to a close the "determined battle" that had "raged between Psalmody and Hymnody." Long undervalued the significant role played by Methodists and Evangelical Anglicans in introducing hymnody to the Church of England. See *The Music of the English Church* (New York: St. Martin's, 1971), 331–332.

18. Horton Davies observed that conservative churchmen were "suspicious of hymns." See his *Worship and Theology in England,* vol. 3, *From Watts and Wesley to Maurice, 1690–1850* (Princeton: Princeton University Press, 1961), 234.

19. Erik Routley described the opposition to hymns as a "quiet reaction." See *The Music of Christian Hymns* (Chicago: G.I.A. Publications, 1981), 83.

England, addressing such questions as: What were the motivations for introducing hymns? What were the reasons for opposing such an innovation? Was the shift from metrical psalms to hymns because of a demand of the laity, or was it an imposition of the clergy? Was there a single locus of origin for this movement or did it emerge concurrently in widely divergent areas?[20]

In the course of this study it will be argued that the central issue regarding the introduction of hymns was their legal status in the rites of the Book of Common Prayer. Although the use of metrical forms (psalms, canticles, and hymns) in congregational worship had been a part of the liturgical life of the Church of England since the early days of the Reformation, toward the end of the eighteenth century many began to question whether specific collections had been duly authorized for such use.

By the end of the eighteenth century it was widely believed that there were two authorized versions of metrical psalms that could be used in the liturgy, that of Thomas Sternhold and John Hopkins and that of Nahum Tate and Nicholas Brady. There was also a growing belief that hymns were not prohibited, though perhaps they were not strictly authorized either. The fact that some believed no metrical version of the Psalms was authorized only added to the complexity of the controversy. Although the issue of the authorization of hymns for use in the liturgy emerged gradually out of a number of other concerns, from 1800 on it became the central issue, eventually becoming the basis for a legal challenge and determination by the courts.

If this judgment is correct, then a strong argument can be made for linking the ritualist controversies of the latter half of the nineteenth century with the controversial development of hymnody in the latter half of the eighteenth century and the first decades of the nineteenth. English ritualists of the nineteenth century believed they had discovered that the

---

20. One recent work that also seeks to explore the development of hymnody is Richard Arnold's *The English Hymn: Studies in a Genre* (New York: P. Lang, 1995). In his study, Arnold examines the unique and complex phenomenon of the genre of the hymn by exploring certain aspects (composition, reception, revision, etc.) within a range of contexts (historical, theological, literary, social, etc.) in eighteenth-century England. This study and his differ in focus (Arnold does not limit his work to the Church of England) and in scope (no attempt is made to link this liturgical innovation with the liturgical changes of the nineteenth century). For a particularly helpful presentation of the evolutionary process of a hymn text, see chapters five and six of Arnold's work. Another important recent work is J. R. Watson's *The English Hymn: A Critical and Historical Study* (Oxford: Clarendon, 1997). In this study, Watson discusses the hymn as a literary form, addresses questions of meaning and interpretation, and looks at hymns as literary texts.

ceremonial of the liturgy in 1549 was far more elaborate than previously had been thought. Through a liberal interpretation of the Ornaments Rubric in the Book of Common Prayer they sought to reintroduce such practices as eucharistic vestments, candles on the altar, crucifixes, genuflection, and so forth, into the liturgy of the Church of England. Their ecclesiastical opponents maintained that a proper interpretation of the rubric disallowed these practices, and they eventually sought to enforce liturgical and doctrinal uniformity in the courts. These opponents of the ritualists held that the character of the Reformation settlement of the Church of England, as they interpreted it, provided the basis for this action, and because it was by acts of Parliament that the church had been established during Elizabeth I's reign and reestablished during Charles II's reign, the stage was firmly set for litigation. If the rubric in question was capable of various interpretations, then the courts would make matters clear.[21]

In similar fashion, those who advocated a far less restrictive congregational song found support in their interpretation of the Elizabethan Injunctions of 1559 and the rubrics of the Book of Common Prayer. Thus, rather than the ritualist controversies being an isolated development that emerged from the Tractarian movement, they were part of a series of liturgical reforms, of which the introduction of hymns was the first and most significant. This reform began in the middle of the eighteenth century and continued into the first two decades of the twentieth. In short, the vast and unprecedented (at least since the sixteenth century) liturgical renewal experienced by the Church of England in the nineteenth century was actually a continuation of a late eighteenth-century liturgical development.

This study seeks to illuminate in part an unexplored topic in English church history by tracing the controversial shift from metrical psalms to hymnody in the Church of England. Beginning with a broad survey of the early development of congregational song in England, the study will proceed with an analysis of the secondary aspects of the shift from metrical psalms to hymns. A detailed examination of the legal issue will follow. It is hoped that by the end of this study a fuller understanding of the rich and complex development of hymnody and its introduction into the liturgical life of the Church of England will emerge. It is also hoped that the rela-

---

21. See James Bentley, *Ritualism and Politics in Victorian Britain: The Attempt to Legislate for Belief* (Oxford: Oxford University Press, 1978). Bentley noted that hymnody played a small role in the ritualist controversies. The two issues raised were the use of hymns during the service and the introduction of hymns containing doctrines believed to be contrary to those of the Prayer Book (36, 58, 63).

tionship between this eighteenth-century innovation and the liturgical innovations of the nineteenth century will be evident.

Finally, if there is a single aim or goal of this study, it is to encourage further work in a field ripe for exploration. Few church historians or musicologists have attended to the struggle involved in the transition from metrical psalm singing to hymns, a transition that in many ways anticipated subsequent controversies and may well have set subsequent positions. Further study could redefine our reading of an important period in English history as well as provide a basis for contemporary liturgical scholars and musicians who are now wrestling with many of the same issues.

Chapter One

English Congregational Song, 1530–1760

> Yea, would God that our minstrels had none other thing to play upon, neither our carters and ploughmen other thing to whistle upon save psalms, hymns, and such godly songs as David is occupied withal! And if women . . . spinning at the wheels had none other songs to pass their time withal, . . . they should be better occupied than with *hey nony nony, hey troly loly,* and such like phantasies.[1]

The beginnings of vernacular English religious song can be dated as early as the mid-fourteenth century, when Latin office hymns and other liturgical texts began to be translated into English for private devotional use, a practice that continued into the sixteenth century. Supporters of the Re-

---

1. Miles Coverdale, *Goostly psalmes and spirituall songes* [c. 1535], preface, cited by Robin Leaver, *'Goostly psalmes and spirituall songes': English and Dutch Metrical Psalms from Coverdale to Utenhove, 1535–1566* (Oxford: Clarendon, 1991), 81. For a more comprehensive analysis of the period under consideration in this chapter, see Nicholas Temperley, *The Music of the English Parish Church,* 2 vols. (Cambridge: Cambridge University Press, 1979), 1:1–202; Louis F. Benson, *The English Hymn: Its Development and Use in Worship* (G. H. Doran, 1915; reprint edition, Richmond, Va.: John Knox, 1962), 19–154, 205–257; Peter le Huray, *Music and the Reformation in England 1549–1660* (New York: Oxford University Press, 1967); Robin A. Leaver, "English Metrical Psalmody," in *The Hymnal 1982 Companion,* ed. Raymond F. Glover, 3 vols. (New York: The Church Hymnal Corporation, 1990–1994), 1:321–348; Nicholas Temperley, "The Tunes of Congregational Song in Britain from the Reformation to 1750," in *The Hymnal 1982 Companion,* 1:349–364; Robin A. Leaver, "British Hymnody from the Sixteenth Through the Eighteenth Centuries," in *The Hymnal 1982 Companion,* 1:365–392; Maurice Frost, ed., *Historical Companion to Hymns Ancient and Modern* (London: W. Clowes and Sons, 1962), 1–111.

formation were quick to grasp the potential of using similar devotional materials as a means for disseminating their message. The first printed primer in English is an example. Published in 1529(?), George Joye's *Ortulus anime* bore a strong resemblance to the earlier Sarum primers but reflected the theological views of the continental reformers, especially Luther.[2] The prominence, for example, given to Mary in the Sarum primers was rejected in favor of a more Christocentric foundation for daily devotions.[3]

In England one of the earliest advocates of congregational song was Miles Coverdale. In 1535 or 1536 Coverdale published a collection entitled *Goostly psalmes and spirituall songes.*[4] "Drawen out of the holy Scripture, for the comforte and consolacyon of soch as loue to reioyse in God and his worde," Coverdale's work, like his English Bible, was intended to make the word of God more accessible to the English people.[5] The collection consisted primarily of Lutheran hymns translated into English (including no less than fifteen metrical psalms)[6] and, it would seem, enjoyed a certain popularity prior to 1546.[7] In that year it was included in the list of books burned at St. Paul's Cross on September 26, having been

---

2. George Joye, *Ortulus anime. The garden of the soule: or the englisshe primers (the which a certaine printer lately corrupted & made false to the grete sclaunder of thauthor & greter desayte of as many as boughte and red them) newe corrected and augmented* (Antwerp: n.p., 1530). The first edition is no longer extant. The sole surviving copy of the 1530 edition is in the British Museum.

3. See Leaver, '*Goostly*', 56–62; Charles C. Butterworth and Allan G. Chester, *George Joye 1495?–1553: A Chapter in the History of the English Bible and the English Reformation* (Philadelphia: University of Pennsylvania Press, 1962), 23–32, 60–67. For a thorough discussion of English primers, see Charles C. Butterworth, *The English Primers (1529–1545): Their Publication and Connection with the English Bible and the Reformation in England* (Philadelphia: University of Pennsylvania Press, 1953).

4. The dating of this work varies among scholars because of the fact that the only complete extant copy (in Queen's College, Oxford) is undated. Maurice Frost gives the date as not earlier than 1543. Peter le Huray and Gustave Reese believe it was written c. 1539–1540. Louis Benson takes a more cautious approach and simply states that it was written some time after 1531. John Julian and Nicholas Temperley do not venture a date. Robin Leaver believes that c. 1535 is more accurate. See Robin A. Leaver, "A Newly-discovered Fragment of Coverdale's Goostly psalmes," *Jahrbuch für Liturgik und Hymnologie* 26 (1982):136–150.

5. Title page, cited by Leaver, '*Goostly*', 68.

6. Of the forty-one items in the collection, sixteen are by Luther. In addition to the hymns, Coverdale included metrical versions of the Magnificat, the Nunc Dimittis, the Creed, the Lord's Prayer, Gloria in excelsis Deo, and the Ten Commandments. For a full discussion of the collection, see Leaver, '*Goostly*', 62–86.

7. Leaver, '*Goostly*', 80–82.

prohibited earlier because (almost certainly) of its contents and the failure of Henry VIII to form an alliance with the Lutheran princes of the Schmalkaldic League.[8]

Robert Crowley's *The psalter of David newely translated into Englysh metre in such sort that it maye the more decently, and wyth more delyte of the mynde, be read and songe of al men* has the distinction of being the first complete metrical psalter.[9] It is speculative to believe that either of these works was used in congregational worship to any significant extent, although it is probable that some experimentation did take place. There seems to be only one account (c. 1551–1552) of metrical psalms being used in congregational worship prior to the return of the Marian exiles, that of John à Lasco. Concerning the singing of metrical psalms, he wrote: "After the Lord's prayer is finished, by order of the minister a psalm is begun by persons specifically appointed for this purpose with a view to avoiding confusion in the singing, the whole congregation soon joining the singing with the utmost propriety and dignity."[10] In discussing this account, Temperley observed, "The question that naturally arises is whether it was tried out in English churches, in imitation of Austin Friars, during the closing months of Edward's reign. It may have been so, though no positive evidence has ever been found."[11] Even though metrical psalmody was off to a less than spectacular start, in the space of a few short years one psalter would dominate English church music: the work of Thomas Sternhold.

It is difficult to state with any certainty when Sternhold, groom of the robes to Henry VIII, first attempted to transpose a prose psalm into metrical form. Others, clearly, had tried their hands in this fashionable enterprise prior to Sternhold.[12] Reportedly, Sternhold's versions were sung at the English

---

8. See Leaver, "Newly-discovered," 136–137; *'Goostly'*, 65. The date of the prohibition is not clear. In the first edition of John Foxe's *Acts and Monuments* the date given is 1539. However, subsequent editions omit the list.

9. The collection was published on September 20, 1549.

10. John à Lasco, *Opera,* ed. A. Kuyper, 2 vols. (Amersterdam: n.p., 1866), 2:83.

11. Temperley, *Music,* 1:18.

12. In addition to Coverdale and Crowley, John Croke (*Thirteen Psalms translated in the Reign of Henry VIII,* c. 1547), Sir Thomas Smith (*Certaigne Psalmes or Songues of David,* 1549), and Henry Howard (*Songes and sonettes,* 1557) had produced some metrical versions of the Psalms along the lines of Clement Marot, the poet of the French court. See Hallett Smith, "English Metrical Psalms in the Sixteenth Century and Their Literary Significance," *Huntington Library Quarterly* 9 (1946):262–263; C. A. Huttar, "English Metrical Paraphrases of the Psalms, 1500–1640" (Ph.D. dissertation, Northwestern University, 1956), 118–122; Leaver, *'Goostly',* 117.

court and had gained the favor of Henry VIII.[13] The first edition of Sternhold's work, containing nineteen psalms in meter, was almost certainly published in 1547,[14] and a second, posthumous, edition of thirty-seven psalms (with seven metrical versions by John Hopkins in an appendix), dedicated to Edward VI, was printed in 1549.[15] While Sternhold and John Hopkins were producing their metrical versions of the Psalms, Thomas Cranmer, archbishop of Canterbury, was actively engaged in revising the liturgy of the English church. The subject of music occupied his thoughts as early as 1544. In an often-cited letter, Cranmer set forth his views concerning what type of congregational song the church should have.

[I]n mine opinion, the song that shall be made thereunto would not be full of notes, but, as near as may be, for every syllable a note; so that it may be sung distinctly and devoutly, as be in Matins and Evensong *Venite,* the hymns *Te deum, Benedictus, Magnificat, Nunc dimittis,* and all the Psalms and Versicles; and in the mass *Gloria in excelsis, Gloria Patri,* the Creed, the Preface, the *Pater noster,* and some of the *Sanctus* and *Agnus.* As concerning the *Salva festa dies,* the Latin note, as I think, is sober and distinct enough; wherefore I have travailed to make the verses in English, and have put the Latin note unto the same. Nevertheless, they that be cunning in singing can make a much more solemn note thereto. I made them only for a proof, to see how English would do in song.[16]

Cranmer's setting of the Latin *Salva festa dies* has not survived, and interestingly Edward VI's two prayer books make no provision for congregational song. It has been argued that Cranmer could not advocate congre-

---

13. This seems to be derived from a statement by George Puttenham (*The Arte of English Poesie,* 1589) that the King "for a Psalmes of *David* turned into English meetre by Sternhold, made him groome of his priuy chamber & gaue him many other good gifts." See G. Gregory Smith, ed., *Elizabethan Critical Essays,* 2 vols. (London: H. Milford, 1904), 2:17. Whether this was an attempt on the part of Puttenham to support this new congregational song by supplying royal approval is unclear, although it is a distinct possibility.

14. *Certayne Psalmes chosen out of the Psalter of Dauid, & drawen into Englishe Metre by Thomas Sternhold grome of ye kynges maiesties Roobes* (London: n.p., [1547]).

15. *Al such Psalmes of Dauid, as T. Sternehold late grome of ye kinges Maiesties Robes didde in his life time draw into English Metre. Newly emprinted* (London: n.p., 1549).

16. Cranmer to Henry VIII, October 7, 1544, cited by F. E. Brightman, *The English Rite,* 2 vols. (London: Rivingtons, 1915), 1:lxi. Robin Leaver believes that the dating of the letter is "problematical but was probably written in 1544." See *The Liturgy and Music: A Study of the Use of the Hymn in Two Liturgical Traditions* (Bramcote, Nottingham: Grove Books, 1976), 3.

gational song while Henry was alive because of the "popularity of hymn singing among the Lutherans."[17] However, if Henry's antipathy toward congregational song restrained Cranmer, such an obstacle was removed at Henry's death. Cranmer certainly had no objection to hymns but was, perhaps, silent because of the "currency of Zwinglian views in the country: silence on the matter would serve to appease both conservative catholics who wanted to retain traditional ceremonial and music and also radical Zwinglians who wanted neither."[18] Another possible explanation, and the simplest, why hymns were not included or mentioned in the Prayer Book was that they were few in number at that point.[19] In any event, however intriguing these speculations are, the reason seems impossible to ascertain.

Even so, the musical setting of Cranmer's *Litany* of 1544 demonstrated how a reformed church music could be achieved; Cranmer's ideal was ably expressed by John Marbeck, who provided the most comprehensive musical setting for the new liturgy.[20] Compositionally, Marbeck's setting was a mixture of adapted plainsong and original melody, and it represented the kind of solution that would have been accepted by many had it survived into a second edition.[21]

Mary's accession halted all liturgical and musical reforms in the English church, including the completion of Sternhold and Hopkins's psalter.[22] But more important, because of the Marian exiles, English psalmody journeyed to the continent.

Metrical Psalmody on the Continent

When the exiles left England during Mary's reign, it is probable that they took with them the 1551 edition of Sternhold and Hopkins and the 1552 Book of Common Prayer.[23] One group of exiles, led by William

---

17. Temperley, *Music,* 1:13.

18. Leaver, *Liturgy and Music,* 6, 10.

19. See John Dowden, *Further Studies in the Prayer Book* (London: Methuen, 1908), 72–78; Brightman, *The English Rite,* 1:lxxxiii.

20. John Marbeck, *The booke of Common praier noted* (London: n.p., 1550); see also Robin Leaver's facsimile edition (Appleford: Sutton Courtenay, 1980).

21. Marbeck's work has had much success since its revival in the nineteenth century.

22. In addition to this title, the work is known as Day(e)'s Psalter, *The Whole Book of Psalms,* and as the "Old Version" (to distinguish it from Nahum Tate and Nicholas Brady's *New Version,* published in 1696).

23. An edition of Sternhold and Hopkins was published on the continent, possibly at Wesel, in 1556. See Temperley, *Music,* 1:31; Robin Leaver, ed., *The Liturgy of the Frankfurt Exiles 1555* (Bramcote, Nottingham: Grove Books, 1984), 4; Leaver, *'Goostly',* 199–206.

Whittingham, reached Frankfurt on June 27, 1554. After forming a congregation, they reached the following conclusions concerning worship.

> [T]hat the answeringe alowde after the Minister shulde not be vsed, the letanye, surplice, and many other thinges also omitted. . . . It was farther agreed vppon, that the Minister (in place off the Englishe Confession) shulde vse an other. . . . And the same ended, the people to singe a psalm in meetre in a plaine tune as was and is accustomed in the frenche, dutche, Italian, Spanishe, and Skottishe churches. . . . After the sermon, a generall praier. . . . At thende off whiche praier, was ioined the lords praier . . . and a rehersall of tharticles off oure belieff . . . whiche ended the people to singe and [an] other psalme as before.[24]

The question concerning the means for putting these conclusions into practice, however, was far from settled. A small group wanted to use the 1552 Prayer Book without changes; others wanted to adopt the English translation of Calvin's Genevan order. Both suggestions were rejected. The calling of John Knox (who favored the Genevan order and was later expelled on March 25, 1555) to be the pastor in September 1554 and the arrival of Richard Cox (who advocated the Prayer Book) in March 1555 only increased the controversy over what form of worship to use in the English congregation.[25] With the expulsion of Knox, Cox, who had been involved in the drafting of the 1549 and 1552 Prayer Books, was able to make sufficient revisions in the 1552 Book of Common Prayer to secure its acceptance in its revised form by the congregation.[26]

In the midst of this controversy, a new psalter was compiled, drawn largely from Sternhold and Hopkins's 1551 edition and containing seven new metrical psalms composed most likely by Whittingham. In the preface of *The forme of prayers* (Geneva, 1556), Whittingham set forth reasons for

---

24. *A Brieff discours off the troubles begonne at Franckford in Germany Anno Domini 1554. Abowte the Booke off common prayer and Ceremonies, and continued by the Englishe men theyre, to thende off Q. maries Raigne, in the which discours, the gentle reader shall see the very originall and beginninge off all the contention that hath byn, and what was the cause of the same* (London: n.p., 1575), 6–7. See also Edward Arber, ed., *A brief discourse of the troubles at Frankfort [sic] 1554–1558 A.D. Attributed to William Whittingham, dean of Durham* (London: E. Stock, 1908), 24–25.

25. Temperley indicated that Cox arrived on March 4, leading a fresh wave of exiles (*Music*, 1:28). Leaver has Cox arriving on March 13 (*Frankfurt*, 3).

26. This liturgy, or the 1552 Prayer Book without revision, was used by the exiles throughout this period. Cox's revised liturgy bore the title *The Order of Common Prayer,* and it contains the earliest reference to singing metrical psalms in an English reformed liturgy. For a complete text, see Leaver, *Frankfurt.*

the use of singing in worship, noting the abuse it had suffered under the papists "partly by strange language, that can not edifie: and partly by a curious wanton sort, hyringe men to tickle the eares, and flatter the phantasies" and reflecting Calvin's understanding that "there are no songes more meete, then the psalmes of the Prophete Dauid, which the holy ghoste hath framed to the same vse, and commended to the churche."[27] The metrical psalms, printed with *The forme of prayers* under its own title *One and Fiftie Psalmes of David in Englishe metre, whereof .37. were made by Thomas Sterneholde: a[n]d the rest by others. Conferred with the hebrewe, and in certeyn places corrected as the text and the sens of the Prophete required* became known as the Anglo-Genevan psalter and appeared in 1556, followed by editions in 1558, [1559], and 1561.[28] This, in addition to the fact that psalmody was becoming well established on the continent prior to the arrival of the Marian exiles, must certainly have influenced their understanding of the role of congregational music in worship.[29]

The First Challenges to Psalmody

When the exiles returned to England, they presented Elizabeth I with a book of Psalms in English (which edition is unknown). As reported by John Strype, the dedication (dated February 10, 1559) read, in part: "They supposed, in their judgments, that no part of the whole scripture was more necessary for her grace than that little book of Psalms, if it were well

---

27. Calvin wrote, "Look where we may, we will never find songs better, nor more suited to the purpose, than the Psalms of David; which the Holy Ghost himself composed. And so, when we sing them, we are certain that God puts the words in our mouth, as if he himself sang in us to magnify his praise." Fol. A7r, A7v, cited by Temperley, *Music,* 1:20. The complete preface to *The forme of prayers* can be found in Leaver, *'Goostly',* 308–313.

28. The significance of this work is in the number of tunes that eventually made their way into the first full music edition of Sternhold and Hopkins in 1562. For a complete analysis of the tunes of the English psalters, see Maurice Frost, *English and Scottish Psalm and Hymn Tunes c. 1543–1677* (London: Oxford University Press, 1953).

29. For a survey of the development of congregational music on the continent, including metrical psalmody, see Walter Blankenburg, "Church Music in Reformed Europe," in *Protestant Church Music: A History,* ed. Friedrich Blume (New York: W. W. Norton, 1974), 509–546. For a discussion of the origin and development of metrical psalms in the reformed churches, see Louis F. Benson, "John Calvin and the Psalmody of the Reformed Churches," *Journal of the Presbyterian Historical Society* 5 (1909):1–21, 55–87, 107–118.

weighed and practised."[30] Although it is not clear what specific book was presented, it is possible that it was the 1558 Anglo-Genevan psalter. If so, it would not be this psalter that would dominate English church life for the next two and one-half centuries, but the work of Sternhold and Hopkins.

With the return of the exiles came the return of the English metrical psalms. From the outset their return was not without controversy, as this description of a graveside service by Henry Machyn reveals:

> there was a gret compene of pepull, ij and ij together, and nodur [i.e., neither] prest nor clarked, the new prychers in ther gowne lyke ley[-men,] nodur syn-gyng nor sayhyng tyll they cam [to the grave,] and a-for she was pute into the grayff a [collect] in Englys, and then put in-to the grayff, and after [took some] heythe [i.e., earth] and caste yt on the corse [i.e., corpse], and red a thynge . . . for the sam, and contenent [i.e., incontinently] cast the heth [i.e., earth] in-to the [grave], and contenent red the pystyll of sant Poll to the Stesselonyans the [ ] chapter, and after thay song *pater-noster* in Englys, boyth prychers and odur, and [women,] of a nuw fassyon, and after on[e] of them whent in-to the pulpytt and mad a sermon.[31]

Challenges were raised concerning whether the provisions of the Act of Uniformity authorized such additions to the prescribed liturgy of the church. One challenge was made from the cathedral at Exeter, where the dean and chapter took every step possible to prevent congregational singing in the cathedral services. Although they had been ordered by the queen's visitors early in 1559 to permit the people to "sing a psalm," by the end of the year it had been reported that

> certain of your [i.e., the cathedral's] vicars have scoffed and jested openly at the godly doings of the people on this behalf, and by divers and sundry ways have molested and troubled them; and that you the canons there, which of all others should most have rejoiced thereat, and should have en-

---

30. John Strype, *Annals of the Reformation and Establishment of Religion and other various occurrences in the Church of England during Queen Elizabeth's Happy Reign together with an Appendix of Original Papers of State, Record, and Letters,* A new edition, 4 vols. (New York: B. Franklin, [1966]), 1, i:164.

31. *The Diary of Henry Machyn, Citizen and Merchant-Taylor of London, From A.D. 1550 to A.D. 1563,* ed. John Gough Nichols (London: Camden Society Publications, 1848; reprint ed., New York: AMS, 1968), 193. There were at least two versions of the Lord's Prayer in metrical form in use at this time. See also W. H. Frere, *The English Church in the Reigns of Elizabeth and James I* (London: Macmillan, 1904), 32.

couraged the people to go forward, have uncourteously forbidden them the use of your choir. . . .[32]

An appeal to the ecclesiastical commissioners removed any doubt concerning the use of metrical psalms when they affirmed that the order stood.[33] Their decision remained unquestioned following the consecration of Matthew Parker as archbishop of Canterbury. Thus, a certain degree of authorization concerning the use of metrical psalms was established.[34]

Before the end of the year (1559), Elizabeth indicated her inclinations toward congregational music in this clause of the Injunctions of 1559:

> And that there be a modest distinct song, so used in all parts of the common prayers in the church, that the same may be as plainly understood, as if it were read without singing, and yet nevertheless, for the comforting of such that delight in music, it may be permitted that in the beginning, or in the end of common prayers, either at morning or evening, there may be sung an hymn, or such like song, to the praise of Almighty God, in the best sort of melody and music that may be conveniently devised, having respect that the sentence of the hymn may be understood and perceived.[35]

The significance of this clause will be discussed fully later. For the moment it is sufficient to note the spirit of compromise that it reflects. The more eager reformers believed that they had permission to sing metrical psalms, although with clear limitations. The more conservative reformers were allowed to continue to use the traditional chants, but also with clear stipulations.

In a letter (March 5, 1560) to Peter Martyr, John Jewel, bishop of Salisbury, described the London scene thus:

> Religion is now somewhat more established than it was. The people are every where exceedingly inclined to the better part. The practice of joining in church music [i.e., metrical psalmody] has very much conduced to this. For as soon as they had once begun singing in public, in only one little

---

32. David Wilkins, *Concilia Magnae Britanniae et Hiberniae,* 3 vols. in 4 (London: n.p., 1737), 4:201. It is most likely that the singing took place as the people assembled for worship or at the close of the service rather than in the service itself. See Leaver, *Liturgy and Music,* 9, 26.

33. See Frere, *English Church,* 43–44. Frere also noted that challenges to the new congregational song continued, nonetheless (*English Church,* 62, 66, 115, 168).

34. See Frere, *English Church,* 43; Frost, *Companion,* 38.

35. W. H. Frere and W. M. Kennedy, eds., *Visitation Articles and Injunctions of the Period of the Reformation,* 3 vols. (London: Alcuin Club, 1910), 3:8. See also Frere and Kennedy, 2:42; Frost, *Companion,* 39.

church in London,[36] immediately not only the churches in the neighbourhood, but even the towns far distant, began to vie with each other in the same
practice. You may now sometimes see at Paul's cross, after the service, six
thousand persons, old and young, of both sexes, all singing together and
praising God. This sadly annoys the mass-priests and the devil. For they per-
ceive that by these means the sacred discourses sink more deeply into the
minds of men, and that their kingdom is weakened and shakened at almost
every note.[37]

It is probable that Jewel was exaggerating the degree of the impact that
the new congregational form had on London churches. Psalters were certainly in short supply, and the time factor for such a level of participation
was remarkably short, less than two years. One must note, however, that
between 1550 and 1554, nine reprints (at least) of Sternhold and Hopkins's
1549 edition were issued. This implies a certain degree of popularity. The
increasing popularity of metrical psalms, in general, can be seen in the
number of publications that were also published during this time: for example, Robert Crowley, Henry Howard, John Croke, Thomas Smith (all
noted previously); John Hall, *Certayn chapters taken out of the Proverbs
of Salomon, wyth other chapters of the Holy Scriptures* (London, c. 1550);
William Hunnis, *Certayne Psalms chosen out of the Psalter of David, and
drawen furth into Englyshe meter* (1550); Frances Seager, *Certayne
Psalmes select out of the Psalter of Dauid, and drawen into Englyshe Metre, wyth Notes to every Psalme in iiij parts to Synge* (London, 1553). The
conclusion that these were prepared as alternatives to the prose versions in
the Book of Common Prayer is inescapable. Nonetheless, one cannot as-
sume that they were sung within the liturgy of the church. It is more likely
that they were used in private households.[38] Yet, Jewel's anticipated acceptance of metrical psalms by the people of England was correct, for by
the end of the next century Sternhold and Hopkins's metrical psalms dom-

---

36. It appears that the first congregational singing took place at St. Antholin's
Church, London, on September 21, 1559. Machyn recorded: "The [ ] day of September be-gane the nuw mornyny prayer at sant Antholyns in Boge-row, after Gen-
eve fassyon, — be-gyne to rynge at v in the mornyng; men and women all do syng,
and boys" (212).

37. Hastings Robinson, ed., *The Zurich Letters, Comprising the Correspondence of Several English Bishops and Others, with some of the Helvetian Reformers, During the early part of the Reign of Queen Elizabeth* (Cambridge: Cambridge
University Press, 1842), 71.

38. See Leaver, *'Goostly'*, 136–140; John Harper, *The Forms and Orders of
Western Liturgy: From the Tenth to the Eighteenth Century* (Oxford: Clarendon,
1991), 186–187.

inated congregational life and would do so for another century even though challenged by Tate and Brady's *New Version* and by other psalters. This dominance, however, was not easily achieved. The debate that troubled the Marian exiles continued in England. Should the church in England conform to the Genevan-style liturgy and polity, accepting the Anglo-Genevan psalter, or remain loyal to Cranmer's Book of Common Prayer and episcopal polity, including metrical canticles and hymns along with the metrical psalms? For those who favored the Anglo-Genevan psalter, a reprint of the fourth Geneva edition was published in London in 1560, including eighty-seven metrical psalms and three canticles. For those who favored the other side, a collection comprising sixty-four metrical psalms and eight canticles was published also in 1560 in London.

By 1561 a compromise had been reached. The *Psalmes of David in English Metre* (London, 1561) contained Sternhold and Hopkins's modified versions as found in the Anglo-Genevan psalter of 1556, along with additional versions by Hopkins, Kethe's version of Psalm 100, and eighteen canticles. In 1562 a companion volume was issued: *The Residue of all Davids Psalmes in metre;* these two collections were combined to produce the basic English metrical psalter: *The Whole Booke of Psalmes, collected into Englysh metre by T. Sternhold, I. Hopkins & others: conferred with the Ebrue, with apt Notes to synge the[m] withal, Faithfully perused and alowed according to thordre appointed in the Quenes maiesties Iniunctions. Very mete to be vsed of all sortes of people priuately for their solace & comfort: laying apart all vngodly Songes and Ballades which tends only to the norishing of vyce, and corrupting of youth.*[39] The inclusion of the phrase "alowed according to thordre appointed in the Quenes maiesties Iniunctions" in the title page played a critical role in the controversy that developed regarding the introduction of hymns into the liturgy. Louis Benson drew attention to the fact that the "title of the editions of 1561–1562 contained the words: 'Very mete to be vsed of all sorts of people priuately.' It was not until 1566 that the title page of the Psalter claimed authorization for its use in church."[40] Although metrical psalms dominated the contents of the volume, it must be noted that two sections of canticles and hymns were

---

39. London: J. Day, 1562.

40. Benson, *English Hymn,* 30. The 1566 title page read: *The whole booke of Psalms, collected into Englysh metre by T. Sternhold, I. Hopkins & others: Newly set forth and allowed to be song in all Churches, of all the people together, before & after morning & euenyng prayer: as also before and after the Sermo[n], and moreouer in priuate houses for their godly solace and comfort, laying aparte all vngodly songes and balades, which tend onely to the norishyng of vice, and corrupting of youth* (London: J. Day, [1566]).

also included.[41] Numbering nineteen, these hymns, based primarily on bib-
lical texts, would seem to provide "a not inconsiderable provision for congregational use in the Church of England."[42] Although Benson has argued
that it is doubtful that they were so used, being rather a convenient way of
providing doctrinal material in metrical form for the poorly educated public, his opinion is not supported by hard evidence.[43] At this time we simply
do not know.

With regard to the place of music in worship, the two positions reflec-
tive of this early period were ably expressed by John Northbrooke and in
a book attributed to John Case. Northbrooke, who like many of the more
conservative reformers was troubled by anything overly ornate or tending
toward Rome, wrote,

> First we must take heed that in music be not put the whole sum and effect of
> godliness and of the worshipping of God, which among the papists they do
> almost . . . think that they have fully worshipped when they have long and
> much sung and piped. Further, we must take heed that in it be not put merit
> or remission of sins. Thirdly, that singing be not so much used and occupied
> in the church that there be no time, in a manner, left to preach the word of
> God and holy doctrine. . . . Fifthly, neither may that broken and quavering
> music be used wherewith the standers-by are so letted that they cannot un-
> derstand the words, not though they would never so fain. Lastly, we must take
> heed that in the church nothing be sung without choice, but only those things
> which are contained in the holy scriptures, or which are by just reason gath-
> ered out of them, and do exactly agree with the word of God.[44]

---

41. These included: *Veni Creator* ("Come Holy Ghost eternal God"), *Te Deum*
("We praise thee, God"), *Benedicite* ("O all ye works of God the Lord"), *Benedictus* ("The only Lorde of Israel"), *Magnificat* ("My soule doth magnifye the Lord"),
Nunc Dimittis ("O Lord be cause my harts desire"), *Creed of Athanasius* ("What
man soeuer he be that"), *Lamentation of a Sinner* ("O Lord turn not away thy
face"), *Humble Sute of the Sinner* ("O Lorde of whom I do depend"), *Lord's Prayer*
(in Double Common Meter [DCM] and 8.8.8.8.8.8.), *Commandments* (in DCM and
Long Meter [LM]), *XII Articles of the Faith* ("All my belief, and confidence"), *A
Prayer before Sermon* ("Come holie spirit the God of might"), *Da pacem* ("Giue
peace in these our daies O Lord"), *The Lamentation* ("O Lord in thee is all my
trust"), *Thanksgiving after receiving the Lord's Supper* ("The Lord be thanked for
his gifts"), and "Preserue vs Lord by thy deare word." For a full discussion of the
hymns included in metrical psalters, see E. D. Parks, *The Hymns and Hymn Tunes
Found in the English Metrical Psalters* (New York: Coleman Ross, 1966), and for
an analysis of the contents of the 1562 psalter see Leaver, *'Goostly',* 316–319.

42. Benson, *English Hymn,* 29.

43. Benson, *English Hymn,* 29.

44. John Northbrooke, *A treatise wherein dicing, dancing, etc. are reproved*
(London: n.p., 1577), 113–114, cited by Temperley, *Music,* 1:41.

It is interesting that Northbrooke did not limit the choice of texts strictly to the Bible. His allowance for material "gathered out of them" represented a greater degree of flexibility than would be exercised in the next two centuries. John Case, while supporting Northbrooke's position concerning what should be sung, allowed a more elaborate style of music to be used in worship. He wrote,

> [O]nly herein we differ, that they would have no great exquisite art or cunning thereunto, neither the noise of dumbe instruments, to fil up the measure of the praises of god [*sic*]: & I alow of both. Wherein if I be not too much affectioned, me thinks they do great iniurie to the word of God, in that they can contentedly permit it to bee song plainly, denying the outward helpes & ornaments of art, to adde more grace & dignity thereunto. . . . The Psalmes may bee used in the church as the authour of them appointed: But the holy Ghost, the author of the Psalms, appointed and commanded them by the Prophet David, to be song, and to be song most cunningly, and to be song with diuerse artificiall instruments of Musick, and to bee song with sundry, seuerall, and most excellent notes & tunes: Therefore in our English church, the psalms may be song, and song most cunningly, and with diuerse artificiall instruments of Musick, and song with sundry seuerall and most excellent notes.[45]

Both viewpoints continued to find expression in the following centuries. Northbrooke's opinion found eager support in parish churches throughout the realm where congregational song had to be simple and accessible if people were to participate, requirements ably met by Sternhold and Hopkins's psalter. Case's position was reflected in the cathedral tradition where medieval choral foundations continued to provide support for professional musicians to sing the praises of God, and that "most cunningly."

The Seventeenth Century

In the years following 1562, Sternhold and Hopkins's dominance continued to increase, although it was challenged by a number of rivals. The most significant rival was George Wither's *Hymnes and Songs of the Church* (1623). Wither's work received support from the crown, and, with tunes composed by the greatest English musician of the day, Orlando Gibbons, it enjoyed a momentary popularity. A more lasting popularity appeared

---

45. [John Case], *The Praise of Musicke: Wherein besides the antiquitie, dignitie, delectation, & use thereof in ciuill matters, is also declared the sober and lawfull use of the same in the congregation and Church of God* (Oxford: I. Barnes, 1586), 136–137.

possible when Wither obtained a patent from the crown requiring that
every copy of Sternhold and Hopkins must include Wither's collection as
a supplement. Opposition to Wither's plan was readily forthcoming and
was ably expressed in a letter from a certain E. R. to Sir Thomas Pucker-
ing (January 23, 1633).

> Upon Friday last, Wither convented before the [Privy Council] Board all or
> most of the Stationers of London. The matter is this. Mr. Wither hath, to
> please himself, translated our singing Psalms into another verse; which he
> counts better than those the Church hath so long used; and therefore he hath
> been at the charge to procure a patent from his Majesty under the broad seal,
> that his translation shall be printed and bound to all Bibles that are sold.[46]
> The Stationers refusing to bind them and to sell them with the Bible, (the
> truth is, nobody would buy the Bible with such a clog at the end of it,) and
> because some of them stood upon their guard, and would not suffer Mr.
> Wither and his officers to come into their shops and seize upon such Bibles
> as wanted his additions, therefore he complained of them for a contempt of
> the Great Seal. After their Lordships had heard the business *pro* and *con* at
> length, their Lordships thought good to dame [*sic*] his patent in part; that is,
> that the translation should not longer be sold with the Bible, but only by it-
> self; and for my part, I think their Lordships have done very well in order-
> ing it in this matter.[47]

Clearly, the time was not right for a book of hymns to be accepted.[48] Opposition from conservative churchmen and from the Stationers' Company,
who denounced the patent as an infringement of its rights, was sufficient
to make the king's patent worthless. As a result, Wither's work never
achieved wide use, although Gibbons's tunes made a lasting contribution
to hymnody.

Other works of lesser distinction contributed to the ongoing development of congregational song but posed no serious threat to Sternhold and
Hopkins's popularity. For example, Henry Dod published his collection in
1620; George Sandys's collection, though not intended for public use, was

---

46. Sternhold and Hopkins was often bound with the Bible and the Prayer Book.

47. Cited by [Jonathan Gray], *An Inquiry into Historical Facts, relative to
Parochial Psalmody, In reference to the Remarks of the Right Reverend Herbert,
Lord Bishop of Peterborough* (York: Printed by J. Wolstenholme, 1821), 79. See
also Leaver, "British Hymnody from the Sixteenth through the Eighteenth Centuries," in *The Hymnal 1982 Companion,* 1:370–373. Leaver argued that the result
of this controversy "had the effect of discouraging the writing of hymns for public
worship" (373).

48. The second part of the collection included hymns for seasons and holy days
in the Prayer Book and hymns for communion time.

published in 1636; and James I's work, *The Psalms of King David*, appeared posthumously in 1637 with the blessings of Charles I, who "allow[ed] them to be song in all the Churches of oure Dominiones."[49]

The passage of *A Directory for The Publique Worship of God*, which came into effect on January 3, 1645, meant the abolishment of the Book of Common Prayer and the legal establishment of metrical psalmody in worship. The *Directory* stated clearly "[i]t is the duty of Christians to praise God publiquely, by singing of Psalmes together in the Congregation, and also privately in the Family."[50] The question was what metrical psalter to use. The version by Sternhold and Hopkins was criticized for its departure from a literal translation of the Hebrew texts, and earlier (1640) the Committee of Peers had recommended that "the meeter in the Psalms should be corrected."[51] One effect of the passage of the *Directory* was to make the revision of the psalter more urgent.

William Barton, minister of St. Martin's, Leicester, was invited to make a revision, and it was published in 1644.[52] Given the criticism of Sternhold and Hopkins, it is surprising that Barton included thirty-five selections from their work in his revision. This number was increased by thirty selections in the second edition in 1645.[53] A third edition was submitted by the House of Commons to a committee where it failed to be sanctioned.

The work of Francis Rous (Rouse), provost of Eton during the Commonwealth, vied with that of Barton for the privilege of being the official psalter. Published first at Amsterdam, Rous revised his metrical versions in 1646 and submitted them to the Westminster Assembly for approval.[54]

---

49. H[enry] D[od], *Al the Psalmes of Dauid: with certeine songes & Canticles of Moses, Debora, Isaiah, Hezekiah & others . . . Nowe faithfully reduced into easie meeter, fitting our common tunes* ([London]: n.p., 1620); G[eorge] S[andys], *A Paraphrase upon the Psalmes of David. And upon the Hymnes dispersed throughout the Old and New Testaments* (London: [A. Hebb], 1636); James I, *The Psalms of King David* (London: T. Harper, 1637), preface.

50. *A Directory for the Publique Worship of God, Throughout the Three Kingdoms of England, Scotland, and Ireland* (London: Printed for E. Tyler, A. Fifield, R. Smith, and J. Field, 1644), 83.

51. Julian, *Dictionary*, 918.

52. W[illiam] B[arton], *The Book of Psalms in metre* (London: M. Simmons, for the Companie of Stationers, 1644).

53. William Barton, *The Book of Psalms in metre, lately translated, with many whole ones, and choice collections of the Old Psalms added to the first impression . . . now much augmented* (London: Printed by G. M., 1645).

54. [Francis Rous], *The Psalms of David, in English meeter* (London: M. Flesher, for the Company of Stationers, 1646).

In April the House of Commons ordered this version, "and none other," "to be sung in all churches and chapels within the kingdom."[55]

Although approved by the House of Commons, Rous's work met with opposition from the House of Lords, whose members either supported the work of William Barton or preferred that no specific version be required. The conflict kept the Commonwealth from establishing a uniform psalmody, because neither work was officially sanctioned for use by both houses. Even so, throughout this period, whether authorized or not, people continued to sing metrical psalms, if not in the proscribed liturgy of the Prayer Book then in their private devotions or in the new services of Parliament.

With the restoration of the monarchy in 1660, the status of the Book of Common Prayer became a pressing concern. The Presbyterians requested that a new liturgy be compiled or, at the least, that the existing book be revised and reformed. To this request, the bishops replied that they were "not against revising of the Liturgy," and Charles II issued a declaration promising to appoint "learned divines of different persuasions to review the Book of Common Prayer."[56] Among the specific requests made by the Presbyterian divines was for a revision of Sternhold and Hopkins or "leave to make use of a purer version."[57] To this concern the "learned divines" responded emphatically, "Singing of psalms in metre is no part of the liturgy, and by consequence no part of our commission."[58] The response indicated a strict interpretation of the Injunctions of 1559 (the permission to sing *before* or *after* the office being

---

55. Julian, *Dictionary*, 918.

56. George Gould, ed., *Documents relating to the Settlement of the Church of England by the Act of Uniformity of 1662* (London: W. Kent, 1862), 17, 35, 73n. See also G. J. Cuming, *The Durham Book: Being the First Draft of the Revision of the Book of Common Prayer in 1661* (London: Oxford University Press, 1961), xvi–xvii; R. C. D. Jasper, *The Development of the Anglican Liturgy 1662–1980* (London: SPCK, 1989), 1–5.

57. *An Account of all the Proceedings of the Commissioners of both persuasions, &c.* (London, 1661), 6, cited by Henry John Todd, *Observations upon the Metrical Version of the Psalms, Made by Sternhold, Hopkins, and Others: With a View to Illustrate the Authority with Which this Collection was at First Admitted, and how that Authority has been since regarded, in the Public Service of the Established Church of England: and Thence to Maintain, in This Venerable Service, the Usage of Such Metrical Psalmody Only as is Duly Authorized. With Notices of Other English Metrical Versions of the Psalms* (London: Printed for F. C. and J. Rivington, 1822), 48. I have been unable to verify this reference.

58. Cited by Temperley, *Music*, 1:84. Temperley does not indicate the source for this quotation.

clearly understood to mean that metrical psalms were not to be included in the liturgy) and the rubrics of the Book of Common Prayer. Concessions to the Presbyterian divines were few and insignificant, and the revised book was authorized by the new Act of Uniformity, which became law on May 19, 1662.[59] References to music were few. The option of saying or singing the appointed canticles was continued. A new rubric in both morning and evening prayer directed that following the third collect "In Quires and places where they sing here followeth the Anthem,"[60] and in the Ordinal the hymn "Veni, creator spiritus" was required to be sung at the ordination of a priest and at the consecration of a bishop or archbishop. Apart from this, the "learned divines" made no other provisions for congregational singing, including metrical psalms.

Nonetheless, the tradition of singing metrical psalms continued to expand, and new collections to satisfy this increasing use were published. In 1671, for example, John Playford put forth his *Psalms & hymns in solemn musick of fovre parts on the common tunes to the Psalmes in metre: used in Parish-chvrches.*[61] This collection was noteworthy for several reasons. First, it consisted of a selection of metrical psalms from a variety of sources. The work of Sternhold and Hopkins, of course, was well represented, but there were also metrical versions of the Psalms by John Cosin, Bishop King, Miles Smyth, George Herbert, William Barton, and several from the Scottish Psalter of 1650. Second, the forty-seven tunes included in the book significantly increased the number available for use. Third, Playford provided a definite place for hymns, both within the body of the book and on the title page.[62] Of the seventeen hymns included in the collection, most were taken from John Austin's *Devotions in the Antient Way of Offices* (Paris, 1668), a Roman Catholic manual of devotions. To borrow from such a source was somewhat surprising, although an Anglican version was available.[63] Less surprising was the generally negative reception that the collection received. The time was still not ripe for hymns to take an equal place alongside metrical psalms. Six years later Playford published a far more successful

---

59. R. C. D. Jasper, *Prayer Book Revision in England 1800–1900* (London: SPCK, 1954), 1.

60. How this rubric was interpreted in parish churches is unclear. It is possible that instead of the choir singing an anthem the congregation may have sung a metrical psalm.

61. London: Printed by W. Godbid, 1671.

62. Frost indicated that Playford's collection was the first to do so (*Companion*, 59).

63. I am indebted to Robin Leaver for drawing my attention to this.

collection.[64] The music was less demanding than that in his earlier work, and the innovative hymnody had been dropped.

Tate and Brady

Although Sternhold and Hopkins continued to be the metrical psalter for the church, it was increasingly criticized: "Their piety was better than their poetry"; "they had drunk more of the Jordan than of the Helicon"; "sometimes they make the Maker of the tongue speak little better than barbarism, and have too many verses in such poor rhime that two hammers on a smith's anvil would make better music."[65]

Although fault could be found, more often than not from the author of a new metrical version of the Psalms, Sternhold and Hopkins had succeeded in establishing itself, in the minds of the people, as the only authorized version.[66] Consequently, any serious challenge to its dominance had to achieve similar status. Thus, Nicholas Brady, a chaplain to William III, and Nahum Tate, the poet laureate, sought royal permission to issue a new collection of metrical psalms. Petitioning the Privy Council in 1696, they received the following decision:

AT the Court at KENSINGTON,
DECEMBER 3, 1696.
PRESENT,
The KING's Most Excellent Majesty in
COUNCIL.

UPON the Humble Petition of Nicholas Brady and Nahum Tate this Day read at the Board, setting forth, that the Petitioners have, with their utmost Care and Industry, compleated *A New Version of the Psalms of David, in English Metre, fitted for Publick Use;* and humbly praying His Majesty's Royal Allowance, that the said *Version* may be used in such Congregations as think fit to receive it.

---

64. John Playford, *The Whole Book of Psalms: with the usual Hymns and Spiritual Songs; together with all the ancient and proper tunes sung in churches, with some of later use. Compos'd in three parts, cantus, medius, & bassus: in a more plain and useful method than hath been formerly published* (London: W. Godbid for the Company of Stationers, 1677).

65. Julian, *Dictionary,* 865. Although not indicated, several of the criticisms (inaccurately quoted) are from Thomas Fuller's *The Church-History of Britain: From the Birth of Jesus Christ, Until the Year M.DC.XLVIII* (London: Printed for J. Williams, 1655).

66. The question of legal status will be discussed fully in Chapter 3.

His Majesty taking the same into His Royal Consideration, is pleased to order in Council, that the said *New Version of the Psalms in English Metre* be, and the same is hereby Allowed and Permitted to be used in all such Churches, Chappels, and Congregations, as shall think fit to receive the same.[67]

Although having secured permission, the first edition came under serious criticism almost immediately, for many felt that the *New Version* was hardly an improvement over the "Old Version." Compare, for example, the opening of Psalm 1:

Sternhold and Hopkins:

The man is blest that hath not lent
  To wicked men his ear,
Nor led his life as sinners do
  Nor sat in scorner's chair.

Tate and Brady:

Happy the Man whom ill Advice
  From Virtue ne'er withdrew:
Who ne'er with Sinners stood, nor sat
  Amongst the scoffing Crew.

This first edition was quickly withdrawn and substantially revised, appearing in its new form in 1698.[68] The second edition was also criticized, withdrawn and revised, and reissued later in the same year. It was this revised second edition that became the rival to Sternhold and Hopkins.

---

67. N[ahum] Tate and N[icholas] Brady, *A New Version of the Psalms of David, Fitted to the Tunes Used in Churches* (London: T. Hodgkin, 1699). This declaration faces the title page and is signed by W. Bridgeman. The first edition (London: M. Clark, 1696) did not include this declaration. It did, however, have the following dedication: "To His Most Excellent Majesty William III. Of Great-Britain, France, and Ireland King, Defender of the Faith, &c. This New Version of the Psalms of David Is most Humbly Dedicated, by His Majesty's Most Obedient Subject and Servants." With the publication of *A New Version,* Sternhold and Hopkins's work began to be referred to as the "Old Version."

68. The revised version of Psalm 1 (1698) read:

How blest is he who ne'er consents
  By ill Advice to walk;
Nor stands in Sinners ways, nor sits
  Where Men profanely talk.

In a subsequent printing, Tate and Brady announced a forthcoming supplement that would contain the "usual Hymns, Creed, Lord's Prayer, Ten Commandments, all set to their proper Tunes; with aditional [sic] Hymns for the Holy Sacrament, Festivals &c."[69] The supplement was published in 1700 and, as promised, contained new material.[70] Of the sixteen new texts, ten were new paraphrases of previous items; the remaining six were the promised "aditional Hymns."[71]

Tate and Brady's work did not escape the opposition that other new versions had experienced, the most significant being that of William Beveridge, bishop of St. Asaph. One of Beveridge's concerns was the possibility, an actuality in his estimation, that the *New Version* had never been "conferred with the *Hebrew* as the others was [i.e., the "Old Version"]."[72]

But the *New Version* also had some ardent supporters. Basil Kennet, for example, praised Tate and Brady for having "answered their good design" and for not failing to "shew themselves equal to a nobler attempt, and capable of all those graces of poetry, which are not vulgar."[73] Thomas Bray held that the decline in psalmody was because of the weak-

---

69. Tate and Brady, 1699. The announcement was in the form of an advertisement at the end of the book.

70. N. Tate and N. Brady, *A Supplement to the New Version of Psalms* (London: F. Heptinstall, 1700).

71. They were: "While Shepherds watch'd their Flocks by Night," "Since Christ, our Passover, is slain," "Christ from the Dead is rais'd, and made," "Thou God, all Glory, Honour, and Pow'r," "All ye, who faithful Servants are," and "To God be Glory, Peace on Earth." Although paraphrases of scripture (except for "To God be Glory," which was a paraphrase of the *Gloria*), the fact that these were authorized by queen and council on July 30, 1703, established a precedent that would be built upon in the coming century.

72. William Beveridge, *Defence of the Book of Psalms, Collected into English Metre, by Thomas Sternhold, John Hopkins and others. With Critical Observations on the late New Version and the Old* (London: n.p., 1710), 39. Probably written in response to this and other criticisms, Tate published *An Essay for promoting of Psalmody* in 1710. In that work, he wrote: "After all, to shew that I speak not for self-interest, let the principal persons of our Church and State, who were pleased to approve and allow the use of that Version wherein I was concerned, be satisfied that a more serviceable performance is produced; and I shall think myself happy in having helped to make way for such a Version: let our Churches be accommodated to satisfaction, and my ambition is answered." See also the criticisms of John Phillips, *A Specimen of some of David's Psalms in metre, with Remarks upon the late Translators* (N.p.: n.p., 1698).

73. Basil Kennet, *An Essay towards a Paraphrase on the Psalms, in English Verse. To which is added a paraphrase on the third chapter of the Revelations [sic]* (London: B. Aylmer, 1706), preface.

nesses of the "Old Version." Thus, the *New Version* became a significant feature in his scheme for the restoration of family religion.[74] The various religious societies that sought to revitalize religion in the nation, including the services of the church, also were concerned about psalmody. Josiah Woodward, for example, noted that "[t]heir zeal hath in many places given new life to the celebration of the *Lord's supper, public prayer, singing of psalms,* and *Christian conference,* duties which were in many places almost disused, or performed in a cool and languishing manner."[75] This support of metrical psalmody and the call for increased attention to this aspect of worship gained an influential voice in the 1720s.

Edmund Gibson, bishop of London, supported efforts to revitalize psalmody, and in 1724 he directed his clergy to "take the Trouble of directing the Choice of proper Psalms."[76] He believed that with an established "course" of singing the "most useful Parts of the Book of Psalms" a reform of congregational singing might be achieved.[77] The liturgy, of which psalm singing (but not hymns) was a part, was the clergy's responsibility, he argued, and they were to see to the "decent and orderly Performance of the publick Worship of God."[78] Ironically, some of those who favored the introduction of hymns appropriated Gibson's ideas to further their cause![79]

Less conservative were those who believed that hymns had a rightful

---

74. Frost, *Companion,* 84.

75. [Josiah Woodward], *An account of the rise and progress of the religious societies in the City of London, &c.,* [2nd ed.] (London: n.p., 1698), 63.

76. Edmund [Gibson], *The Excellent Use of Psalmody, with a Course of Singing-Psalms for half a year* (1724), reprinted in *Religious Tracts, Dispersed by the Society for Promoting Christian Knowledge,* 12 vols. (London: F. and C. Rivington, 1800), 1:3. Gibson's thoughts on psalmody were quoted often throughout the eighteenth century.

77. Gibson, 1:3–4. A number of editors and compilers followed Gibson's lead. One compiler did so, but did not limit his selections to the "Old Version," preferring the greater variety of meters of the *New Version.* See *A Course of Singing Psalms, Beginning On the First Sunday in January, And again On the First Sunday in July: And also proper Psalms for particular Days and Occasions. Agreeable To the Directions given by the late Lord Bishop of London to the Clergy of his Diocese, in the Year 1724. Together With the Tunes adapted to each Psalm* (London: n.p., 1767).

78. Gibson, 1:7.

79. See, for example, R. W., *The excellent use of Psalmody, with a course of Singing Psalms for half a year* (Nottingham: n.p., 1734). This work contains twenty-eight hymns that are incorporated in the rota.

place in the Christian life, though not in the church's liturgy. In 1727 *A Collection of Psalms, and Divine Hymns, suited to the great festivals of the Church, for morning and evening, and other occasions* was published. Although the title page made reference to "Parish-Clarks," the preface stated the compiler's intentions clearly: "I have no thought of proposing the Use of any Part of this *Collection* in the Publick Service."[80]

Although the Injunctions of 1559 continued to remain in force, by this time they were not observed. Organ voluntaries had replaced the metrical psalms before and after the service, that is, in the appointed place, and the custom had developed of singing metrical psalms between the litany and the communion service as well as before and after the sermon and occasionally after the second lesson, a practice that troubled some greatly.[81] Such violations of the Injunctions and the rubrics of the Book of Common Prayer were noted with dismay and later would be included in the arguments against the introduction of hymns into the liturgy.

During the first three decades of the eighteenth century, the church was slow to accept even the limited number of hymns made available in the *Supplement* of 1700 by Tate and Brady. The most significant change in the music of the church was brought about by the number of new tune books that were published. One of the more important books was the work of John Chetham.[82] In addition to reviving older tunes, Chetham included several tunes in a new style. These new tunes, treated in a separate section of the book, were more florid in character and would, as they developed later in the century, become a source of concern in some segments of the church. Many of these tune books contained a small number of hymns in appendixes. These hymns numbered from zero to eighteen and were drawn from a variety of sources, "While shepherds watched their flocks by night" being about the only common choice.[83]

---

80. Cited by Benson, *English Hymn,* 342.

81. See, for example, Tho[mas] Bisse, *The Beauty of Holiness in the Common-Prayer: As set forth in Four Sermons Preach'd at the Rolls Chapel* (London: Printed by W. B. for H. Clements, 1716), 95–96.

82. John Chetham, *A book of psalmody, containing variety of tunes for all the common metres of the Psalms in the old and new versions and others for particular measures* (London: Printed by W. Pearson, 1718). This work was in wide use for more than a century. The other significant collection was John Arnold's *The compleat psalmodist: or, The organist's, parish-clerk's and psalm-singer's companion* (London: Printed by R. Brown, 1739).

83. Frost, *Companion,* 94.

Isaac Watts

Although opposition was readily forthcoming, the use of hymns in worship, as distinct from metrical psalms, became increasingly accepted during the eighteenth century. Contributing significantly to this development was the acceptance of hymns by the Dissenting churches. Benjamin Keach, pastor of the Particular Baptist Church in Horselydown, Southward, was probably the first[84] to challenge the domination of the metrical psalters when he introduced communion hymns to his congregation in 1673.[85]

It was the work, however, of Isaac Watts, a Congregationalist, that proved to be one of two significant factors in the development of hymnody in the eighteenth century.[86] In 1707 Watts published his first collection, *Hymns and Spiritual Songs*. Divided into three sections: 1) Paraphrases, 2) Hymns on Divine Subjects, and 3) Hymns for the Lord's Supper, the work enjoyed enormous success, running into sixteen editions in Watts's lifetime.[87] Included in this collection was an essay that indicated clearly the direction Watts would take. Watts did not intend to lay aside the Psalms of David, for they were God's word to humanity. Rather than singing them in paraphrase, the Psalms should be read in prose in order to be as faithful as possible to the Hebrew original. Thus, the song of Christians was not to be metrical psalms, but "evangelical hymns," poetry of human composition that expressed the thoughts and feelings of the individual and the community of

---

84. Whitley credits Katherine Sutton's *A Christian womans [sic] experiences of the glorious working of Gods [sic] free grace. Published for the edification of others* (Rotterdam: n.p., 1663) with the honor of being the first hymn book for congregational use, noting that the book contained many hymns. However, there seems to be little evidence to support the conclusion that it was intended for congregational use. See William Thomas Whitley, *A History of British Baptists,* 2nd ed., revised (London: Kingsgate, 1932), 186.

85. According to most authorities, Keach is credited with publishing the first hymn book, *Spiritual Melody,* in 1691. His verse, however, leaves much to be desired, being either feeble rhyme, at best, or mere doggerel. The earliest Baptist worship included no music or singing. By the 1670s some Baptist congregations had begun to use metrical psalms. The introduction of hymns provoked serious discussion, and many congregations split over the issue. To give Keach his due, he is best seen as a poet in the heroic couplets of *The Glorious Lover* (1679) and *War with the Devil* (1673). See J. R. Watson, *The English Hymn: A Critical and Historical Study* (Oxford: Clarendon, 1997), 110–114.

86. See, for example, Robin A. Leaver, "Isaac Watts's Hermeneutical Principles and the Decline of English Metrical Psalmody," *Churchman* 92:1 (1978):56–60.

87. Such success must certainly have been in part because of the collection being used outside of Watts's own communion.

faith.[88] Even so, material from the Old Testament could be used insofar as it was brought within the understanding of the New Testament.

> You will always find in this Paraphrase dark Expressions enlighten'd, and the Levitical Ceremonies, and Hebrew Forms of Speech chang'd into the Worship of the Gospel, and explained in the language of our Time and Nation; and what would not bear such an Alteration is omitted and laid aside. After this manner should I rejoice to see good part of the Book of Psalms fitted for the use of our Churches, and David converted into a Christian.[89]

This "Christianizing" of the Psalms was the first step; the second step was to compose new texts that would be in compliance with the New Testament commandment found in Ephesians 5:19–20 (". . . as you sing psalms and hymns and spiritual songs among yourselves, singing and making melody to the Lord in your hearts, giving thanks to God the Father at all times and for everything in the name of our Lord Jesus Christ.") and similar passages.

By 1719 David's conversion was complete. In the preface to *The Psalms of David Imitated,* Watts underscored what he had written earlier:

> [S]ince I believe that any *Divine Sentence* or *Christian Verse* agreeable to Scripture may be sung, tho' it be composed by Men uninspired, I have not been so curious and exact in striving every where to express the antient Sense and Meaning of *David,* but have rather exprest myself as I may suppose *David* would have done, had he lived in the Days of *Christianity.* And by this means perhaps I have sometimes hit upon the true Intent of the Spirit of God in those Verses, farther and clearer than *David* himself could ever discover, as St. *Peter* encourages me to hope. 1 *Pet.* 1. 11, 12. . . . In all Places I have kept my grand Design in View, and that is *to teach my Author to speak like a Christian.*[90]

One has only to examine Psalm 1 to find evidence of David's conversion. It begins in a manner not unlike Sternhold and Hopkins or Tate and Brady:

> Blest is the Man who shuns the Place
>   Where Sinners love to meet:
> Who fears to tread their wicked Ways,
>   And hates the Scoffer's Seat.

By stanza six, however, Watts has, in his words, "borrowed a Line or two

---

88. Isaac Watts, *Hymns and Spiritual Songs. In three books . . . With an essay towards the improvement of christian [sic] psalmody, by the use of evangelical hymns in worship, as well as the Psalms of David* (London: J. Lawrence, 1707), 241–254.

89. Watts, *Hymns and Spiritual Songs,* preface.

90. I[saac] Watts, *The Psalms of David Imitated in the Language of the New Testament, And apply'd to the Christian State and Worship* (London: Printed for J. Clark, R. Ford, and R. Cruttenden, 1719), xix–xx.

from the New Testament, that the excellent and inspired Composures of the Jewish Psalmist may be brighen'd by the clearer Discoveries of the Gospel:"

> Sinners in Judgment shall not stand
>   Amongst the Sons of Grace,
> When *Christ* the Judge at his Right-hand
>   Appoints his Saints a Place.[91]

It is difficult to comprehend fully the radical character of Watts's work. For almost a century and a half English worshipers had been Christians in their prayers and "little better than Jews" in their praises. This observation led two commentators to note that "[m]any an eminent believer, who joined in the public worship for fifty years, never sang the name of Jesus till he arrived in heaven."[92] Within a very short time, Watts became the daily solace of many. Philip Doddridge, Independent minister of Northampton, described in a letter a conversation between two worshipers: "'What if Dr. Watts should come to Northampton!' said one. 'The very sight of him would be like an ordinance to me,' was the reply of another."[93]

The enormous success of Watts's work[94] brought forth a host of imitators, not so much from a demand for more hymns, but from ministers' desire to write their own hymns in order to illustrate their sermons better.[95] Watts's popularity, furthermore, was not limited to Dissenters, for clergy in the Church of England came to incorporate some of his hymns in their collections as the desire to sing something other than metrical psalms grew.[96]

John and Charles Wesley

The second influence on hymnody in the early years of the eighteenth century, and for Anglicans of greater significance, was the work of John and

---

91. Watts is drawing from Matthew 25.33: "He shall set the Sheep at the Right-hand." Watts, *Psalms of David,* 2–3.

92. The commentators were Bennett and Bogue. No other identification is given. Cited by J. Spencer Curwen, "Early Nonconformist Psalmody," *The British Quarterly Review* 71 (January 1880):86.

93. Cited by Curwen, "Early Nonconformist Psalmody," 86.

94. By 1720, seven editions of Watts's *Hymns* had been published.

95. For example, Philip Doddridge wrote hymns to reinforce the content of his sermons. These hymns (370) were published after his death in 1755. See *Hymns founded on Various Texts in the Holy Scriptures. Published from the Author's Manuscript by Job Orton* (Salop: J. Orton, 1755).

96. John Wesley included several of Watts's hymns in his first hymnal: *A Collection of Psalms and Hymns* (Charleston: n.p., 1737). Among those included (in altered form) were: "I'll praise my Maker" and "Come we that love the Lord." This hymnal was discovered by William Thomas Brooke in 1878.

Charles Wesley. Both Wesleys were well acquainted with the tradition of metrical psalmody, and both may have questioned its adequacy before their departure to Georgia in 1735. If they had not done so, their encounter with the hymn singing of the Moravians during the journey certainly demonstrated a different alternative to the metrical psalms of both the "Old Version" and the *New Version*.

In 1737 John Wesley published anonymously his *Collection of Psalms and Hymns*. The collection consisted of seventy hymns and included items drawn from Austin's *Devotion* (edited by George Hickes), George Herbert, Isaac Watts, Joseph Addison, and five translations from German by Wesley.[97] The collection was probably used only a few times, because in August 1737 Wesley was charged with, among other things, "introducing into the church and service at the altar, compositions of Psalms and Hymns not inspected or authorized by any proper judicature."[98] Interestingly, although the grand jury responded to most of the charges, they did not respond to the charge of introducing hymns into the services of the church. Returning to England the following year, Wesley published another collection with the same title, and he published a third collection, commended for use in public worship, in 1741.

In 1739 Wesley purchased an abandoned foundery in Moorgate Fields with the aid of friends. The Foundery became an important chapel in the Wesleyan movement, and in its services hymn singing played an important role. In 1742 Wesley published a collection of the tunes sung there. The variety of meters and the setting of each hymn to its own tune (only one tune being repeated) was a bold step away from the extremely limited meters of the metrical psalters and the number of tunes in the common repertoire.[99]

Although Wesley had commended the 1741 collection for use in worship, conclusive evidence of its use in the services of the church is lacking. This lack of use may have been because of the fact that Wesley's followers preferred the simpler "Preaching Service," which consisted of two

---

97. Franz Hildebrandt and Oliver A. Beckerlegge, eds., *A Collection of Hymns for the use of the People called Methodists,* vol. 7, *The Works of John Wesley* (Nashville: Abingdon, 1983), 22–23; Faith Ingles, "The Role of Wesleyan Hymnody in the Development of Congregational Song" (D.M.A. dissertation, Combs College of Music, 1986), 125; Frost, *Companion,* 96.

98. W. Reginald Ward and Richard P. Heitzenrater, eds., *The Works of John Wesley,* vol. 18 (Nashville: Abingdon, 1988), 555. The charges resulted from Wesley's relationship with Sophia Hopkey. In Virginia, Archibald McRoberts was charged with singing unauthorized hymns c. 1779, and in Maryland, William Briscoe Jr. was charged with the same offense in 1808. See Robert W. Prichard, *A History of the Episcopal Church* (Harrisburg, Pa.: Morehouse, 1991), 65.

99. [John Wesley], *A collection of tunes, set to music, as they are commonly sung at the Foundery* (London: A. Pearson, 1742).

hymns, sermon, and prayer, even though Wesley urged the use of the daily offices of the Prayer Book. In fact, the rules that governed the societies included instructions for the sessions to begin and end with singing.[100]

As early as 1746, however, it was evident that the singing of hymns would not remain within the class meetings or private devotions. In that year *Hymns on the Great Festivals and Other Occasions* was published.[101] As suggested in the title, the collection contained hymns appropriate for various occasions in the church year from Christmas to Trinity.[102] Because the observance of these feasts was part of the Book of Common Prayer, the hymns were designed for use on those days in the parish services.

In the same year the subject of singing occupied a portion of the discussion at the Methodist annual conference. The record, in the form of question and answer, reads:

Q.   How shall we guard more effectually against formality in public singing?

A.   (1) By the careful choice of hymns proper for the congregation; (2) In general try choosing hymns of praise or prayer, rather than descriptive of particular states; (3) By not singing too much; seldom a whole hymn at once, seldom more than five or six verses at a time; (4) By suiting the tune to the hymns; by often stopping short and asking the people, 'Now do you know what you said last? Did it suit your case? Did you sing it as to God with the spirit and with the understanding also?'[103]

In 1753 John Wesley anonymously published the first distinctively Wesleyan collection.[104] This collection consisted of selections of material written by John and Charles, drawn from three volumes of hymns published

---

100. See Trevor Dearing, *Wesleyan and Tractarian Worship: An Ecumenical Study* (London: Epworth and SPCK, 1966), 47; R. C. D. Jasper, *The Development of the Anglican Liturgy 1662–1980* (London: SPCK, 1989), 19–20. Later, hymns would also play a significant role in the Watch-night and communion services.

101. Charles Wesley, *Hymns on the Great Festivals and Other Occasions* (London: Printed for M. Cooper, 1746). The original tunes in this collection were composed by John Frederick Lampe.

102. Of the twenty-four hymns in the collection, seventeen were by Charles Wesley, all of them for various feast days in the church year.

103. Cited by James T. Lightwood, *Methodist Music in the Eighteenth Century* (London: Epworth, 1927), 19–20. It is interesting to note that in 1747 Wesley told his preachers "not to sing any hymns of their own composing" (Lightwood, *Methodist,* 26).

104. [John Wesley], *Hymns and Spiritual Songs, Intended for the Use of Real Christians Of all Denominations* (London: W. Strahan, 1753).

by them in 1739, 1740, and 1742, each with the title *Hymns and Sacred Poems*. Although the collection contained only eighty-four hymns, the fact that it contained their hymns rather than the works of other authors set it apart from the earlier collections. Lamenting the "immoderate Attachment to particular Opinions or Modes of Worship" (an indication that Wesley was conscious of the need to reform congregational music?), it was Wesley's hope that

> the ensuing Collection of Hymns, may in some measure contribute, thro' the Blessing of God, to advance this glorious End [i.e., the removal of "immoderate Attachment"], to promote this Spirit of free Love, not confined to any one Opinion or Party. There is not an Hymn not one Verse inserted here, but what relates to the Common Salvation; and what every serious and unprejudiced Christian, of whatever Denomination, may join in.[105]

For the people involved in the societies, two distinct types of singing were experienced. In the societies, the faithful sang the powerful hymnody of the Wesleys and other evangelical authors. At the Sunday parish service, however, they sang the metrical psalms of either the "Old Version" or the *New Version*. Such could not continue for long, and by 1757 the use of hymns had expanded beyond the meeting house to the Church of England. In a letter, John Wesley wrote that the Eucharist was "enlivened by hymns suitable to the occasion."[106]

The 1780 *Collection of Hymns, for the Use of the People Called Methodists* brought to a suitable conclusion Wesley's desire to provide a hymnbook for his societies. This book, however, was more than a mere collection of appropriate materials. It was in its organization a "spiritual biography of the sort of person whom [Wesley] called . . . a real Christian." In the beginning sinners were exhorted to return to God and, if they persevered, they

---

105. J. Wesley, 1753, iv.

106. John Wesley, *The Letters of the Rev. John Wesley,* 8 vols., ed. John Telford (London: Epworth, 1931; reprint ed., 1960), 3:228. The letter, directed to a friend, is dated September 20, 1757. Dearing's claim that "Wesley was the originator of the Sung Eucharist in which the ancient hymns contained in the Liturgy are set to 'modern' music and rendered by the whole congregation" is far too bold (24, fn. 120). The impact of the Wesleys upon hymnody cannot be challenged; however, singing the eucharistic liturgy as the normal practice on Sunday in any significant number of parishes would not be achieved until the 1930s. It should also be noted that as early as 1769 at least one parish was singing the responses in the communion service. See James Woodforde, *The Diary of a Country Parson: The Reverend James Woodforde, 1758–1781,* 5 vols., ed. John Beresford (London: H. Milford, 1924), 1:92. Further, in 1792 a clergyman had to file articles against his churchwardens for attempting to stop the chanting of the service. A report of this action is found in *The Christian Remembrancer* 11 (1829):376–379.

would know salvation and sing the hymns of "corporate life."[107] For Wesley, hymns were "a means of raising or quickening the spirit of devotion; of confirming the believer's faith; of enlivening his hope; and of kindling and increasing his love to God and man."[108] Like others in this period, Wesley desired to offer an alternative to the "formal drawl of the parish clerk, the screaming of boys who bawl out what they neither understand or feel."[109]

A Period of Transition

The singing of the Wesleyan societies, often described as "hearty," could not fail to attract attention. Some saw the potential of financial gain and rushed forward with collections to benefit the singing societies and those parishes where hymns had begun to be introduced; others saw nothing but potential danger and argued in the following years against the "methodistical" innovation.[110]

---

107. Bernard Lord Manning, *The Hymns of Wesley and Watts* (London: Epworth, 1943), 11–12.

108. John Wesley, *A Collection of Hymns, for the Use of the People Called Methodists* (London: J. Mason, [1780]), preface. In the introductory essays found in volume seven of *The Works of John Wesley,* which is devoted to this collection, it is interesting that the authors, Franz Hildebrandt, Oliver A. Beckerlegge, and James Dale, do not seem to be aware of any controversy regarding the development of hymnody in the eighteenth century. It is also interesting that there is no discussion of the impact of this collection upon the Church of England.

109. Telford, *Wesley,* 3:227 (September 20, 1757). In a later letter (September 11, 1765), Wesley described the type of tune which should not be used: "They sing all over CORNWALL a tune so full of repetitions and flourishes that it can scarce be sung with devotion. It is to those words, 'Praise the Lord, ye blessed ones.' Away with it! Let it be heard no more. They cannot sing our old common tunes. Teach these everywhere. Take pains herein" (Telford, *Wesley,* 4:311–312).

110. One of the first collections to be printed was the anonymous *The Divine Musical Miscellany* (N.p.: n.p., c. 1755?). George Whitefield prepared a collection for his congregation at the Tabernacle, *A Collection of Hymns for Social Worship, More particularly designed for the Use of the Tabernacle Congregation, in London* (London: W. Strahan, 1753). For a lengthy (740 pages) attack on hymn singing, see George Lavington, *The Enthusiasm of Methodists and Papists Compar'd* (1749). I am indebted to Richard Arnold for drawing my attention to this work (*The English Hymn: Studies in a Genre,* 69). See also William Riley's *Parochial Music Corrected. Containing Remarks on the Performance of Psalmody in Country Churches, and on the ridiculous and profane Manner of Singing practised by the Methodists; Reflections on the bad Performance of Psalmody in London, Westminster, &c. with some Hints for the Improvement of it in Public Worship; Observations on the Choice and Qualifications of Parish-Clerks; the Utility of Teaching Charity-Children Psalmody and Hymns; the Use of Organs, and the Performance of Organists* (London: n.p., 1762) in a section entitled "The Methodists' profane Manner of Singing."

With the growth of Methodism came an increasing hostility on the part of the Church of England toward such "enthusiasm." Urged to be faithful attenders of the local parish, members of the Methodist societies were often excluded because of the suspicions of clergy. This hostility was also extended toward Evangelicals. Commonly despised by bishops, those Evangelicals seeking ordination were often refused and, if successful, often found themselves unable to secure an appointment.[111] One identifying badge was the use of hymns.[112]

The early advocates of hymnody were clearly of an evangelical persuasion.[113] James Hervey, for example, was a participant in the Holy Club and a member of Lincoln College, Oxford.[114] Hervey graduated in 1736, was ordained by Potter of Oxford, and assumed a curacy under his father, rector of Weston Favell (in the Midlands) and Collingtree. In 1738 he exchanged this curacy for another, took a leave of absence because of ill health, assumed the curacy at Bideford (North Devon) for three years (being dismissed by the new rector who disapproved of his teaching), and returned to Weston Favell and Collingtree in 1743.[115]

At Collingtree, Hervey introduced hymn singing sometime between 1752 and 1754. A visitor reported his impressions of this innovation:

> Last Sabbath-day, after preaching in the morning at Olney, with three others, I rode to hear one Mr. Hervey, a minister of the Church of England, who preached at Collingtree, and, to my great surprise as well as satisfaction, having never seen such a thing before, in prayer-time, instead of singing psalms, they sung two of Dr. Watts's hymns, the clerk giving them out line by line.[116]

---

111. See Kenneth Hylson-Smith, *Evangelicals in the Church of England, 1734–1984* (Edinburgh: T. and T. Clark, 1989), 33, 50, 67.

112. Davies noted that the "very success . . . of hymnody was sufficient argument for the conservatives to be suspicious of hymns" (*Worship and Theology,* 3:234).

113. The term *evangelical,* when not capitalized, refers to the broad religious revival that occurred in the eighteenth century in England. When capitalized, it refers specifically to the revival within the Church of England.

114. The Holy Club was a rigorous society founded by Wesley at Oxford that included a rule of life, a pattern of self-examination, mutual oversight and good works. It was this organizational structure that gave them the abiding name of *methodists.*

115. L. E. Elliott-Binns, *The Early Evangelicals: A Religious and Social Study* (Greenwich: Seabury, 1953), 141–148.

116. [A. C. H. Seymour], *The Life and Times of Selina, Countess of Huntingdon,* 2 vols. (London: W. E. Painter, 1844), 1:192. The visitor was one of Lady Huntingdon's preachers. For a discussion of Lady Huntingdon's support of hymns, including the important collection of 1780, see S. E. Boyd Smith, "The Effective Countess: Lady Huntingdon and the 1780 edition of *A Select Collection of Hymns,*" *The Hymn* 44:3 (July 1993):26–32.

Two observations made by this visitor are significant. First, the fact that he had never witnessed the use of hymns during "prayer-time" implies that, at least in this region, Hervey was an early advocate for supplementing metrical psalms with hymns. Second, by selecting hymns from Watts's collection, Hervey demonstrated a willingness to embrace non-Anglican material for use in the services of the church, an attitude that would not become widely shared until the latter half of the nineteenth century. Hervey died in 1758, and no indication of how hymnody continued to be received in the parish has been found.[117]

Throughout the eighteenth century numerous proposals for the revitalization of parochial church music were suggested by advocates for reform. Charity choirs, itinerant singing masters, various revisions of existing psalters as well as new versions, singing galleries,[118] the publication of singing methods,[119] and the rise of village bands,[120] were all designed to remedy the perceived defects of the performance of metrical psalmody.

---

117. It is possible that Hervey's embrace of hymnody was because of his friendships with Watts and Doddridge at Northampton and the famous Baptist, John Ryland, all of whom were intimates. According to Elliott-Binns, Hervey was completely estranged from Wesley by 1758, owing to Wesley's criticism of Hervey's *Dialogues between Theron and Aspasio* (1755), which was decidedly Calvinistic. See Elliott-Binns, *Early Evangelicals,* 146–147.

118. Between 1737 and 1799 licenses were granted for the construction of galleries in fifty-one churches. The construction of galleries was primarily to accommodate increased congregations. Some galleries were constructed for choirs, however, and others were taken over by parish musicians. For an excellent survey of church architecture, see Nigel Yates, *Buildings, Faith, and Worship: The Liturgical Arrangement of Anglican Churches 1600–1900* (Oxford: Clarendon, 1991).

119. For a survey of instruction materials available, see Bernarr Rainbow, *English Psalmody Prefaces: Popular Methods of Teaching, 1562–1835* (Kilkenny, Ire.: Boethius, [c. 1982]). The two most popular methods used during the eighteenth century were William Tans'ur's *A compleat melody: or, The harmony of Sion, the whole is composed in two, three, and four musical parts, according to the most authentick rules for voice or organ* (London: Printed by W. Pearson, for J. Hodges [c. 1735]), and John Arnold's *The complete psalmodist*. See also David Hunter, "English Country Psalmodists and Their Publications, 1700–1760," *Journal of the Royal Musical Association* 115, 2 (1990):220–239, and Sir John Stainer, "On the Musical Introductions Found in Certain Metrical Psalters," *Proceedings of the Royal Musical Association* 27 (November 1900):1–50.

120. See K. H. MacDermott, *The Old Church Gallery Minstrels* (London: SPCK, 1948). For an engaging but limited discussion of the conflicts concerning village bands, see Vic Gammon, "'Babylonian Performances': The Rise and Suppression of Popular Church Music, 1660–1870," in *Popular Culture and Class Conflict, 1590–1914: Explorations in the History of Labour and Leisure,* ed. Eileen Yeo and Stephen Yeo (Sussex: Harvester, 1981), 62–88.

The introduction of hymns into the liturgy was viewed by some to be
yet another means for restoring congregational song to its proper place.
Those who favored the introduction of hymns, however, faced enormous
difficulties. The temper of the age was one that distrusted extremes,
viewed change (when rational opposition was wanting) as "Popery,"[121]
and deemed "enthusiasm" as an attack upon reason and common
sense.[122] Hannah More captured the mood of the century when she
wrote,

> A cheerful knight [Sir Gilbert] of good estate,
> . . .
> He dreaded nought like alteration,
> Improvement still was innovation;
> . . .
> He thought 'twou'd shew a falling state,
> If STERNHOLD should give way to TATE.[123]

Although a small number of hymns had been in existence and in use
from the earliest days of the Reformation in England, it was the events of
the first half of the eighteenth century that set the stage for the shift from
metrical psalms to hymns. The struggle for dominance would not be between the "Old Version" and the *New Version,* but between metrical
psalms and hymns.

As Dissenters embraced hymns and as their use by the Methodists and
Evangelicals became known, those anxious to maintain the continued use
of metrical psalms and the exclusion of hymns sought ways to achieve their

---

121. Chetham described opposition to change thus: "What terrible outcries do they
make . . . against any alterations; and if their understanding does not help 'em to any
arguments against the thing itself, they immediately cry out Popery!" (preface)
122. Elliott-Binns, *Early Evangelicals,* 20–21.
123. [Hannah More], *Florio: A Tale, For Fine Gentlemen and Fine Ladies*
(London: T. Cadell, 1786). In the version cited by Elliott-Binns (*Early Evangelicals,* 374), the verse reads:

> [F]ear'd 'twould show a falling State,
> If Sternhold should give way to Tate:
> The Church's downfall he predicted,
> Were modern tunes not interdicted.

These additional lines, although not in the 1786 version, support the perception
that change had dire consequences. They apparently were known, because Neale
cited the first two lines in an article published in 1849. See [John Mason Neale],
"English Hymnology: its History and Prospects," *The Christian Remembrancer*
18, n.s. (October 1849):306. Whether the author of the added lines is More or an
unknown hand has not been determined.

goals. Likewise, those in favor of increasing the use of hymns in the church and the consequent reduction of the use of metrical psalms sought support for their efforts. From the middle of the eighteenth century onward, the arguments both for and against the inclusion of hymns in the liturgy of the church became more pronounced.

Chapter Two

The Early Controversies, 1760–1810

As there are some persons who explode all music whatever, and others that reject only the aid of instruments, so there are many who have violent prejudices against the use of HYMNS in religious worship.[1]

By 1760 hymns were in wide use in Dissenting congregations and had made some modest inroads into the Church of England primarily because of the work of John and Charles Wesley and, to a lesser extent, that of George Whitefield, Martin Madan, Augustus Toplady, and others (although the whole impact of "Anglican" collections on Anglican congregations has not been thoroughly researched). The majority of Anglican clergy, however, viewed the inclusion of hymns in the liturgy with dismay for several reasons. Most prominent was the still strong belief that hymns of human composition were inappropriate in the liturgy, a belief that had its origins in the Reformation's stress on the centrality of the Bible for the church. The clergy also cared little for Dissenters and viewed their hymns as a potential threat to Anglican theological integrity. Methodists[2] were viewed as fanatics, and their hymns were deemed to be colored with enthusiasm; both fanatics and enthusiasm were to be avoided. For these reasons the hymnody of the Dissenters and the Methodists was viewed with extreme suspicion by most

---

1. David Simpson, *Select Psalms and Hymns,* A new edition (Macclesfield: Printed and Sold by E. Bayley, 1795), x.

2. Methodism had not yet become a separate denomination, although there were separate society meetings. The term *methodist* was used rather indiscriminately to describe any Christian displaying any signs or tendencies toward "enthusiasm" during most of the eighteenth century. It also referred to followers of John Wesley (Arminian methodists) as well as to those who looked to Whitefield or the Countess of Huntingdon for guidance (Calvinistic methodists).

Anglicans, and their advocacy of hymnody provided far more material for use by those opposed than those in favor of hymns.

As the eighteenth century progressed, the call for the reform of parochial psalm singing increased dramatically. Examples of the poor quality of congregational singing abounded, and every advocate for reform drew attention to them. Even those who may not have advocated reform noted with dismay the low level of congregational singing. James Woodforde, for example, commented in his diary: "We went to Church this morning [April 16, 1775] at Weston. . . . My clerk is a shocking Hand. The worst singing I ever heard in a Church, only the Clerk and one man, and both intolerably bad."[3] Some of those calling for reform included the introduction of hymns as a means for achieving reform. Others continued to advocate the reform of psalm singing without any change or additions, preferring to maintain the use of either the "Old Version" or the *New Version* in the parish.[4] Some argued for completely new metrical versions of the Psalms or collections of metrical psalms drawn from existing psalters, and by the end of the century a few brave souls advocated the use of hymns only. Richard Cecil, for example, compiled a collection of metrical psalms (no hymns) that included the work of John Denham, Luke Milbourne, Nahum Tate and Nicholas Brady, Christopher Smart, James Merrick, Isaac Watts, John Milton, Joseph Addison, Elizabeth Rowe, Anne Steele, and Elizabeth Tollet. He noted that "as the desire of discontinuing the Old Version was pretty general, nothing prevented its removal but the different opinions which prevailed respecting the *best* of succeeding ones."[5] In contrast, the anonymous *A Collection of Hymns, for Public Worship* (Totnes: Cleave and Fisher, 1797) included no metrical psalms.

Those who argued for either new metrical versions of the Psalms or for the inclusion of hymns were, in part, responding to the poor poetry of Sternhold and Hopkins and other psalters as well as the obscurity of the language. For example, Richard De Courcy, observed:

> Whoever possesses the smallest taste for *poetical* composition, will easily perceive, that *Sternhold* and *Hopkins,* (the versifiers of our psalms) were bet-

---

3. James Woodforde, *The Diary of a Country Parson: The Reverend James Woodforde, 1758–1781,* 5 vols., ed. John Beresford (London: H. Milford, 1924), 1:152. If Woodforde desired a reform of congregational singing, he did not mention it in his diary.

4. Generally, rural congregations continued to line out and sing Sternhold and Hopkins, whereas urban congregations had embraced Tate and Brady.

5. Richard Cecil, *The Psalms of David Selected from Various Versions, and adapted to Public Worship* (London: Sold by J. Mathews, 1785), advertisement.

ter acquainted with the truths of *Divinity,* than conversant in the beauties of *Poetry;* and that a wreath of *laurel* did by no means suit *their* brow; or, as Fuller in his Church-History facetiously observes, "they drank deeper of the *waters of life,* than of the streams of *Helicon.*"[6]

De Courcy inaccurately quoted Thomas Fuller, who noted that Sternhold and Hopkins "had drank more of *Jordan,* than of *Helicon.*" Fuller continued, "Since, later men have vented their just exceptions against the baldnesse of the translation, so that sometimes they make the Maker of the Tongue to speak little better than barbarisme, and have in many Verses such poor rhime, that two hammers on a Smith's anvill would make better musick."[7]

One person, evidently, was thoroughly convinced that the language of Sternhold and Hopkins was so obscure that he wrote a reference work to explain the difficult and obtuse words.[8]

As the use of hymns increased, arguments for and against their introduction into the liturgy of the church also increased. These arguments stemmed from a variety of concerns, often overlapped, and were repeated at various times throughout the period under consideration, often without elaboration or additional insight. In fact, some of the arguments continued to be expressed substantially in their original form well into the nineteenth century, and even a few were still being used in the opening decades of the twentieth century. Although there was a wide range of arguments used, some far more substantial than others, a few concerns dominated the discussion in the controversy. Before turning to those concerns, a brief discussion of the earliest significant use of hymns is in order.

Hospitals, Asylums, and Charity Children

Opposition to the use of hymns was minimized at first because of the fact that hymns were introduced in hospital chapels and other charitable institutions by their Evangelical chaplains rather than in parish churches, thus

---

6. Richard De Courcy, *A Collection of Psalms and Hymns, Extracted from different Authors,* 2nd ed. (Shrewsbury: T. Wood, 1782), iii–iv.

7. Thomas Fuller, *The Church-History of Britain: From the Birth of Jesus Christ, Until the Year M.DC.XLVIII* (London: Printed for J. Williams, 1655), Book VII, Cento XVI, paragraphs 31, 32.

8. See W. C[ole], *A Key to the Psalms, Being an Easy, Concise and Familiar Explanation of Words, Allusions, and Sentences in Them, Selected from Substantial Authorities, Tending to Promote Expeditiously the Better Understanding of Them Among the Ignorant in General, and for the Information of the Lower Class of People in Particular* (Cambridge: F. Hodson, 1788).

avoiding potential ecclesiastical strictures.[9] By choosing this venue, advocates of hymnody also avoided the hostility of those who supported the long-established custom of singing metrical psalms. This decision, however, did little to advance the cause of hymnody, except for one notable instance.

Martin Madan enjoyed great success when he introduced hymns in his London chapel. Educated at Westminster and Christ Church, Oxford, Madan began his career at the bar in 1748. In response to a challenge (in order later to do a burlesque of the sermon), Madan went to hear John Wesley preach and, as a consequence, left his legal career to take holy orders.

From 1750 to 1780 Madan was chaplain of the chapel attached to Lock Hospital (founded in 1746 for the rehabilitation of "fallen women"), near Hyde Park in London. A man of considerable learning and musical talent and a strong preacher, Madan made the chapel a "fashionable place of worship."[10] In 1760 he published *A Collection of Psalms and Hymns, Extracted from various Authors* for use in the chapel.[11] The collection was essentially a reediting (and expansion) of George Whitefield's collection of 1753.[12] Madan, like Whitefield, borrowed and adapted freely the work of others, and there is no evidence that he wrote any of the texts in this collection. Madan also compiled a collection of tunes for use in the chapel that influenced subsequent tune books.[13] Because of his editorial skill, the literary quality of the texts, and his musical skill, both collections enjoyed

---

9. Singing became a marked feature in these institutions, and a considerable number of hymns, anthems, and odes were written and published in collections for their use.

10. Robin A. Leaver, "British Hymnody from the Sixteenth through the Eighteenth Centuries," in *The Hymnal 1982 Companion,* ed. Raymond F. Glover, 3 vols. (New York: The Church Hymnal Corporation, 1990–1994), 1:388.

11. M[artin] Madan, *A Collection of Psalms and Hymns, Extracted from various Authors* (London: n.p., 1760). Given the difficulties that faced Evangelicals in securing livings or curacies in London, proprietary chapels offered a means of expanding their influence. These chapels were controlled by the person who erected them and were aimed at meeting the needs of an expanding population, but only those who could pay pew rents, not the poor. Securing a popular preacher enabled the proprietor to fill the chapel and recover his expenses. The system was open to numerous abuses. The Lock Chapel was one of the most famous in the early years of the movement.

12. First compiled for the Moorfields chapel, it later was used in the new Tottenham Court Road chapel built by the Countess of Huntingdon in 1756.

13. Martin Madan, *A Collection of Psalm and Hymn Tunes, never before Published* (London: n.p., 1769).

considerable success.[14] During the next one hundred years, many of the collection's 170 hymns were reprinted in subsequent collections.[15]

The innovation of introducing hymns into the services at the Lock Hospital also occurred at other charitable institutions in London, though perhaps without the same fashionable crowd in attendance.[16] Some of these institutions soon had their own collections, though none could match the standards set by Madan. In these collections the hymns focused more on the clientele of the institution, the verses often being pointedly written to underscore either their status,

> When Parents deaf to Nature's Voice
> Their helpless Charge forsook;
> Then Nature's God who heard our cries
> Compassion on us took,[17]

their good fortune,

> Father of Mercy, hear our Pray'rs
> For those who do us Good;
> Whose Love for us a Place prepares,
> And kindly gives us Food,[18]

the course their lives should take,

> Ye Worshippers of Jacob's God,

---

14. See Leaver, "British Hymnody," 1:388.

15. See John Julian, *A Dictionary of Hymnology: Setting Forth the Origin and History of Christian Hymns of All Ages and Nations,* revised edition, with new supplement (London: J. Murray, 1907), 709–710. See also Donald E. Demaray, *The Innovation of John Newton (1725–1807): Synergism of Word and Music in Eighteenth Century Evangelism* (Lewiston, N.Y.: E. Mellen, 1988), 216.

16. James Woodforde noted in his diary (October 8, 1786) the "excellent singing at Magdalen Chapel" (2:275). Magdalen House or Hospital was founded in 1758 for penitent prostitutes. Apparently, Magdalen Chapel maintained an excellent music program into the nineteenth century. William Jones recorded in his diary in 1803 that he was "very much affected with the whole service, particularly the singing." See *The Diary of the Revd. William Jones, 1777–1821,* ed. O. F. Christie (London: Brentano, 1929), 159.

17. *Psalms, Hymns, & Anthems Used in The Chapel of the Hospital for the Maintenance & Education of Exposed & Deserted Young Children* (N.p.: n.p., [177?]), 1. This "hymn" is based upon Psalm 27.

18. [William Riley], *Psalms and Hymns, for the use of The Chapel of the Asylum for Female Orphans* (London: H. Bunce, 1773), 24.

> All ye of Isr'el's Line,
> O praise the Lord, and to your Praise
> Sincere Obedience join,[19]

or one's place within the divine plan,

> The good Man's Way is God's delight,
> He orders all the Steps aright
> Of him that moves by his Command;
> Tho' he sometimes may be distress'd,
> Yet shall he ne'er be quite opprest,
> For God upholds him with his Hand.[20]

The hymnody of the various charitable institutions in London did not affect the parish church immediately. As people experienced Madan's hymns, in particular, they may have urged their consideration by the parish clergy. Unless a clergyman was already inclined toward or in sympathy with Evangelicalism, it is doubtful if such urging effected any change in the congregational song of the parish. The collections themselves, especially Madan's, contributed to the development of hymnody as they became known and as other editors and compilers drew upon their work for new collections.[21]

The Inadequacy of Metrical Psalms

The most often cited reason for the use of hymns was to supplement the metrical versions of the Psalms. The perceived inadequacy of metrical psalms to meet the needs of the worshiping community was not new. Isaac Watts had demonstrated clearly that both metrical psalms and hymns could work to-

---

19. Riley, *Psalms and Hymns*, 6.

20. *The Hymns used at the City of London Lying-in-Hospital, in the City-Road, at the Baptism of Infants, Born There* ([London?]: Printed for Henry Thorowgood, musical instrument-maker and music printer, [1770?]), 20. Another collection published for children was designed to "impress devotional feelings as early as possible." See [A. L. Barbauld], *Hymns in Prose for Children* (London: n.p., 1781), v.

21. For example, Richard Conyers's *A Collection of Psalms and Hymns, From Various Authors: For the Use of Serious and Devout Christians of Every Denomination* (London: n.p., 1767) incorporated nearly two-thirds of Madan's collection. Conyers, Vicar of Helmsley in the North Riding of Yorkshire, was converted to an Evangelical ministry in 1758. Subsequent revisions (1774 and a fifth edition published in York in 1788) provided a solid foundation for the growth of hymnody in the north of England.

gether in singing the praises of God and that both were necessary in the life of the church, each fulfilling their appropriate role. Dissenting churches had embraced this expansion but not without some controversy. For the Church of England, however, the question was far more controversial.[22]

While Madan was introducing hymnody in London, John Berridge (1716–1793) was doing the same in his parish of Everton. Presented to the living of Everton with Tetworth in 1755, Berridge became committed to the Evangelical revival shortly thereafter. In 1760 he compiled a collection for the use of his parish. The collection was divided into nine sections, each section containing selections for specific areas as indicated:

    I. Hymns to be sung in Society
    II. Hymns to be sung before Preaching
    III. Hymns for those who are seeking Redemption through Christ's Blood, even the Forgiveness of their Sins
    IV. Hymns for Believers, that is, for those who have the Knowledge of Salvation by the Forgiveness of their Sins
    V. Hymns for those who have started aside from the Path of God's Commandments, or are in Danger of sliding back through manifold Temptations
    VI. Hymns for Morning and Evening, and for the great Festivals
    VII. Hymns for the Sacrament
    VIII. Hymns for the Sick, and funeral Hymns
    IX. Hymns before and after Eating, Travelling, &c.[23]

Drawn chiefly from the Wesleys, with some hymns from Watts and a few original texts, the collection was designed to satisfy several needs. First, it provided a wealth of material for use in the society meetings, more than one-half of the collection being so designated.[24] Second, the collection included a number of items for private and family use. And third, Berridge provided material for use in the liturgy of the church, including hymns to be sung during communion, before the sermon, and for feast days.

The overall effect of including selections from this collection in the liturgy, coupled with Berridge's preaching, must have enlivened wor-

---

22. This is a tentative assessment of the degree of controversy within various denominations in the eighteenth century. Additional research is needed before one can make a judgment in this area.

23. John Berridge, *A Collection of Divine Songs, Designed chiefly for the Religious Societies of Churchmen, In the Neighbourhood of Everton, Bedfordshire* (London: n.p., 1760).

24. Of the 376 hymns in the collection, 204 were designated for use in society meetings.

ship. In the following years Berridge's doctrinal views changed, moving away from those of John Wesley.[25] As a result Berridge attempted to suppress his first collection.[26] Although he believed that his early work was "tunable enough," the fact that the hymns had been "chiefly cast in a celebrated Foundery" (a reference to Wesley) limited their ability to sound a "clear gospel tone. . . . Human wisdom and strength, perfection and merit," in Berridge's estimation, gave "Sion's bells a Levitical twang, and [drowned] the mellow tone of the gospel outright." During a six-month illness in 1773, Berridge wrote new hymns and edited existing ones to reflect more accurately his theological views, publishing them twelve years later in 1785.[27] Berridge's hymns (there were no metrical psalms) contributed little to the development of hymnody. His work, however, indicated how willing some were to abandon the use of metrical psalms entirely and to embrace with equal vigor the use of hymns.

Not everyone was as eager as Berridge to replace metrical psalms with hymns. The majority of advocates preferred to take a more deliberate and cautious approach to the introduction of hymns. For example, Thomas Cannon did not wish to exclude the metrical psalms from use in "our Established Church" (that is, the Church of England). He granted "that there was some Gospel Light in the Days of David, as is to be seen in his Book of Psalms, . . . yet the Light of the Gospel in and under the New Testament exceeds that as far as the Light of the Sun does the Light of the Moon."[28] He did wish, however, to remove those portions of the Psalms of David not applicable to the Christian state. Selected hymns would supplement the remaining metrical psalms.

Equally cautious was John Smith, rector of Nantwich. The title of his collection, *Select Portions of the Psalms appointed to be Sung in Churches: Taken chiefly from the New Version; with Hymns Collected*

---

25. A good number of Evangelicals were offended by Wesley's belief that the offer of salvation was for all (Arminianism). By the 1770s Berridge became a strong supporter of the Calvinist doctrine of election.

26. According to Benson, Berridge destroyed "every copy he could secure." See Louis F. Benson, *The English Hymn: Its Development and Use in Worship,* (G. H. Doran, 1915; reprint edition, Richmond, Va.: John Knox, 1962), 331.

27. John Berridge, *Sion's Songs, or Hymns: Composed For the Use of them that love and follow the Lord Jesus Christ in Sincerity* (London: Printed for Vallance and Conder, 1785), preface. The use of hymns to convey particular theological views became a point of controversy as their use increased.

28. T[homas] Cannon, *Select Psalms and Hymns, for the use of St. John's Chapel, West-Lane, Walworth, and the City Chapel, London,* 2nd ed. revised and corrected (London: Minerva, [1793?], preface.

from various Authors, and intended occasionally to be sung in public Worship, succinctly stated the attitude expressed by many toward hymnody as well as suggested the issue that would become the center of the controversy in the next century.[29] First, the singing of metrical psalms still occupied the "noblest Part of divine Worship," as indicated by its placement in the title.[30] Second, hymns were primarily to be used as supplements to the psalters; and third (eventually the central issue), metrical psalms were "appointed to be Sung in Churches."

Many of the reasons given by Smith for producing his collection were shared by other compilers: The performance of psalmody was in need of reformation; the "injudicious Choice of Verses" and the "lifeless Manner of singing them" raised concerns; the fact that only a few participated in the praise of God was an affront to God's glory.[31] Smith also argued that unless one was willing to sing "here below" how could one be "duly qualified to enter the Regions of the Blessed, and join with the heavenly Choir above[?]"[32]

Smith's selections came primarily from the *New Version,* which he believed to be "well calculated to shew forth the Praises of our God, and to edify our Souls." Moreover, if any portion of the "Old Version" was desired for use, one could "find them at the End of your Common Prayer Books."[33] While recognizing the priority of the Psalms, Smith also saw the need for a more Christological hymnody.[34]

Richard De Courcy also acknowledged that the book of Psalms had "proved a rich fund for hymnal composition," yet regretted that those that had little bearing upon the Christian life continued to be made available,

---

29. John Smith, *Select Portions of the Psalms appointed to be Sung in Churches: Taken chiefly from the New Version; with Hymns Collected from various Authors, and intended occasionally to be sung in public Worship,* 2nd ed., with additions (Nantwich: E. Snelson, 1786).

30. Smith, *Select Portions,* 1.

31. Smith, *Select Portions,* 1. Interestingly, Smith, in a somewhat similar fashion to S. S. Wesley in the nineteenth century, held that unless a person could sing well it might be better not to sing at all: "Some of you perhaps may not be qualified to perform this Duty [i.e., singing] properly at present: You had better therefore content yourselves by joining with the rest rather in Heart than Voice" (*Select Portions,* 2).

32. Smith, *Select Portions,* 2. See also the preface to *A Collection of Psalms & Hymns, from various authors; adapted chiefly to Public Worship* (Lancaster: H. Walmsley, 1780): "Singing is the grand employment of Heaven."

33. Smith, *Select Portions,* 2. Because a number of various printings of the Book of Common Prayer included the "Old Version," some found support for their arguments that it was the "appointed" version for use in the liturgy.

34. Smith, *Select Portions,* 2.

thus limiting the opportunity for including metrical versions of other passages of scripture.[35] De Courcy believed that through "versification" of a more comprehensive range of scripture the deficiencies of psalmody could be overcome. De Courcy, however, was unable to recognize how thin the line was that separated "versification" of scripture and hymns from "*human* composition."[36] The first was entirely acceptable, whereas the second was highly questionable. Even so, De Courcy included in his collections items that, although containing scriptural allusions, were closer to the latter than the former, for example, "Hark, the herald-angels sing," "Jesus, the all-atoning Lamb," "Come ye that love the Lord," and "Christ the Lord is ris'n today!"

Whereas Cannon, Smith, and De Courcy represented the more conservative approach to modifying the prevailing practice of singing only metrical psalms,[37] others were not as conservative. R. Elliot, for example, responding to those who held that "nothing ought to be sung in Public Worship" except that provided by the "inspired Word," argued,

If this Objection against the Use of Psalms, &c. Composed by private Christians, and which are not recorded in the Old and New Testament, is of any Weight, it must be owing to some divine Prohibition, or scriptural Disapprobation of them. But I know of no such prohibition in the Word of God, either directly or indirectly.[38]

35. Richard De Courcy, *A Collection of Psalms and Hymns, Extracted from different Authors,* 2nd ed. (Shrewsbury: T. Wood, 1782), iii. De Courcy published the first edition in 1775. The prefaces in both editions are identical. In 1801 Robert Banister attempted to provide his congregation with metrical versions of the whole of scripture, from Genesis to Revelation, in 451 selections. There were only thirty-three metrical versions of the Psalms included. See Robert Banister, *Scriptural Hymns, Selected for the Congregation of All Saints' Church, Liverpool* (Liverpool: H. Forshaw, 1801).

36. De Courcy, 1782, vi.

37. Even more conservative was the work of Richard Cecil. Cecil compiled his collection apparently at the request of his congregation, who desired to discontinue the "Old Version," but apparently did not desire to sing hymns since none were included. See also *Select Portions of the Psalms, Both old and new Version: Also. A Collection of Hymns and Anthems, As they are sung in the Parish Church of Cranbrook* (Cranbrook: S. Waters, n.d.). This collection included all 150 Psalms and only nine hymns.

38. R. Elliot, *Psalms and Hymns and Spiritual Songs: in Two Parts. The First being a Collection from Various Authors. The Second Part, Together with a Preface on the Nature, Use and Benefit of Divine Psalmody* (London: Printed for the author, 1769), viii.

Sharing Elliot's views, David Simpson, St. John's College, Cambridge, published his first collection in 1776.[39] After ordination, Simpson took his first curacy in Macclesfield (Midlands) and "had the unusual experience of being violently ejected from the pulpit by his rector."[40] As a consequence a new church was built for him, and in 1776 Simpson published a collection for his congregation.[41] Simpson recognized the pastoral necessity for continuing to make available selections from the "Old Version" and the *New Version*.[42] Simpson also recognized that metrical psalms alone were inadequate to meet the needs of the faithful. Hymns drawn from the riches of scripture (not the Psalms alone) and hymns congruent with scripture (though not strict paraphrases) used in the praise of God could produce "more lasting and permanent Impressions in the Mind, than those which accompany any transient Form of Words that are uttered in the ordinary Method of religious Worship."[43] Evidence was sufficiently abundant, Simpson argued, to satisfy "serious and candid Christians that there is no Impropriety in our making use of Hymns as well as Psalms in our religious Adoration of almighty God."[44]

The foremost reason, in Simpson's estimation, for employing hymns in the praise of God was grounded in scripture itself. Numerous passages in the New Testament provided examples of what kind of songs Christians should sing, songs clearly not restricted to the Psalms of David. Moreover, the fact that the early church maintained the practice gave further support to the use of hymns in "reasonable Service of the Gospel."[45]

---

39. David Simpson, *Select Psalms and Hymns* (Macclesfield: n.p., 1776). A second edition was published in 1780 and a new edition in 1795. The collection of 1780 included 150 metrical psalms and 491 hymns.

40. L. E. Elliott-Binns, *The Early Evangelicals: A Religious and Social Study* (Greenwich: Seabury, 1953), 305.

41. Benson, *English Hymn*, 335.

42. Benson is less than accurate in stating that Simpson and others were not concerned "with the old metrical Psalmody" (*English Hymn*, 335). The fact that these editors continued to include metrical psalms in their collections indicates a certain appreciation of the esteem that selected metrical psalms enjoyed. See also William Bromley Cadogan, *Psalms and Hymns*, 2nd ed. (London: W. Justins, 1787). Cadogan maintained an equal balance between metrical psalms and hymns, including 150 of each.

43. D[avid] Simpson, *A Collection of Psalms and Hymns And Spiritual Songs: For the Use of Christians Of Every Denomination*, 2nd ed., with an appendix (Macclesfield: T. Bayley, 1780), xi.

44. Simpson, 1780, xviii.

45. Simpson, 1780, xiv–xviii.

Despite this support, Simpson had certain concerns with regard to
hymnody. Most important was the character and type of tune to be used.
For him,

> Brisk, solemn, lively Tunes, [were] best adapted to awaken holy Affections.
> Avoid therefore such as are light, frothy, and fantastic; and let all the Con-
> gregation join together in one grand Chorus. Such Words, such Tunes, such
> Singing as leaves us dull, stupid, and languid, answer no valuable End what-
> ever. They are neither pleasing to God, nor profitable to Man.[46]

Although the arguments employed by Simpson in support of hymns aided
their increasing use, the arguments were not unique. Simpson's collection,
however, played an important role in the transition, introducing several
new hymns of lasting merit.

As the number of collections increased, a number of supporters of
hymnody believed that there was still room for improvement. Edward
Smyth, making no attempt to hide his opinion of his work, is representative. He wrote,

> Though many different Publications of this kind have already appeared, yet
> as the composition of some of them greatly disparages the dignity of the sub-
> ject, and as none of them contain such a number of Hymns as is necessary for
> the several occasions that present themselves, the Editor of this Work has
> taken uncommon pains to render it complete, and, on an impartial examina-
> tion, he thinks it will be acknowledged it has many advantages above others
> of a similar nature.[47]

As others had before him, Smyth argued that "singing has been always
considered as a part of divine worship," drawing from scripture to sub-
stantiate his position. He acknowledged, however, that some objected,
"What need is there of introducing new hymns? Are not the Psalms of
David fully sufficient for us?"[48] In reply, Smyth stated, "We are commanded to sing *hymns,* as well as *psalms,*" for "fine Music . . . has the

---

46. Simpson, 1780, v. This was probably an attack upon the increasing use of secular tunes adapted to sacred texts as well as his dislike of the "methodistical" tunes.

47. Edward Smyth, *A Choice Collection of Hymns, Psalms, and Anthems; Principally designed for the Congregation attending Bethesda-Chapel; but calculated
for all Denominations of Christians, who desire to worship God in spirit and in
truth* (Dublin: B. Dugdale, 1785), iii.

48. Smyth, 1785, vii.

power of raising grateful sensations, and engaging the heart in *God's* service." Moreover,

> though it be allowed that *David*, that sweet *Singer of Israel*, was moved by the *Holy Ghost*, when he composed his Psalms, and that they were sung in the Temple, yet, as we are under a dispensation widely different, more spiritual and evangelical . . ., which was only *the shadow of good things to come*, being now abolished, the *shadow*, consequently, gives place to the *substance*, the *prophecies* to their *fulfilment*, and the *types*, to their great *Antitype*.[49]

Although many Evangelicals were strong supporters of hymnody, at least one Evangelical voice, William Romaine, was raised in strong opposition. His views were expressed in an essay designed "to restore the singing of them [i.e., metrical psalms] in the congregation to their primitive usefulness."[50] Like others before him, Romaine "lamented, that all singing of psalms at present is not upon the right plan, and does not answer the end of its institution." His lament, however, was not based upon the "contempt, with which it is treated by the age, or of the neglect of it by many professors, but of the prevailing abuses of it among them, who would be thought altogether Christians."[51]

In closely reasoned arguments, Romaine challenged those who would see the metrical psalms laid aside in favor of hymns. To those who argued that the New Testament church needed hymns that reflected the glories of Christ, Romaine responded that that "is the subject of the book of psalms."[52] In addition to the prevailing lack of understanding regarding the content of the Psalms, Romaine deplored the fact that not every one joined in the singing. He wrote,

> It [i.e., psalm singing] was to be the service of the whole church. All were to join; whereas among us it is performed by some few, and they are sometimes set by themselves in a singing gallery, or in a corner of the church, where they sing to be admired for their fine voices, and others hear them for their entertainment. This is a vile prostitution of church music, and contrary to the letter and spirit both of the old testament and also of the new.[53]

Contrary to those who found support for the singing of hymns in Paul's injunction to sing "psalms, hymns, and spiritual songs," Romaine argued that

---

49. Smyth, 1785, vii–viii.
50. [William Romaine], *An Essay on Psalmody* (London: n.p., 1775), iii.
51. Romaine, 87.
52. Romaine, 8–9.
53. Romaine, 95–96.

this referred to three distinct types of Psalms.[54] In fact, he noted, the reformers of the sixteenth-century English church

> certainly understood those proper psalms to be descriptive of Christ, and took them in the same sense our Lord and his apostles did, who have quoted the book of psalms eighty-two times. Their manner of quoting it demonstrates, that they took it for granted it was written concerning Christ.[55]

To those who would lay the metrical psalms aside, Romaine countered that this would be to lay aside the divinely inspired word of God.[56] He noted that, already,

> [t]hey [i.e., metrical psalms] are quite rejected in many congregations, as if there were no such hymns given by the inspiration of God, and as if they were not left for the use of the church and to be sung in the congregations. Human compositions are preferred to divine. Man's poetry is exalted above the poetry of the holy Ghost. Is this right? The hymns, which he revealed for the use of the church, that we might have words suitable to the praises of Immanuel, are quite set aside: By which means the word of man has got a preference in the church above the word of God, yea so far as to exclude it entirely from public worship.[57]

The reasons, according to Romaine, for this development were twofold: First, people had "lost sight of the meaning of the psalms," and second, the "general complaint against Sternhold and Hopkins."[58] Thus,

---

54. This is based on Romaine's interpretation of three Hebrew words *Thebilim, Zemer,* and *SHeR:* "These three names take in the subject of the whole book [i.e., the book of Psalms]—the *hymns* contain the praises of Immanuel, our sun of righteousness—the *psalms* treat of his taking our nature, and in it being cut off for his people, that through his death they might live—the *songs* celebrate the glories of his kingdom, both in earth and heaven, in time and eternity" (30–31). Romaine may have based his interpretation upon the work of E. H., *Scripture Proof for Singing of Scripture Psalms, Hymns and Spiritual Songs: or, An Answer to several Queries and Objections frequently made use of to stumble and turn aside young Christians from their Duty to God in Singing of Psalms, Gathered out of the Scriptures of Truth. To which is added The Testimony of some Learned Men, to prove that Scripture Psalms are intended by all those three words, Psalms, Hymns and Songs, used by the Apostle* (London: Printed by J. Astwood, 1696).

55. Romaine, 11. Romaine based his argument on the manner in which the reformers used the Psalms in the lectionary cycle of the Prayer Book.

56. Romaine, 10.

57. Romaine, 110–111.

58. Romaine, 111. With regard to the "Old Version" Romaine wrote, "Their translation was treated, as poor flat stuff. The wits ridiculed it. The prophane [*sic*] blasphemed it. Good men did not defend it."

hymn-makers . . . suffered to thrust out the psalms to make way for their own compositions: of which they have supplied us with a vast variety, collection upon collection, and in use too, new hymns starting up daily—appendix added to appendix—sung in many congregations, yea admired by very high professors to such a degree, that the psalms are become quite obsolete, and the singing of them is now almost as despicable among the modern religious, as it was some time ago among the prophane.[59]

Romaine was not entirely opposed to the use of human compositions by Christians; such were not sinful when used in private devotion. They were, however, not fit to replace the Psalms. His "complaint" was

against preferring mens [*sic*] poems to the good word of God, and preferring them to it in the church. I have no quarrel with Dr. Watts, or any living or dead versifier. I would not wish all their poems burnt. My concern is to see christian [*sic*] congregations shut out divinely inspired psalms, and take in Dr. Watts's flights of fancy, as if the words of a poet were better than the words of a prophet, or as if the wit of a man was to be preferred to the wisdom of God. . . . Why should Dr. Watts, or any hymn-maker not only take the precedence of the holy Ghost, but also thrust him entirely out of the church?[60]

Although Romaine was willing to make certain concessions in the use of nonbiblical material, he drew the line at supplementing the metrical psalms with hymns and certainly at their removal from the services of the church entirely.[61] Romaine did "not desire to see any innovation in our public worship," observing that the present moment was "no favorable season for it."[62] Although Romaine's work provided support to those who continued to favor metrical psalms and who opposed the introduction of hymns, it did not stem the tide. As the century progressed, the inadequacy of metrical psalms to address the needs of the congregation became increasingly apparent. The use of hymns to supplement metrical psalms and to address their perceived deficiencies likewise increased.

---

59. Romaine, 111–112.

60. Romaine, 112–113.

61. Romaine was so opposed to hymnody that his collection not only contained no hymns, it did not include even those hymns (e.g., "While Shepherds watched their flocks by night") that had won almost universal acclaim, even by those opposed to the use of hymns.

62. Romaine, 134.

An Enlivened Worship

A number of those who saw a need for supplementing metrical psalms with hymns also expressed the belief that the use of hymns would enhance the services of the church. For them the contrast between the vigor of the Methodist society meetings and the often noted dryness of the parish liturgy could not be ignored any longer. Hymns, in their opinion, would not only alleviate the deficiencies of metrical psalms but would enliven the liturgy.

Although many Evangelicals embraced hymnody as a means of revitalizing parish worship, none, perhaps, did so with more enthusiasm than Thomas Haweis, rector of All Saints, Aldwinkle, Northamptonshire.[63] In his collection of 1792, Haweis argued strongly for a hymnody that reflected the "power of vital Christianity."[64] Haweis observed that a vast difference existed between the present age and the age of the "primitive" church: "Hymns to the Saviour's praise then gladdened the hearts of the faithful, and prepared them for the crown of martyrdom. The glorious subject of their songs was a crucified Jesus."[65] In his opinion, the metrical psalms of Sternhold and Hopkins and Tate and Brady, were far removed from the poetry of the "primitive" church.

Arguing against the "more enlightened modern divines," who had "discovered" that the "joy" of the early church was "enthusiasm, and their religious delusion," Haweis sought to enable every worshiper to share in Christ's "incommunicable glory."[66] Haweis, like many (including those who were not in favor of hymns), lamented the prevailing standards of congregational song:

---

63. A devout Evangelical, Calvinist in theology, Haweis was a regular preacher in the Countess of Huntingdon's proprietary chapels. When the countess was forced to register them as Dissenting Congregations under the Toleration Act, Haweis remained with her while others returned to the Church of England. The transition did not change his understanding of the power of hymnody but gave him more freedom to express it. It should also be noted that Haweis was Madan's assistant at the Lock Hospital.

64. T[homas] Haweis, *Carmina Christo; or, Hymns to the Saviour: Designed for the Use and Comfort of those who Worship the Lamb that was Slain* (Bath: S. Hazard, 1792), preface. A second edition was published in 1795 containing 141 hymns, only two more than the first edition, and a new edition in 1808 contained 256 hymns. See also W. Day, *A Collection of Psalms and Hymns, for Public Worship* (Evesham: J. Agg, 1795).

65. Haweis, 1792, preface.

66. Haweis, 1792, preface. It is possible that Haweis was referring to Bishop Porteus as one of the "enlightened modern divines," because Porteus, in his *Charge* of 1790, had argued against hymnody in favor of metrical psalms.

Even in our public worship the voice of joy and gladness is too commonly silent, unless in that shameful mode of psalmody, now almost confined to the wretched solo of a parish clerk, or to a few persons huddled together in one corner of the church, who sing to the praise and glory of themselves, for the entertainment, or oftener for the weariness of the rest of the congregation: an absurdity too glaring to be overlooked, and too shocking to be ridiculous.[67]

The use of hymns, Haweis believed, would do much in achieving a reform in parochial psalmody and bringing the joy of the early church into the present church. Haweis, apparently, found additional support for this departure from custom in the Injunctions of 1559 (the relevant clause being printed on the second page of the collection), although he did not state this explicitly.[68]

The use of hymns was also seen by many as a means of complementing the observance of the feast days appointed in the Book of Common Prayer. The lack of suitable portions of the Psalms for these feasts was stated often as the reason for including hymns in the liturgy of the church. Thomas Biddulph, for example, made this clear in the preface to his collection and in the title.[69] James Stewart also made it clear that his selection of hymns was based upon "either . . . the subject of our Festivals, or from some part of the Services of the Day."[70]

---

67. Haweis, 1792, preface.

68. This view was shared by others. The anonymous compiler of a collection published in 1798 also cited the Injunctions of 1559 on the facing page of the hymn section of his work. See *Select Portions of Psalms, taken from The Old and New Versions, and that of Mr. Merrick: to which are added A Few Hymns from approved Authors: Compiled for the use of the Congregation of the Holy Trinity Church in Halifax* (Halifax: E. Jacobs, 1798).

69. Tho[mas] T. Biddulph, *Portions of the Psalms of David, Together with a Selection of Hymns, Accommodated to the Service of the Church of England, on Sundays and other Holy Seasons of Public Worship Which She Observes* (Bristol: W. Pine and Son, 1802). See also [John W. Cunningham], *Select Portions of Psalms, Extracted from Various Versions, and adapted to Public Worship. With an Appendix, containing Hymns for the Principal Festivals of the Church of England* (London: Ellerton and Henderson, 1811) and [John Venn], *Select Portions of Psalms, Extracted from Various Versions, and Adapted to Public Worship, With an Appendix, Containing Hymns for the Principal Festivals of the Church of England*, 2nd ed. (London: March and Teape, 1802). Richard Cecil published his *Psalms of David* in 1785, but it was not until 1806 that he added an appendix titled: *Hymns for the principal festivals of the Church of England*.

70. James H. Stewart, *A Selection of Psalms & Hymns, Adapted to the Service of the Church of England; Revised for the use of Percy Chapel, Charlotte Street, Fitzroy Square* (London: W. M. Thiselton, 1813), preface.

Basil Woodd, apparently, was the first to conceive the plan of compiling a hymnal that would be a companion to the Prayer Book. Published in 1798, the purpose given in the title, *The Psalms of David, And other Portions of the Sacred Scriptures, Arranged according to the order of the Church of England, For every Sunday in the Year; also for the Saints' Days, Holy Communion, and other Services,* was meticulously executed in the contents.[71] For every appointed day, Woodd provided a metrical psalm for the introit (as provided for in the rubrics of the 1549 Prayer Book). Hymns were selected to reflect the proper of the day; other hymns were chosen for use at communion, for Baptism and other occasions, and a few for general use. The effect of this collection was significant, for it demonstrated that hymnody could reflect the character of the liturgy of the Church of England.[72]

The desire to enliven the liturgy of the church through the introduction of hymns also brought forth concerns regarding the appropriateness of certain kinds of hymns and tunes. William Riley, for example, was among the first to note the dangers posed by the growing use of hymns, especially the music being used. Echoing others, Riley

---

71. Basil Woodd, *The Psalms of David, And other Portions of the Sacred Scriptures, Arranged according to the order of the Church of England, For every Sunday in the Year; also for the Saints' Days, Holy Communion, and other Services* (London: Watts and Bridgewater, [c. 1798]). Woodd may have been inspired by the work of John Jones, vicar of Alconbury. In 1749 Jones published anonymously his proposals (*Free and Candid Disquisitions relating to the Church of England, and the Means of advancing Religion therein*) for reforming the liturgy of the church. Jones was a disciple of Samuel Clarke, who had proposed revisions of the Prayer Book in 1724. See Alexander Elliott Peaston, *The Prayer Book Reform Movement in the Eighteenth Century* (Oxford: B. Blackwell, 1940); Norman Sykes, *Church and State in England in the Eighteenth Century* (Cambridge: Cambridge University Press, 1934):386–388. Among the proposals was a plea for the inclusion of hymns and New Testament passages for singing. Although Convocation failed to consider his proposals, Jones's work was widely known (Peaston, 5–7).

72. Benson argued that it established the future course by demonstrating that hymns could be an integral part of liturgical worship (*English Hymn,* 351). In marked contrast to the organizational principles of Woodd's collection, Charles Simeon's *A Collection of Psalms and Hymns from Various Authors, chiefly designed for the use of Publick Worship* (Cambridge: J. Archdeacon and J. Burges, [1795]) continued to follow a topical pattern (e.g., "Times and Seasons"). The trend toward a liturgical collection ultimately prevailed in the Church of England.

was concerned over the neglect of psalmody as well as its bad performance.[73] Of greater concern to him was the type of music that was becoming increasingly popular. Riley charged the Methodists with full responsibility for this grievous development:

> It may not be improper to make some Observations on the Tunes which are used by the *Methodists,* especially as some of them are creeping into the Churches, being introduced chiefly at Morning and Evening Lectures, where the Congregations, being mostly of that Cast, not only choose such Lecturers as suit their own Turn of Mind, but will also pay the Clerk and Organist to stay away, that Two of their own People may supply their places; by which Means they have every Thing performed in their own Way: It is true they have not yet ventured to sing Ballad-Tunes, as at the Tabernacle, Foundery, and elsewhere; because by such a Procedure they would doubtless be forbid the Use of the Church, but the Tunes they commonly use are generally too light and airy for Church-Music; and consequently have nothing in their Composure that may excite a true Spirit of Devotion.[74]

Although objecting to a certain style of tune, that is, tunes that had dotted rhythms (e.g., a dotted quarter note followed by an eighth note), a broad vocal range, and repeated phrases, Riley gave qualified support to hymnody, yet preferred metrical psalms.[75] Riley held that "Church-Music," in contrast to the "light and airy" tunes of the Methodists, "ought to be grave, serious, noble and divine; to raise the Affections of the Soul, with the proper Passions of Devotion; *viz.* Joy, Reverence and Admiration; and

---

73. William Riley, *Parochial Music Corrected. Containing Remarks on the Performance of Psalmody in Country Churches, and on the ridiculous and profane Manner of Singing practised by the Methodists; Reflections on the bad Performance of Psalmody in London, Westminster, &c. with some Hints for the Improvement of it in Public Worship; Observations on the Choice and Qualifications of Parish-Clerks; the Utility of Teaching Charity-Children Psalmody and Hymns; the Use of Organs, and the Performance of Organists* (London: n.p., 1762), 1.

74. Riley, *Parochial Music,* 3.

75. The tune HELMSLEY first appeared in John Wesley's *Sacred Melody: or a choice Collection of Psalm and Hymn Tunes,* 2nd ed. (London: n.p., 1765). Thomas Olivers supposedly had heard a melody whistled on the street and reworked it into a hymn tune for the text "Lo, he comes with clouds descending" by Charles Wesley. The first line of the tune bears a marked similarity to a tune in Thomas Arne's *Thomas and Sally,* an *opera buffa.* It is an excellent example of what came to be known as a "methodistical" tune.

not the rapturous Strains of unhallowed Love, which pollute the Soul, and fire it with a wanton Passion."[76] Riley concluded,

> Since Music then is capable of being made acceptable and well-pleasing to GOD, and an Help to Devotion, I hope the Established Church will never follow the Example of these frantic Enthusiasts, in *stripping the carnal Lover of his* MOVING *Strains and* MELTING *Measures;* especially as there is such a Variety of Compositions which are far more suitable to the all-pure Worship of Him, who will not accept of that which is devoted to his Enemy.[77]

Although differences regarding what congregational song should or should not be used in the liturgy of the church existed, the expression of concern indicates that the eighteenth-century church was more interested in the performance standards, content, character, and implementation of worship than has been recognized by many scholars.[78]

---

76. Riley, *Parochial Music,* 6. The tunes included in this collection conformed to the typical metrical psalm tunes of the day.

77. Riley, *Parochial Music,* 10. Riley related this exchange between a Methodist and an acquaintance who asked, "How they [i.e., the Methodists] could act so inconsistently, and be so profane, as to sing Hymns to the Deity in such wanton Strains? received this for Answer; That 'All Sounds are in themselves innocent, unless made otherwise by corrupt or profane Words; which he looked upon to be the Case with all Ballad-Tunes; but by applying other Words to them, those innocent Melodies are rescued from the Service of Sin and Satan, and lifted into the Causes of GOD and Religion'" (*Parochial Music,* 6). Compare Charles Wesley's verse:

> Who on the part of God will rise,
>   Innocent sound recover,
> Fly on the prey, and take the prize,
>   Plunder the carnal lover;
> Strip him of every moving strain,
>   Every melting measure,
> Music in virtue's cause retain,
>   Rescue the holy pleasure?

Cited by Nicholas Temperley, *The Music of the English Parish Church,* 2 vols. (Cambridge: Cambridge University Press, 1979), 1:210.

78. William J. Gatens, for example, described worship at the start of the nineteenth century thus: "Services were conducted in a perfunctory and listless fashion. Parish music, if any, was often confined to metrical psalmody dispensed from a west gallery, often inharmoniously, to a generally silent congregation." See his *Victorian Cathedral Music in Theory and Practice* (Cambridge: Cambridge University Press, 1986), 6. Although there was much to complain about in the performance of psalmody, evidence indicates that many were passionately concerned and sought vigorously to bring about improvements.

Doctrinal Concerns

Many who advocated hymns saw clearly the enormous possibilities for strengthening a congregation's understanding of the faith. Nonconformist hymn writers during the first half of the century had used hymns as a means of reenforcing the themes of their sermons.[79] The Wesleys valued hymnody's ability to teach the essentials of the Christian faith.[80] John Berridge, who disagreed with John Wesley's views, sought to make clear his theological views through his second collection of hymns. The power of hymnody to convey religious truths was duly noted by Thomas Haweis:

> I am persuaded also that no other method of communicating the knowledge of religious truths hath been attended with happier effects, or serves to leave deeper impression of them on the memory and conscience of the common people, than sacred songs. And for whom should we delight to labour but for these? 'To the poor the Gospel is preached.'[81]

Many recognized the ability of hymns to communicate the Evangelical message even if there were differences regarding what that message was. Hymns were especially suitable for those who, because of limited education, had difficulty in grasping abstract theological concepts when expressed in written form or in reasoned sermons. The repeated use of simple expressions of basic doctrine in the poetry of hymns, in contrast, brought home the teachings given through other forms.[82] Perhaps no one expressed this understanding more clearly than the author of the preface to Philip Doddridge's collection, Job Orton:

79. As late as 1782 this was still being done by at least one Nonconformist minister. See John Fawcett, *Hymns: Adapted to the Circumstances of Public Worship, and Private Devotion* (Leeds: G. Wright and Son, 1782). Nonconformists, however, were not the only ones to use congregational song to stress a particular view. The clerk of one parish supported his vicar's views on the Bill for the Naturalization of Jews (1753) by "selecting staves proper for the occasion." See Charles J. Abbey, *The English Church and its Bishops 1700–1800,* 2 vols. (London: Longmans and Green, 1887), 1:215.

80. See Ted A. Campbell, *The Religion of the Heart: A Study of European Religious Life in the Seventeenth and Eighteenth Centuries* (Columbia: University of South Carolina Press, 1991), 121–122; Erik Routley, *The Musical Wesleys* (New York: Oxford University Press, 1968), 30; D. W. Bebbington, *Evangelicalism in Modern Britain: A History from the 1730s to the 1980s* (London: U. Hyman, 1989), 68.

81. Haweis, 1792, preface. Several scholars have noted the Evangelicals' use of hymns to convey religious teaching. See, for example, Kenneth Hylson-Smith, *Evangelicals in the Church of England, 1734–1984* (Edinburgh: T. and T. Clark, 1989) 54, 99; Bebbington, 61, 68.

82. See Hylson-Smith, 54.

These Hymns being composed to be sung, after the Author had been preaching on the texts prefixed to them, it was his Design, that they should bring
over again the leading Thoughts in the Sermon, and naturally express and
warmly enforce those devout Sentiments, which he hoped were then rising in
the Minds of his Hearers, and help to fix them on the Memory and Heart.[83]

It was perhaps inevitable that the didactic capacity of hymnody would become a point of controversy.[84] Why should the church use anything but
scripture to teach the faith, many asked, failing to see that the metrical
psalms themselves were one step removed from scripture.[85]

Whereas Haweis and Berridge were representative of the extremes, it is
probable that most took a more conservative approach toward the use of
hymns to teach doctrine. Charles Abbot, for example, introduced Miller's
collection of metrical psalms into his parish, but found it inadequate:

Having used every effort in my power to establish an Evening Lecture in my
Parish [St. Mary's, Bedford], . . . I found the want of a second Psalm for my
Lecture—These hymns were written with a view to supply that defect—It is
hoped that if a want of poetical merit should be discovered in them, that the
candid Critic will consider the views with which they were written, a desire
of advancing the doctrines of our Church, and at the same time of furthering
the general interest of Christianity.[86]

---

83. Philip Doddridge, *Hymns founded on Various Texts in the Holy Scriptures.
Published from the Author's Manuscript by Job Orton* (Salop: J. Orton, 1755), iv.
Charles Simeon also supported the use of hymns to illustrate doctrine expressed in
sermons and to underscore its appeals. See his *A Collection of Psalms and Hymns
from Various Authors, chiefly designed for the use of Publick Worship* (Cambridge:
J. Archdeacon and J. Burges, [1795]).

84. For a discussion of the theological content of hymns in the eighteenth century,
see Lowell B. Harlan, "Theology of Eighteenth Century English Hymns," *Historical
Magazine of the Protestant Episcopal Church* 48:2 (June 1979):167–193.

85. For an extremely conservative approach, see, for example, *An Introduction
to Reform Singing: Being An Essay to Sing the Holy Scriptures; Or Repeat them
Melodiously in Churches, Instead of Singing Erroneous Rhymes and Human Compositions* (London: n.p., [1791?]). The anonymous author of this work argued for
the exclusive use of scripture.

86. Charles Abbot, *Hymns Composed for the Use of St. Mary's Church, in the
Town of Bedford* (Bedford: W. Smith, 1791), preface. Abbot probably had introduced
to his parish George [W. A.] Drummond and Edward Miller's *Select Portions of the
New Version of Psalms, For every Sunday throughout the year; with the Principal
Festivals and Fasts for the use of Parish Churches. The words selected by the Rev.
George Hay Drummond; the music selected, adapted, and composed by Edward
Miller* (London: W. Miller, 1790). The seventh edition was published in 1791.

The fifty-four hymns in the collection may have served Abbot's purpose, but they lacked sufficient "poetical merit" to commend them to a wider audience. Even so, the fact that Abbot produced a collection of hymns for the use of his parish indicated that attitudes toward hymns were shifting as the end of the century drew near.

A different approach toward the use of congregational song to further the teachings of the church was taken by Beilby Porteus, bishop of London. Like many others, Porteus was distressed by the poor level of psalmody in both rural and city parishes. In his *Charge* of 1790 to the clergy, Porteus added his voice to those who called for reform. His reasons for addressing this issue were expressed in his notebook (May 10, 1790):

> With respect to our Psalmody it was [at?] so low an ebb both in London and in the Country that it became highly necessary to recommend a little more attention to it: especially as Dr. Burney had in his History of Music very insidiously taken great pains to ridicule and discredit the rise of Psalmody in our Churches, and to introduce Choral and Cathedral Music in the Room of it. Many Churches and Chapels in London had already adopted his ideas, and at their Charity Sermons Men and Women Singers, from [ ], Vauxhall, the Play-Houses and Operas were brought to sing Hymns and Anthems for the benefit of the Children. [ ] in one or two Churches there had been Musical Entertainment on a Tuesday Evening without either Prayers or Sermon. To prevent therefore our Churches from being turned into Concert Rooms it seemed highly requisite to put some stop to this musical Madness, and to bring back our Psalmody if possible to its antient Purity and Simplicity.[87]

In his opinion, one avenue for achieving the much sought after reform had not been considered. Sunday schools, he argued, provided a ready vehicle for improving parochial psalmody:

> This, I know, has been already done in several parishes with great success, especially in those where Sunday-Schools have been established; in which it is often a part, and a most useful part of their education to exercise and improve the scholars in psalm-singing, with which they are in general much delighted, and in more respects than one greatly benefited. By these means a considerable choir of well taught young people may in a few years be formed in every church, who will serve as guides and instructors to the rest of the congregation; and when it is considered that there are now near 300,000 sunday [sic] scholars in various parts of the kingdom, if one third of them can be taught to perform the best Psalm tunes tolerably well, these useful institutions

87. MS 2103 (Lambeth Palace Library), 28–29.

will contribute no less to the improvement of our parochial Psalmody, than to the reformation of the lower orders of the people.[88]

Unfortunately, from Porteus's perspective, some Sunday schools used hymns in their instruction. The Manchester Sunday School (founded in 1784), for example, included "a selection of Watts's hymns" in their worship services.[89] With repeated exposure to materials (texts and tunes) that were markedly different than the "Old Version" and the *New Version,* it is not inconceivable that those who grew up in such an environment developed a taste for them. As adults attending the parish church, they may have demanded their favorite hymns, perhaps to the consternation of the clergy.[90]

Porteus was concerned also by those (i.e., the Methodists) who "separate from our communion" and who knew "perfectly well the use and force of

---

88. Beilby Porteus, *A Charge Delivered to the Clergy of the Diocese of London, at the Primary Visitation of that Diocese in the year MDCCXC* (London: J. F. and C. Rivington, 1790), 18–19. One wonders if the recent events in France led Porteus to suggest that learning psalmody would not only improve congregational song but would also reform "the lower orders of the people." This *Charge* encouraged a number of well-meaning authors to produce new books to instruct children in singing. One example is that of Henry Heron, who provided a work that, if used according to his instructions, would have thoroughly prevented anyone from learning how to sing. Heron, while paying homage to earlier instructional books, failed to understand the purpose of the solfa system, which was designed to relate a given note to its tonic. See Henry Heron, *Parochial music corrected: intended for the use of the several charity-schools in London, Westminster, &c., as well as for all congregations: being plain and distinct rules for the more pleasing and correct performance of psalmody, by the children, &c., in their respective parish-churches. With psalms, hymns, and anthems, set to music. . . . To which is added an easy introduction to singing* (London: W. Richardson, 1790). Heron was organist at St. Magnus, London Bridge.

89. W. R. Ward, *Religion and Society in England 1790–1850* (New York: Schocken, 1972), 13. The forms for worship were eclectic in Manchester as a result of a collaborative effort by the ministers of the Church of England, the Unitarians, the Roman Catholics, and other Dissenters. At Almondbury, a division occurred when the Anglican clergy prohibited the singing of hymns: "This arbitrary prohibition as might be expected, resulted in disaffection, strife, and ultimately division. Many of the teachers indignant at the insult offered to the hardworking Methodists protested against the injustice. But the protest was unheeded. And as they would not submit to be wholly ignored in the conduct of a school in which they had toiled so patiently and assiduously, they resolved themselves into a committee for the purpose of establishing a purely Methodist school." See Richard Roberts, *History of Methodism in Almondbury,* 28–29, cited by Ward, *Religion and Society,* 44. See also *Select Psalms, from different Versions; to which are added a few Occasional Hymns* (Cambridge: J. Archdeacon, 1789), which was prepared for use in Sunday schools and contained fifteen hymns.

90. The collection by the Reverend Thomas Cannon was made specifically at the request of the congregation.

this commanding instrument of devotion."[91] William Vincent, too, had noted with great concern the threat to the Church of England posed by the hymnody of the Methodists:

> It is not rashness to assert, that for one who has been drawn away from the Established Church by preaching, ten have been induced by Music. And many who have primarily had no other attraction, have, by their attendance on it, given an opportunity to have their affections estranged from the Established Church, which they would not otherwise have been exposed to.[92]

---

91. Porteus, 19. John Randolph, bishop of Bangor, echoed Porteus's concern eighteen years later. In his *Charge* he wrote: "I would also suggest, whether an attention to the Psalmody of the Church would not be a likely means of keeping your congregations regular in their attendance, and earnest in their worship. Our adversaries, as is well known, and they are much to be commended in this particular, render their meetings attractive by a careful attention to this custom, and by the skilful [*sic*] practice of it." See *A Charge delivered to the Clergy of the Diocese of Bangor* (Bangor: Printed by J. Broster, 1808), 23. Temperley argued that Porteus was an example of those clergy who adopted methods similar to the Evangelical clergy as "a defensive measure against the inroads of Methodism and other dissenting bodies" (*Music*, 1:213). For an analysis of episcopal perspectives toward Methodism and revivalism, see Richard Allen Soloway, "Episcopal Perspectives and Religious Revivalism in England, 1784–1851," *Historical Magazine of the Protestant Episcopal Church* 40 (March 1971):27–61. See also Anthony Armstrong [Willis], *The Church of England, the Methodists and Society, 1700–1850* (London: University of London Press, 1973), 80, who noted that "[i]t is clear that music contributed greatly to the success of the Methodist movement, and that it provoked a great deal of envy from the Church of England."

92. William Vincent, *Considerations on Parochial Music*, 2nd ed., with additions (London: Printed for T. Cadell, 1790), 14–15. The danger had been noted as early as 1765. See *Thoughts on the Use and Advantages of Music, and Other Amusements* (London: Printed for J. Dodsley, 1765), 85. Writing in 1801, Charles Daubeny noted: "[P]roper attention will never be wanting to that part of it [i.e., congregational singing] to which we are now alluding; and that the excuse, bad as it is, for frequenting irregular places of worship, for the sake of that sacred harmony which, if you are not wanting to yourselves, may at all times be found within these walls, will never be suffered to have place in your minds." See his *Psalms and Hymns, Appointed to be Sung by The Congregation assembled at Christ Church, Bath* (Bath: Wood, 1816), preface. As late as 1819, it was observed that the hymns of the Methodists were "of an enthusiastic and rapturous strain, abounding often with false and dangerous doctrine." See W. X. Y., "On the present State of the Methodists," *The Christian Remembrancer* 1 (October 1819):602. Vincent's description of the powerful attraction of Evangelical singing may have been the source for A. J. B. Beresford-Hope's comment that "the impatient spirits who followed the politic Wesley and the fiery Whitefield into secession, reanimated each other's spirits, and multiplied tenfold their converts by the power of their hymn-singing." See his *The English Cathedral of the Nineteenth Century* (London: J. Murray, 1861), 119–120.

By following their lead in stressing the importance of congregational singing but not their forms (i.e., hymns), Porteus believed that "[i]t would render your congregations more numerous and more constant, it would enliven and animate their devotion, it would add one charm more to our excellent form of worship."[93] Moreover,

> Psalmody . . . from its connection with religion, from its forming an ancient and essential part of our public service, from its known and powerful influence on the minds and morals of the great mass of the people, is of more *real* and *national* and *practical* importance, than even those sublime and elaborate compositions of our great masters which are so generally and so justly admired.[94]

The concern over the dissemination of false doctrine through the use of hymns must have caused a number of clergy to pause momentarily as they considered whether or not to introduce hymns into their parish. The ability of hymnody to reenforce positively the teachings of the church must have also encouraged a number of clergy to support the use of hymns. The problem was to ensure that the hymns selected for use contained teaching fully in accordance with the formularies of the Church of England. Some believed that this was achievable; others held that the potential dangers outweighed any potential benefits.

The Methodist Threat

Public attention to the increasing use of hymns was focused more sharply when six students were expelled from Edmund Hall, Oxford, in March 1768, in part, for "taking upon them to . . . sing hymns in private houses."[95]

---

93. Porteus, 20. At least one person responded almost immediately to Porteus's call for a selection of metrical psalms from the *New Version* as a means of revitalizing congregational singing. In fact, the preface is taken almost word for word from Porteus's *Charge* (19–20). See [John Hutchins], *Select Psalms and Hymns, for the use of the Parish Church of St. Botolph without Aldersgate, London* (London: n.p., 1790). The collection contained twenty-six metrical psalms and six hymns. See also George [W. A.] Hay Drummond and Edward Miller, *Select Portions of the New Version of Psalms, For every Sunday throughout the Year; with the Principal Festivals and Fasts. For the Use of Parish Churches,* 7th ed. (London: n.p., 1791). Although this is a reprinted collection, the authors cite in the preface the bishop of London's *Charge.*

94. Porteus, 20–21.

95. *The Gospel Magazine* 3 (March 1768):140–141. According to the journal, the full list of charges was "for holding methodistical tenets, and taking upon them to pray, read, or expound the scriptures, and sing hymns in private houses."

The six undergraduates (Benjamin Kay, Thomas Jones, Thomas Grove, Erasmus Middleton, Joseph Shipman, and James Matthews) had been gathering at the home of a certain Mrs. Durbridge along with a number of other people, some of whom were fellows in various colleges, for mutual support in their Christian living.[96]

Although it was only a part of the reason for expulsion, the fact that hymn singing was included among the offenses is clear evidence of the concern felt in some sections of the church regarding this development. The event generated considerable correspondence, including the following published in the London *Chronicle:*

> Ye jovial Souls, drink, whore, and swear,
>   And all shall then go well:
> But O take heed of Hymns and Pray'r,
>   These cry aloud—EXPEL![97]

By May, George Whitefield had entered the fray and in so doing focused almost entirely on the subject of hymn singing. In a letter to the vice chancellor, he wrote:

> Singing, composing, or reading hymns composed by others, and doing this in company, seems to be as little criminal as praying extempore. . . . to teach and admonish one another in psalms, and hymns and spiritual songs [is] . . . truly a scriptural command.[98]

---

96. Elliott-Binns, *Early Evangelicals,* 353–354. The fact that Elliott-Binns does not mention the issue of hymn singing in his account of this incident is indicative of the general oversight of various aspects of church music by church historians.

97. Cited by *The Gospel Magazine* 3 (March 1768):142. Elliott-Binns, citing *The Clerk of Oxford in Fiction* (312), gives the verse thus (*Early Evangelicals,* 355):

> So drink, ye jovial souls, and swear,
>   And all shall then go well;
> But oh! take heed of Hymns and Prayer,
>   These cry aloud—E-X-P-E-L.

Sir Richard Hill prolonged the controversy by dashing off a powerful pamphlet (*Pietas Oxoniensis, or a full and impartial account of the expulsion of six students from St. Edmund Hall By a Master of Arts of the University of Oxford,* 1768), which, among other charges, held that the Articles of the Church of England taught predestination. Dr. Thomas Nowell, in his reply (*An Answer to a Pamphlet entitled Pietas Oxoniensis,* 1768), held that such was not true. Augustus Toplady responded with his *Church of England Vindicated from the Charge of Arminianism.* The pamphlets continue until 1774, when Toplady published his *Historic Proof of the Calvinism of the Church of England.*

98. Cited by *The Gospel Magazine* 3 (May 1768):236.

The editor of *The Gospel Magazine* joined the controversy in July, writing, "[I]t is to be much lamented that their distinguished piety for praying extempore, and for reading and singing hymns, should be the great occasion of their expulsion."[99] Even the great Dr. Johnson was provoked to comment:

> BOSWELL: "I talked of the recent expulsion of six students from the University of Oxford, who were methodists, and would not desist from publickly praying and exhorting." JOHNSON: "Sir, that expulsion was extremely just and proper. What have they to do at a University, who are not willing to be taught, but will presume to teach? Sir, they were examined, and found to be mighty ignorant fellows." BOSWELL: "But, was it not hard, sir, to expel them, for I am told they were good beings?" JOHNSON: "I believe they might be good beings; but they were not fit to be in the University of Oxford. A cow is a very good animal in the field; but we turn her out of a garden.[100]

For those who opposed hymnody, especially the "methodistical" type, the increasing social unrest in England must have provided tangible support for their cause.[101] The events in France had created a crisis mentality that further strengthened opposition to change and innovation.[102] The Georgian church was not inclined to react positively to any movement that posed a challenge to its authority and, in fact, resisted strongly until it was eventually forced to make concessions in the 1830s.[103] It is possible that the movement toward a legal solution to the inclusion or exclusion of

---

99. *The Gospel Magazine* 3 (July 1768):324. For a full account of the incident, see Hill's *Pietas Oxoniensis;* another pamphlet was printed in 1769 entitled *The Oxford Expulsion condemned by a real member of the church of England.* Both works are cited by *The Gospel Magazine* 4 (March 1769):128.

100. April 14, 1772, cited by Elliott-Binns, *Early Evangelicals,* 355–356.

101. This unrest erupted forcefully in numerous food riots and wage disputes in 1795.

102. Ward, *Religion and Society,* 2. Compare Hylson-Smith's analysis that "English society was seen as established, firm and solid" prior to the fall of the Bastille in 1789, but changed rapidly in the years following (63). See also R. C. D. Jasper, *The Development of the Anglican Liturgy 1662–1980* (London: SPCK, 1989), 23–24.

103. See Peter Virgin, *The Church in an Age of Negligence: Ecclesiastical Structure and Problems of Church Reform 1700–1840* (Cambridge: J. Clarke, 1989), passim. Hylson-Smith contended that the Georgian church "was seen not so much as the custodian of the keys of heaven and hell, and the proclaimer of the gospel of salvation, as the religious counterpart of civil society, wherein churchmanship was complementary to citizenship" (8).

hymns resulted from the attempt to use legal means to restrict itineracy and other perceived threats to the Church of England.[104]

The affront to the Church of England posed by Methodism, especially the use of hymns, was also duly noted by Isaac D'Israeli. In his estimation, the singing of metrical psalms that had occupied its rightful place in the life of the whole congregation at the time of the Reformation had by the latter half of the eighteenth century "degenerated into those scandalous compositions which, under the abused title of *hymns,* are now used by some sects [i.e., Moravians and Methodists]."[105] D'Israeli held these compositions in such low esteem that to provide the reader with examples would pollute the pages of his work with "ribaldry, obscenity, and blasphemy."[106]

A Divided Church

By the middle of the 1780s the division of attitudes with regard to the inclusion of hymns in the liturgy reached such a degree of intensity that one writer, William Jones (of Nayland), had no difficulty in stating that the church was "now divided into parties for the old and the new Music, in which there is undoubtedly a great diversity of Style and an attention to different effects, some of which will be preferred to the others, according to the Studies and tempers of different hearers."[107]

Like others, Jones believed that music had "its origin from God himself; whence it will follow, that so far as it is God's work, it is his property, and may certainly be applied as such to his service."[108] Such an origin made it imperative that only "the best music, performed in the best manner we are

---

104. Ward described the bishop of Rochester, Samuel Horsley, *Charge* (1800) as "a howl designed to replace the broken weapon of brute force with legal authority to act" (*Religion and Society,* 51). The rise of clergy in the nominal magistracy also may have strengthened this movement. See Ward, *Religion and Society,* 3; Virgin, 43; Hugh McLeod, *Religion and the People of Western Europe 1789–1970* (Oxford: Oxford University Press, 1981), 25.

105. I[saac] D'Israeli, *A Second Series of Curiosities of Literature; Consisting of Researches in Literary, Biographical, and Political History; Of Critical and Philosophical Inquiries; and of Secret History,* 2nd ed., corrected, 3 vols. (London: J. Murray, 1824), 1:192.

106. D'Israeli, 1:192n.

107. William Jones (of Nayland), *A Treatise on the Art of Music* (Colchester: W. Keymer, 1784), iii.

108. William Jones (of Nayland), *The Nature and Excellence of Music. A Sermon Preached at the Opening of a New Organ, in the Parish Church of Nayland in Suffolk; on Sunday, July the 29th, 1787* (London: G. G. J. and J. Robinson, 1787), 4.

able" should be used in the praise of God.[109] The question that was asked was who decides what is best for the church? Jones's response was "[t]he authority of the minister is competent to direct such music as is proper, and to keep the people to the ancient forms [i.e., metrical psalms]."[110] This authority derived from Elizabeth I's Injunctions: "Queen Elizabeth . . . took what care she could by her injunctions, that affectation, which spoils all other things, should not be permitted to spoil the music of the Church."[111] The proper song of the church, Jones argued, was the metrical psalms and "all the hymns of the morning and evening service; to the words of which, such strains of harmony are adapted in this our Church of England, that the world cannot shew the like."[112] The clergy were obligated to see that the proper song of the church was maintained. Moreover, they had authority to do so. They did not, however, have authority to introduce material not sanctioned for use in the church.

Described as a representative of the "high and dry" eighteenth-century cleric, Jones demonstrates, as does Romaine, that party affiliation did not necessarily dictate one's position with regard to hymnody.[113] His desire to see all of the congregation participate in the singing mirrored that of many Evangelicals at a time when other high church clerics supported (or at least did not oppose) the development of stronger choral programs that often took complete control of all music in the parish. In this, Jones was going against the mood of the day. An anonymous correspondent wrote in 1781 that metrical psalms were

certainly better calculated for the spiritual consolation of tallow-chandlers and taylors, than for the pious uses of the liberal and intelligent. Psalm-singing and

---

109. Jones, *Nature,* 14–18. Further, "Church music has a proper character of its own, which is more excellent than that of secular, or profane music, and should always be preserved. Without the restraints of discretion, wisdom, and authority, the art of man is apt to run out into excess and impropriety; and while it affects to be too fine, and too powerful, becomes ridiculous." Jones echoes here some of the sentiments regarding church music that would be expressed later by the Tractarians and those involved with the Ecclesiological Society.

110. Jones, *Nature,* 18. Perhaps to demonstrate what he considered to be proper music, Jones wrote *Ten Church Tunes for the Organ with Four Anthems in Score* (London: n.p., 1789). The one tune that remains in use, ST. STEPHEN, was first paired with a metrical version of Psalm 23.

111. Jones, *Nature,* 15.

112. Jones, *Nature,* 13. "Hymns" here refers to the canticles of the Prayer Book offices. It is clear that Jones was not opposed to anthems in the liturgy, citing such works as Tallis's "I call and cry," Farrant's "Call to remembrance, O Lord," and Purcell's "Thou knowest Lord the secrets of our hearts."

113. Temperley, *Music,* 1:224.

Republicanism naturally go together. They seem both founded on the same levelling principle. The Republican Calvin appears to have been of opinion, that all people should *sing* in the church, as well as *act* in the state, without distinction or inequality. Hence his necessity of a *vulgar* and *popular* psalmody. There is much philosophical truth in a ludicrous saying of King Charles the Second, that *the Presbyterian worship was not fit for a gentleman.*[114]

Jones's opposition to hymns, however, brought him into a closer affinity with the majority of the church. With regard to the style of music to be used in worship, Jones went against the trend toward a popular style derived from the theater, preferring the traditional psalm tunes.[115]

Like others, Jones recognized many of the difficulties of the age, especially the low degree with which religion was held. And like them, Jones argued that music could play a role in overcoming those difficulties.[116] The fact that he disagreed concerning the character and type of music to be employed contributed to the controversies of the day and demonstrated that the issues surrounding church music were beginning to be addressed by a wider spectrum of the church.

A Shift in the Controversy

Augustus Toplady published his first collection of hymns in 1776. In the preface, he noted:

> Some worthy persons have been of opinion, (and what absurdity is there, for which some well-meaning people have not contended?) that it is "*Unlawfull* to sing *Human Compositions* in the House of God." But, by the same rule, it must be equally unlawfull, to *preach,* or publicly to *pray,* except in the very words of Scripture. Not to observe, that many of the best and greatest Men, that ever lived, have, both in antient and modern times, been *Hymn-Writers;* and that there is the strongest reason to believe, that the best Christians, in all ages, have been *Hymn-Singers.* Moreover, the singing of hymns is an Ordinance, to which

---

114. "Psalmody," *Gentleman's Magazine* 51 (August 1781):369–370.

115. Jones held the work of Ravenscroft in high esteem (*Nature,* 4).

116. Jones wrote, "It must be our own fault, if our music doth not contribute to our reformation, and we shall have it to answer for in common with the other means of grace which we have abused" (*Nature,* 19). Jones achieved a reformation of psalmody in his parish by using a collection entitled *Select Portions of the Psalms of David, for the Use of Parish Churches.* I have not been able to identify the compiler. A work with this title was published c. 1780 and a second edition in 1786. See Temperley, *Music,* 1:378, PC #245.

God has repeatedly set the Seal of his own Presence and Power; and which He deigns eminently to bless, at this very day. It has proved a *converting* Ordinance, to some of his people; a *recovering* Ordinance, to others; a *comforting* Ordinance, to them all; and one of the divinest Mediums of communion with God, which his gracious benignity has vouchsafed to his church below.[117]

Toplady dismissed those who argued against hymns, for example, William Romaine ("some well-meaning people"), believing that hymn singing was an ordinance of God and was certainly not "Unlawfull" (an early and clear reference to what would become the central issue). The collection was decidedly Calvinistic in its theological stance, yet eclectic. Drawing as he did from numerous sources, "between forty and fifty," Toplady's work played a crucial role in the development of the modern hymn book by bringing together a wide diversity of authors in a single collection. It is somewhat surprising to discover a number of hymns by Charles Wesley as well as many Nonconformists.[118]

Although Toplady noted the legal question regarding the use of hymns in the liturgy, he did not pursue it. That question, however, became the central issue in the opening decades of the nineteenth century. The development of the periodical press in the early years of the nineteenth century contributed to the controversy by expanding the audience and by focusing attention on the legal question.[119] Because this shift will be the subject of the next chapter, one example will be sufficient for now.

In a lengthy letter to the editor of *The Christian Observer,* T. J. offered a "few observations" on "Christian Psalmody" to the journal's readers.[120]

---

117. Augustus Toplady, *Psalms and Hymns for Public and Private Worship* (London: Printed for E. and C. Dilly, 1776), preface. Toplady's most famous hymn, "Rock of Ages," first appeared in the March 1776 issue of *The Gospel Magazine.*

118. Toplady, however, altered many of the texts he borrowed in order to make them doctrinally "correct." For example, Wesley's "all-atoning Lamb" becomes the "sin-atoning Lamb." An anonymous work that also brought together a wide diversity of authors was *A Collection of Psalms & Hymns, from various authors; adapted chiefly to Public Worship* (Lancaster: H. Walmsley, 1780). The compilation's editor wrote in the preface: "It was thought expedient and desirable to unite, in one cheap and portable Volume, the labors of many, whose poetic talents have been happily devoted to the service of the Sanctuary." This collection contained 341 hymns and metrical psalms, representing a wide range of materials.

119. For a survey of this development, see Josef L. Altholz, *The Religious Press in Britain, 1760–1900* (New York: Greenwood, 1989).

120. T. J., "Observations on the Intellectual Part of Christian Psalmody," *The Christian Observer* 4 (August 1805): 464. T. J.'s article was in response to the "judicious remarks" of L. R., whose "On the due Regulation of Instrumental Music in Public Worship" had appeared earlier. See *The Christian Observer* 4 (April 1805):212–214.

In his observations, T. J. argued for a wider selection of material for use in worship than the "perpetuation . . . of the two versions in common use [i.e., Sternhold and Hopkins and Tate and Brady]."[121] He held that if "we pin our taste for what is poetic or evangelical to the performance of a Sternhold or a Tate, we must forget that a Watts, a Doddridge, a Merrick, and a Cowper have lived and laboured."[122]

Contrary to those who argued for using only the most literal versifications or those believed to be authorized, T. J. asked his readers to reflect upon the example set by the reformers of the sixteenth century with regard to the judicious selection of materials for worship in the English church:

> I will only appeal to you whether those prayers and collects which were composed by Catholics when the Romish Church was little less corrupt than now, and which, at this hour, adorn the Breviary no less than the Common Prayer Book, ought not, for a similar reason, to be expunged from our Liturgy. But, Sir, the wise compilers of that inimitable system of devotion thought far otherwise. They held, that whatever was intrinsically excellent, even in that form of worship, which they rejected as unscriptural, ought to be retained; and at a time when prejudices must necessarily have been most violent, were actuated by the spirit of him, who could rejoice that Christ was preached, though he was preached of contention.[123]

T. J., however, was not an "advocate for the *indiscriminate* introduction of hymns into our Church Service:"

> To this very circumstance I attribute many evils, against which it is my main object to guard your readers. The practice is dangerous, because it has no limit but the fallible, and often erroneous, judgment of an individual. It moreover opens a door for the admission of false doctrine. The sound creed, and upright intentions, of one clergyman, who selects a number of hymns for the use of his own Church, can afford no security against the enthusiasm, or heterodoxy, of a neighbouring minister; and though the same objection may be thought valid against sermons, I will venture to affirm, that false doctrine comes in a less suspected and more durable form, when introduced under the guise of sacred poetry, than when it is boldly uttered in the pulpit.[124]

The solution proposed by T. J. was a "collection of sacred songs" authorized by "our Bishops." The bishops, he reasoned, would not withhold their

---

121. T. J., 464–465.

122. T. J., 465.

123. T. J., 465. The similarities between this and the arguments in the ritualist controversies in the latter half of the nineteenth century are remarkable.

124. T. J., 466.

"sanction" of such a collection, especially if it contributed to the "edification of the Church." The dangers of not doing so, he believed, were obvious: "Till this desireable [*sic*] event can take place, many errors are likely to continue in some Churches where hymns have been introduced."[125]

Summary

The use of hymns, as evidenced in this limited survey (the examples could easily be multiplied), continued to gain ground as the century drew to a close and increased significantly in the first two decades of the nineteenth century. Although the introduction of hymns was, at first, cautious, the evidence indicates that it was not restricted to any one locale or to any particular segment of the church. Such is also true for those who opposed this development.

There was an almost universal desire in the eighteenth century to improve congregational singing (and the character of worship in general), even though there was significant disagreement concerning the method for achieving such reform. For some, an improvement in the performance of metrical psalms was all that was needed. For some, metrical psalms were inadequate regardless of how well they were sung. Thus, many advocated the use of hymns to supplement metrical psalms. These hymns, it was argued, provided the worshipper with Christological themes. From there it was a logical step to seek to provide texts that reflected the themes of the liturgical year. In both cases, these hymns often were introduced with the desire to enliven worship and to strengthen the teachings of the church.

Opposition to this development was at first focused on the Reformation's stress on the centrality of the word of God in worship. As this argument proved to be less than convincing to a number of hymnody's advocates, the focus shifted to additional arguments against this innovation, including the inappropriate character of the tunes used. Thomas Hirst, for example, abhorred the number of new tunes being introduced, believing that they prevented "many from singing that would wish to sing."[126] For others, those tunes composed by amateurs succeeded "only in being grotesque" rather than contributing positively to parochial wor-

---

125. T. J., 466. As reasonable as his proposal was, it proved to be impossible to implement. To the present day, the Church of England has no authorized collection of hymns. Each congregation is free to determine what collection it will use in its worship.

126. T[homas] Hirst, *Familiar Dialogues, In which an attempt is made To Shew the Use and Abuse of Sacred Music, in Divine Worship* (Nottingham: E. Hodson, 1816), 13.

ship.[127] To this argument concerns about the authorship of the texts (i.e, Dissenters and fanatics), the taint of "enthusiasm," the dangers of disseminating false doctrine, and, when all else failed, the fact that hymnody was innovative, were put forth in opposition. As impassioned as they were, such arguments failed to stop the increasing use of hymns.[128]

Numerous collections of metrical psalms, hymns, and some containing both in various proportions were published during this period.[129] Often described as "unexceptionable" (i.e., the contents were of such quality that no one could possibly take exception), these collections were intended by the editor(s) or compiler(s) as a supplement to whatever collection a parish was currently using. In doing so they attempted to avoid "obscure and controverted" points, references to "peculiar" situations, and, in general, to make available the "labors of many" to as many parishes as possible.[130] These collections enjoyed a certain measure of success, often being reprinted for the original parish and being used by neighboring parishes. The number of these indicates a far wider use of hymns in the latter half of the century than some scholars have noted.

Benson, for example, implies that only a small number of collections

---

127. Donald MacArthur, "Old Village Church Music," *The Musical Times* 64 (April 1923):265.

128. In Demaray's estimation, opponents of hymnody knew "they fought a losing battle." See Donald E. Demaray, *The Innovation of John Newton (1725–1807): Synergism of Word and Music in Eighteenth Century Evangelism* (Lewiston, N.Y.: E. Mellen, 1988), 190.

129. For an extensive, but incomplete, list of materials published between 1801–1820, see Julian, *Dictionary,* 333–334. For a more comprehensive list, including non-Anglican materials, see Robin A. Leaver, ed., *Bibliotheca Hymnologica (1890)* (London: C. Higham, 1981). Originally compiled as a sale catalogue by William Thomas Brooke, it is a valuable listing of hymn books published between 1750 and 1850.

130. See, for example, *A Collection of Hymns for Public Worship: On the General Principles of Natural and Revealed Religion* (Salisbury: n.p., 1778); *Select Psalms and Hymns, for the use of the Parish Churches in the town of Huntingdon* (Huntingdon: A. Jenkinson, 1774); *A Collection of Psalms & Hymns, from various authors; adapted chiefly to Public Worship* (Lancaster: H. Walmsley, 1780); *[A] Collection of Psalms and Hymns for Christian Worship* (Newry: J. Gordon, 1783); *A Collection of Psalms and Hymns for Divine Worship,* 2nd ed., with considerable additions (Exeter: W. Grigg, 1779); W. Parry, *A Selection of Psalms and Hymns* (London: n.p., 1791); [Septimus Hodson], *Psalms & Hymns selected for Congregational Use* (London: W. Smith, 1801); Thomas Scott, *A Selection of Psalms and Hymns* (London: W. McDowall, 1804); *Select Psalms and Hymns, Designed Chiefly for the Use of Public Worship* (Shrewsbury: J. and W. Eddowes, 1807); *A Collection of Psalms and Hymns, Selected for Divine Worship* (Chichester: W. Mason, n.d.).

were available in this period.[131] The evidence, however suggests the opposite conclusion. For example, supportive evidence for concluding that a larger number of collections was available for use is found in comments made by contemporary historians of hymnody. Thomas Hartwell Horne, for example, noted in 1847 that "within the last fifty or sixty years, during which increased attention has been given to the improvement of church-psalmody, very numerous collections and selections have been published, which are now used in various churches and chapels throughout England."[132] Although apparently restricting his observations to the first part of the nineteenth century, Horne noted that this development began as early as 1774 with a collection published in York. Unfortunately, he is not more specific. Surely, Horne would not have used the phrase "very numerous" if he were referring only to twelve collections. Julian's work may have established the belief that only a small number of collections were available and in use. In a sermon, Julian stated,

> These earnest men [i.e., clergy who supported the use of hymns] produced during the eighteenth century twelve different hymnbooks for use in the Established church. At the opening of the nineteenth century, of the 10,000 parishes in the kingdom, not more than, if as many as, 200 had adopted those collections.[133]

The evidence seems to point to the opposite conclusion.

Collections, however, were not the only avenue for introducing hymnody into the life of the church. In a number of instances, hymns were written for specific occasions. This modest introduction must have resulted in either of two reactions: opposition to the use of hymns or a desire to seek further occasions for their use.[134]

---

131. Benson, *English Hymn,* passim.

132. Thomas Hartwell Horne, *Historical Notices of Psalmody* (London: C. F. Hodgson, 1847), 9. Much earlier, Romaine complained that "collection upon collection, and in use too, new hymns starting up daily" had made metrical psalms obsolete. Surely he would not have used such language if there were only a few collections available (Romaine, 111–112).

133. John Julian, *Modern Hymnody and Hymns: A Sermon Preached in Christ Church, Scarborough on Sunday, September 6, 1903* (London: SPCK, 1909), 4.

134. See, for example, [G. Wakefield?], *A Serious Lecture, Delivered at Sheffield; February 28, 1794. Being the Day Appointed for A General Fast; to which are added a Hymn and Resolutions,* 2nd ed. (London: n.p., 1794). The introductory notes indicated that the "Hymn prepared for this solemnity, was then [i.e., after the lecture] sung in full chorus, by the whole assembly." Sung to the tune OLD 100TH, the opening stanza read:

> O God of Hosts, thine Ear incline,
>   Regard our Prayers, our Cause be thine;
> When Orphans cry, when Babes complain,
>   When Widows weep—can'st thou refrain?

Collections of metrical psalms continued to dominate, although even those compilers opposed to hymnody had begun to include hymns in their collections. For example, John Venn, rector of Clapham from 1792 to 1813 and a prominent Evangelical, published a collection for his congregation in 1806.[135] The preface made clear Venn's dedication to the continuing use of metrical psalmody in the liturgy, citing at length portions of Porteus's *Charge* and noting that his selections were from "approved Versions of the Psalms, as appear to be best adapted to the general Use of Congregations."[136] Yet Venn included thirty-seven hymns to enrich the liturgy of the church, thus implying that metrical paraphrases of the Psalms of David alone were not able to meet the needs of the faithful.[137] In contrast, the collection prepared by John Bewsher for his parish contained only hymns. An extremely conservative selection, the collection included several hymns now considered standards.[138]

Venn's collection was used by other parishes and, along with similar works, furthered the transition from an exclusive metrical psalmody in the liturgy to the diversity of congregational song exemplified by the first edition of *Hymns, Ancient and Modern* (1861). These collections assisted in bridging the gulf between those who favored hymns only, those who desired to retain metrical psalms supplemented by hymns for various occasions, and those who wished to adhere to metrical psalms only.

---

135. [John Venn], *Select Portions of Psalms, Extracted from Various Versions, and Adapted to Public Worship, With an Appendix, Containing Hymns for the Principal Festivals of the Church of England* (London: W. Thorne, 1806). See also Hylson-Smith, 83–85.

136. Venn, 1806, iv–v.

137. Septimus Hodson stated this explicitly: "To a selection from the psalms, the addition of unexceptionable hymns, adapted to the occasion of days of peculiar celebration, seems to be necessary for the use of public worship; as the prophetic allusions in the psalms are hardly sufficient for the purposes of commemoration and christian gratitude" (v). The collection contained fifty-four hymns. Hodson was representative of those who readily acknowledged that there were "two versions of the psalms, now in use by authority," but were unwilling to be bound to their use in worship. His metrical psalm selections were drawn largely from Tattersall's version, and the authors of hymns included Watts, Wesley, Addison, and Cowper, to name but a few.

138. [John Bewsher], *A Selection of Hymns for the use of the Parish Church, St. Neots (Hunts)* (N.p.: J. C. Sharp, 1792). The collection consisted of only twenty-two hymns, including Ken's "Awake my soul," Addison's "The spacious firmament," Wesley's "Love divine," "Lo, he comes, with clouds descending," "Hark! the herald angels sing," and Watts's "Before Jehovah's awful throne." A handwritten note at the end of the copy examined at the British Museum indicated that Bewsher, vicar of the parish, died on June 3, 1806.

In 1791 Edward Miller, following the lead of Porteus, offered to the clergy "a few more hints for . . . consideration" toward "a reformation in the performance of Parochial Psalmody."[139] Miller echoed Vincent's and Porteus's observations concerning the powerful singing of the Methodists and admonished the clergy for not learning from them:

> To show how little we are influenced by their example, if any one should step into a parish church while the psalm is singing, would he not find the greater part of the congregation totally inattentive? Irreverently *sitting*—talking to each other—taking snuff—winding up their watches, or adjusting their apparel?[140]

Hymns, however, were not the answer. Rather, the removal of the "Old Version" and a diligent teaching of the *New Version* would achieve the much sought after reformation in congregational singing. Miller preferred using other versions of the Psalms, but felt compelled to use the *New Version* because it was "licensed by authority."[141]

For the greater part, Miller's arguments concerning the use of hymns for congregational singing were not new. His criticisms of the "Old Version," the analysis of the present situation, the deprecation of "detached" singers, the inattentiveness of the clergy, all had been expressed by others previously. The focus, however, was shifting. The previously sufficient argument that nothing except the Psalms of David (and sometimes other select passages from scripture) could be sung in the liturgy was no longer adequate. Now the concern was not simply the use of material from scripture but the use of only those collections "licensed by authority."[142]

Implicitly, or in a few instances, explicitly (though without realizing the

---

139. Edward Miller, *Thoughts on the Present Performance of Psalmody in the Established Church of England, Addressed to the Clergy* (London: Printed for W. Miller, 1791), 1.

140. Miller, *Thoughts,* 5. Miller argued that the reason the Methodists sang well was because they "are taught to believe that singing praises to God is a part of their duty, which they are *bound* to perform. They are also more encouraged to meet frequently for private practice, to correct their pronunciation, and to sing with energy and effect" (*Thoughts,* 4).

141. Miller, *Thoughts,* 32. Versions that Miller thought superior were those of Merrick and Christopher Smart. Miller, along with George Drummond, published a metrical psalter drawn from the *New Version* that reached a seventh edition in 1791.

142. The anonymous author of *An Introduction to Reform Singing: Being An Essay to Sing the Holy Scriptures; Or Repeat them Melodiously in Churches, Instead of Singing Erroneous Rhymes and Human Compositions* held that the only words authorized for use in the liturgy were those taken from scripture. To sing anything else was criminal! See especially pages 237–246.

full implications of their observation), many believed that hymns had no authoritative position within the church. How then could they be used? For those who attempted to support their use through New Testament passages, others (e.g., Romaine) offered differing interpretations of the same passages.[143]

The question of authority began to emerge clearly in the 1790s, especially as a result of the work of William Vincent. Authority proved to be the key issue in the development of hymnody in the Church of England, and it is there that we turn our attention.

---

143. As late as 1843, at least one person still argued that there was no New Testament support for the use of hymns. See Robert Wilson Evans, *A Day in the Sanctuary: with an Introductory Treatise on Hymnology* (London: J. G. F. and J. Rivington, 1843).

Chapter Three

By What Authority? 1790–1825

You will confer a great obligation upon me, and upon many of your readers, if you, or any of your correspondents, will inform me, how far a minister has a right to discontinue the use of the version of the Psalms by Sternhold and Hopkins, or Tate and Brady, and to appoint the psalms or hymns, which he may wish to have sung in his church.

Sternhold and Hopkins are only *allowed*. Tate and Brady are *permitted*. The question is, Are all other versions *excluded*, and by what prohibitory act? And further, Is a clergyman bound, under pain of suspension, or otherwise, to obey the bishop's mandate, to use in his church the old and new versions *only?*[1]

At various times throughout the seventeenth, eighteenth, and nineteenth centuries questions regarding the legal status of Sternhold and Hopkins (and in the eighteenth and nineteenth centuries of the *New Version*) were raised. Those who supported the use of metrical psalms in the liturgy of the Church of England held that the Injunctions of 1559 were intended to allow their use "in the beginning, or in the end of common prayer, either at morning or evening." They based this position upon a rather liberal interpretation of the phrase "an hymn, or such like song." The fact that the title of the 1562 edition of Sternhold and Hopkins included the phrase *alowed according to thordre appointed in the Queenes maiesties Iniunctions* supported such a claim. This position was strengthened in 1566 when the title was changed to read, in part: *Newly set forth and allowed to be song in all*

---

1. W. H. W., "Inquiry as to Psalms and Hymns," *The Christian Observer* 14 (February 1815):95.

Churches, of all the people together, before & after morning & euenyng
prayer: as also before and after the Sermo[n].

No one challenged the practice of congregational metrical singing.
Some did question, however, whether Sternhold and Hopkins could claim
the authority of any positive enactment for use in the services of the Church
of England. Did the word *allowed* in the title mean *required,* as asserted
by some, or did it mean *permitted,* as asserted by others? If Sternhold and
Hopkins was required to be used in the liturgy, what authority had established that requirement? Parliament? Convocation? Crown? Was this the
only version authorized for use, or did the Injunctions of 1559 grant permission to any metrical version of the Psalms? Moreover, the Injunctions
made no reference to the use of metrical psalms or hymns within the liturgy
but only to the use of hymns "or such like song . . . in the beginning, or in
the end of common prayer." The title of the 1566 edition, however, had expanded their use to *before and after the Sermon.* By what authority had this
change been made? George Wither, writing in 1624, commented,

> those metrical Psalms were never commanded to be used in divine service, or
> in our public congregations, by any canon or ecclesiastical constitution, though
> many of the vulgar be of that opinion. But whatsoever the Stationers do in their
> title page pretend to that purpose, they being first allowed for private devotion
> only, crept into public use by toleration rather than by command.[2]

Peter Heylyn, a seventeenth-century historian, dismissed the supposed
authorization of Sternhold and Hopkins in more pointed language. In his
estimation,

> the singing of those Psalms so translated in Rythme and Meeter would work
> some alteration in the executing of the publique liturgy. For though it be exprest
> in the Title of those singing Psalms that they were set forth and allowed to be
> sung in all Churches before and after morning and evening Prayer; and also be-
> fore and after Sermons; yet this allowance seems rather to have been a Con-
> nivence [*sic*] then an approbation: no such allowance being any where found by
> such as have been most industrious and concerned in the search thereof.[3]

At first, he argued, metrical psalms were "recommended to the use of private Families; next brought into the Church for an entertainment before the

---

2. George Wither, *The Schollers Pvrgatory* (N.p.: n.p., [1624]), preface.
Wither's opinions were echoed throughout the course of the next two centuries.

3. Peter Heylin [Heylyn], *Examen Historicum: or A Discovery and Examina-
tion of the Mistakes, Falsities, and Defects In some Modern Histories. Occasioned
By the Partiality and Inadvertencies of their Severall Authours,* 2 vols. (London:
Printed for H. Seile and R. Roysten, 1659), 1:119.

beginning of the Morning and Evening Service."[4] Later The Stationers' Company bound them with the Book of Common Prayer and then added them at the end of the Bible. As a result of these developments, the metrical psalms of Sternhold and Hopkins came to be "esteemed the most divine part of Gods [sic] publique service," thrusting the proper canticles of the office from their appointed place.[5] Even though Sternhold and Hopkins's work was bound with the Book of Common Prayer and sometimes also with the Bible, thus giving weight to the idea that some kind of authorization had been given for use in the liturgy of the church, Heylyn argued that no such authorization existed.[6] Thomas Fuller, a contemporary of Heylyn and no friend of the poetry of Sternhold and Hopkins, took a more open position regarding its legal status, noting that metrical psalms were "if not publicly commanded, generally permitted to be sung in all Churches."[7]

The concern over the legal status of Sternhold and Hopkins (and, by extension, over any metrical version of the Psalms) diminished during the seventeenth century as its popularity increased. By the end of the century it had succeeded in establishing itself, in the minds of the people, as the only version authorized for use in the services of the church, although at

---

4. Peter Heylyn, *Aërius Redivivus: or the History of the Presbyterians. Containing The Beginnings, Progresse, and Successes of that Active Sect. Their Oppositions to Monarchical and Episcopal Government. Their Innovations in the Church; and their Inbroilments of the Kingdoms and Estates of Christendom in the pursuit of their Designs. From the Year 1536 to the Year 1647*, 2nd ed. (London: Printed by R. Battersby for C. Wilkinson, 1672), 215.

5. Heylyn, *Examen Historicum*, 120. See also Heylyn, *Aërius Redivivus*, 215. Heylyn believed that the growing strength of the "Puritan faction" lay behind this development. In the eighteenth century Thomas Warton and Isaac D'Israeli echoed Heylyn's assessment. C. J. Abbey and J. H. Overton noted that many believed that "all ancient hymns were Popish and all modern hymns were Puritan." See *The English Church in the Eighteenth Century*, 2 vols. (London: Longmans and Green, 1878), 2:51.

6. Heylyn, *Aërius Redivivus*, 215. Louis Benson argued that this development blurred any "legal niceties" and "handicapped" the opponents of hymn singing, since hymns were now "within the sacred covers of the Prayer Book itself." See his *The English Hymn: Its Development and Use in Worship* (H. Doran, 1915; reprint edition, Richmond, Va.: John Knox, 1962), 349. Conrad Donakowski wrongly stated that the addition of "a few psalms for congregational singing and a few hymns bound into the back of an edition of the . . . *Book of Common Prayer*" first occurred in 1828! See *A Muse for the Masses: Ritual and Music in an Age of Democratic Revolution, 1770–1870* (Chicago: University of Chicago Press, 1972), 222.

7. Thomas Fuller, *The Church-History of Britain: From the Birth of Jesus Christ, Until the Year M.DC.XLVIII* (London: Printed for J. Williams, 1655), Canto XVI, Book VII.

least one person challenged that view.[8] The belief that authorization was necessary for the use of metrical psalms in public worship may have been foremost in the minds of Tate and Brady when they determined to challenge the dominance of Sternhold and Hopkins with their version in 1696. Prior to publication, they petitioned the king for permission to issue a new collection, and in December of that year the king in council "permitted [their version] to be used in all such Churches . . . as shall think fit to receive the same."[9] Tate and Brady's version of the Psalms also received endorsement from several influential clergymen, including the archbishop of Canterbury and the bishop of London. Royal and ecclesiastical support, however, did not protect the *New Version* from opposition, although this did not produce any immediate challenges to its legal status.

The question whether metrical psalms were authorized for use in the liturgy of the Church of England, and if so, what version(s), began to be asked with renewed vigor during the eighteenth century and continued to be asked well into the nineteenth century.[10] As the number of different metrical versions of the Psalms increased toward the end of the eighteenth century, the question of the legal status of metrical psalms became more prominent. Likewise, as the number of hymn collections multiplied and the use of hymns in the liturgy of the church increased toward the end of the eighteenth century, the question of their legal status began to be included in the debate over hymns, especially because of the work of William Vincent.

Early Legal Challenges

Vincent, dean of Westminster, underscored the legal question with regard to the choice of texts and music to be used in the liturgy of the Church of England. In a treatise published first in 1787 and reprinted with additions in 1790, Vincent opposed the introduction of hymns primarily on two

---

8. See Richard Goodridge, *The Psalter or Psalms of David set to New Tunes,* 2nd ed. (Oxford: n.p., 1684), preface.

9. Nahum Tate and Nicholas Brady, *A New Version of the Psalms of David, Fitted to the Tunes Used in Churches* (London: T. Hodgkin, 1699). The first edition (1696) did not include this royal approval.

10. Apparently some questions were still being raised in the first two decades of the twentieth century. Percy Dearmer, the noted liturgical scholar, observed that "[t]here is a very common idea that hymns are an illegal addition to the Prayer Book services." Dearmer argued that hymns had been "legally sanctioned" during Elizabeth I's reign and "duly licensed" after the Restoration. See his "Hymn Books and the English Hymnal," *Ecclesia* (October 1913):218.

points.[11] First, to all who argued that the Psalms of David were inadequate to express the praises of a New Testament church, Vincent made a rather ingenious counter:

> Christ has not, by means of his Apostles or Evangelists, supplied this deficiency; we may presume therefore it is only imaginary; and if a dispensation of this kind had been absolutely requisite for his Church, we may reasonably conclude he would have granted it.[12]

For Vincent, metrical versions of the Psalms of David were more than sufficient for the church: "[W]hat subject of Religion is there which these cannot supply?"[13] The difficulty, Vincent argued, was not in the metrical psalms, but in the improper selection of them for the liturgy. Second, and far more important, Vincent held that any collection used in public worship had to be "sanctioned by Royal and Episcopal Authority," such as existed for the *New Version*. The introduction of unsanctioned hymns was unnecessary and dangerous:

> In regard to Hymns and all compositions not authorized by the Church, great caution is required. The extravagancies introduced by some of the sectarists on this head, ought to be a sufficient warning how we deviated from the established custom. The Church of England, in compliance with the principles of the reformation, has restricted us to the use of scripture language.[14] And where this has not been the case, and men have indulged their private fancies, you may find a text of scripture indeed at the head of the Hymn or in the margin; but the induction from it in the body, wandering into the wildest licences, recommendatory of particular tenets; and glaring contradictions, confound the perspicuity of the text.
>
> That the mischief of this sort might be introduced into the Established Church, is much to be apprehended.[15]

The question of legal status, for Vincent, was not simply a minor technicality. At the heart of the issue was a passionate concern for the "purity

11. William Vincent, *Considerations on Parochial Music* (London: Printed for T. Cadell, 1787).

12. William Vincent, *Considerations on Parochial Music*, 2nd ed., with additions (London: Printed for T. Cadell, 1790), 39.

13. Vincent, 1790, 38.

14. Vincent was following the argument made in John Brown's *A Dissertation on the Rise, Union, and Power, The Progressions, Separations, and Corruptions of Poetry and Music* (London: Printed for L. Davis and C. Reymers, 1763), 213.

15. Vincent, 1790, 37–38.

of public worship."[16] Hymns could be used by the faithful in private, but to introduce them into the liturgy threatened the well-being of the community of faith. In tones evocative of the arguments used in the ritualist controversies of the next century, Vincent held that the "decency and propriety of public worship" was of great consequence. The introduction of hymns, and especially unauthorized ones, might drive people "from Church by disgust."[17] With due care and the use of appropriate music, that is, the authorized *New Version* (in Vincent's estimation), in public worship, Vincent believed that the interests of "national religion" would be promoted and that "our Church may become as illustrious for Sacred harmony, and Religious decorum, as for Christian purity and genuine Faith."[18]

Vincent was not alone in his concern. Robert Wharton (rector of Sigglesthorne), for example, also objected to anything that deviated from the prescribed liturgy of the Church of England:

> The observation of the strictest decency and propriety in every part of public worship is a matter of so great consequence to religion itself, that it cannot but be highly interesting to all persons who think seriously on that most important subject. If then any abuses have crept into any part whatever of the service of our Church, it is the duty of every friend to it, so far as he can, to endeavour to remove them.[19]

In similar terms, M. T. H., writing more than a decade later, indicated that

---

16. Vincent, 1790, 39. See also Henry John Todd, *Observations upon the Metrical Version of the Psalms, Made by Sternhold, Hopkins, and Others: With a View to Illustrate the Authority with Which this Collection was at First Admitted, and how that Authority has been since regarded, in the Public Service of the Established Church of England: and Thence to Maintain, in This Venerable Service, the Usage of Such Metrical Psalmody Only as is Duly Authorized. With Notices of Other English Metrical Versions of the Psalms* (London: Printed for F. C. and J. Rivington, 1822); Walker Gray, *Select Portions of Psalms and Hymns, Entirely Extracted from the Prayer-Book, without alteration or addition, for the use of Cullumpton Church* (N.p.: Printed for the editor, 1815); Rann Kennedy, *Thoughts on the Music and Words of Psalmody, As At Present in Use Among the Members of the Church of England* (London: Longman, Hurst, Rees, Orme, and Brown, 1821), all of whom shared the same concern as Vincent.

17. Vincent, 1790, 39–41.

18. Vincent, 1790, 37, 43. Vincent viewed the *New Version* as a temporary solution. It was his hope that Tattersall's version based upon Merrick's work would receive "royal authority for admitting it into the service of the church" (1790, 36).

19. [Robert Wharton], *An Essay on Psalmody, Considered as a Part of the Public Worship* (York: W. Blanchard, 1789), i. A second edition was printed in 1791.

the liturgy of the church was of such value that nothing "indecorous in the manner of conducting it" should be permitted.[20]

The concerns expressed by Vincent, Wharton, and M. T. H. and their arguments against the introduction of hymns moved the controversy in a new direction. Previously, the overriding concern was the question of using hymns of human composition versus texts derived from scripture. Having failed to stem the tide of the increasing use of hymns, those opposed to the development, of necessity, had to find other means of support for their opposition. Although the legal question, at least with regard to metrical psalms, had been raised earlier, it came to the fore in the 1790s as perhaps a more effective means of stopping this development. In the opinion of these three opponents (and others), the use of anything not sanctioned by due authority was to be avoided. Wharton stated, "[W]hy it [i.e., the *New Version*] is to be superseded by the unauthorised compositions of dissenters [*sic*] not superior in merit, much more by the unchastised rants of Enthusiasts, I confess, I cannot understand, except it be that some of the established clergy chuse [*sic*] rather to flatter sectaries than pay due respect to their own church."[21]

The question of what constituted due authority was raised in 1792 when the church wardens of St. Botolph, Aldersgate, attempted to obstruct the singing of certain portions of the service. The curate of the parish, John Hutchins, had introduced "singing and chanting by the parish clerk and children of the ward, and congregation, accompanied by the organ."[22] The wardens, who opposed this innovation, argued that as "they paid the or-

---

20. M. T. H., "Letter to the Editor," *The Christian Observer* 3 (January 1804):17–18. In these three authors, Vincent, Wharton, and M. T. H., there is a remarkable similarity to the language and tone used by those opposed to an increasing use of a more elaborate ceremonial in the nineteenth century. Compare, for example, William Bentinck Hawkins, *A Few Plain Words, suggested by some Recent Proceedings in the Diocese of Exeter, addressed to Members of the Church of England* (London: F. and J. Rivington, 1845); Alexander Dallas, *What says the Rubric? The Present Truth* (London: J. Nisbet, 1843); *The Rubric: Its Strict Observance Recommended* (London: J. Burns, 1839).

21. Wharton, 1789, iii–iv.

22. "Upon the Power of Officiating Ministers to Direct the Manner in which Singing shall be Conducted in Parish Churches," *The Christian Remembrancer* 11 (1829):376–379. See also [Robert Druitt], *Conversations on the Choral Service; Being an Examination of Popular Prejudices Against Church Music* (London: T. Harrison, 1853), 74–79; "On the Duties of Churchwardens, and on Psalmody," *The Christian Remembrancer* 5 (August 1823):498–500. Hutchins was the editor of *Select Psalms and Hymns, for the use of the Parish Church of St. Botolph without Aldersgate, London* (London: n.p., 1790).

ganist and managed the children, they were to direct when the organ should or should not play, and when the children should or should not chant."[23] With the wardens opposed to his decisions regarding music, Hutchins sought to remove their interference by instituting a proceeding by articles against them in the courts (*Hutchins v. Denziloe and Loveland*).

In rendering his decision, Sir William Scott first addressed the issue of whether the wardens had authority to interfere in the conduct of the service of the church. Scott determined that the duties of the warden were confined to the care of property, and, with respect to worship, their office was one of "observation and complaint, but not of control."[24] If, in the wardens' opinion, the curate introduced "any irregularity into the service," the law did not give them a right to interfere but only to "complain to the Ordinary of his conduct."[25] With regard to the complaint of the wardens concerning the chanting of portions of the liturgy, Scott acknowledged that at the Reformation the choral service in cathedrals and collegiate chapels was retained. Parishes, in contrast, developed a simpler style of music, one that was "performed in a plain way, and in which all the congregation nearly take an equal part."[26] This division of musical styles had continued to the present. But, Scott argued, modern usage alone was not sufficient grounds for prohibiting a parish from deviating from custom. No law existed that restrained cathedrals to use one style of music and parishes another. In fact, "authority sufficient, in point of law and practice, to support the use of more music even in a Parish Church or Chapel" existed.[27] Thus, Scott concluded that "to sing with plain congregational music [i.e., chanting] is a practice fully authorized."[28]

Although declaring that the wardens were not entitled to interfere and that the practice of chanting was legal, Scott admonished both parties to seek "accommodation," hopefully avoiding further discord within the parish and possible conflict between the curate and the bishop. Scott, therefore, suspended the admission of the articles until the next term, his final ruling being dependent upon the reaching of an "accommodation" between the parties. Such was achieved, and the parties dismissed.[29]

---

23. "Upon the Power," 376.

24. "Upon the Power," 376.

25. "Upon the Power," 377.

26. "Upon the Power," 378.

27. "Upon the Power," 378. The basis for Scott's decision was the rubrics in the Book of Common Prayer, which direct the saying or singing of various portions of the service without distinction between cathedral or parish.

28. "Upon the Power," 379.

29. "Upon the Power," 379.

This incident, although it did not involve the use of hymns, is significant, for it indicates an intensification in the controversies regarding the role and place of music in worship, the style and forms to be used, and the authority for its use.[30] Moreover, the use of the courts to determine the legal status of the curate's actions intimate the path that later advocates and opponents of liturgical change would take for determining other additions to the liturgy not specifically dictated by the rubrics of the Book of Common Prayer.[31]

Additional Sources for Opposition

As the debate increased in intensity, those in favor of metrical psalms and opposed to the introduction of hymns looked for additional support for their positions regarding the legal status of certain metrical versions and the lack of such for hymns. William Dechair Tattersall (incumbent of both Wootton-under-Edge and Westbourne), for example, believed that authorization for the public use of metrical psalms in the church came from statutes 2 and 3 Edw. VI. These statutes contained a proviso that read, in part, "that it shall be lawful for all men as well in Churches, Chapels, Oratories, or other places, to use openly any Psalm or Prayer taken out of the Bible, at any due time, not letting or omitting the Service of any part thereof mentioned in the said

---

30. G. J. Cuming, in his reference to this case, uses the term *hymn* imprecisely, extending it to embrace hymns and chanting. See his *A History of Anglican Liturgy* (London: Macmillan, 1969), 194; 2nd ed. (London: Macmillan, 1982), 149. From the published accounts of the case, it is clear that chanting certain portions of the liturgy was at issue, not the singing of either metrical psalms or hymns. It is possible, however, that the wardens also objected to that as well, because the terminology now used to describe various musical portions of the service was often used differently in the eighteenth century. It is possible that Cuming relied upon the account given in a 1906 report, which also implies that the case involved the singing of either metrical psalms or hymns. See *Report of the Royal Commission on Ecclesiastical Discipline,* 5 vols. in 3 (London: Printed for H. M. Stationery Office by Wyman and Sons, 1906), 1:8.

31. Present research indicates that this is the earliest instance of a court case regarding congregational singing. Cases regarding the financial provision for music, e.g., the salary of an organist, maintenance of an organ, or the purchase of an organ, occurred throughout the latter half of the eighteenth century and into the nineteenth century. See Nicholas Temperley, *The Music of the English Parish Church,* 2 vols. (Cambridge: Cambridge University Press, 1979), 1:106–107.

Book."[32] Tattersall argued that if this was the legal authority by which Stern-hold and Hopkins's metrical version of the Psalms was used in public worship, then these statutes also "granted" the same indulgence to "every other Version, and even to all Prayers and Selections, provided they are really translated from the inspired writings."[33] Confirmation of this interpretation was found by Tattersall in this passage from a Book of Ceremonies published in 1539: "The sober, discreet, and devout singing, music, and playing with organs, used in the Church, in the service of God, are ordained to move and stir the people to the sweetness of God's word, the which is there sung."[34] For Tattersall this was sufficient support for the inclusion of metrical psalms in the liturgy of the church. Moreover, this interpretation did not exclude any particular version or versions so long as they conformed to the requirement

---

32. William Dechair Tattersall, *A Version of the Psalms . . . by the late Reverend James Merrick, divided into stanzas, and adapted to the purpose of public or private devotion* (London: n.p., [1797?]), preface. See also William Dechair Tattersall, *Improved Psalmody. Vol. 1 The Psalms of David, from a Poetrical [sic] Version originally written By the late Reverend James Merrick, A.M. Fellow of Trinity College, Oxford. Divided into Stanzas for the purpose of Public and Private Devotion, With New Music Collected from the most Eminent Composers* (London: T. Skillern, 1794). Volume Two was never published. James Merrick had published his work, *The Psalms, translated or paraphrased in English verse*, in 1765. A scholarly work, which Merrick never intended for public worship, it nevertheless was highly regarded and used by those who desired something other than the rhymes of Sternhold and Hopkins or Tate and Brady. The most significant version of Merrick's psalms adapted for worship was made by Tattersall.

33. Tattersall, *Version*, preface. Tattersall may have derived his argument from the interpretation of this clause by Gilbert Burnet, who held that "[t]he *Proviso* for the *Psalms* and *Prayers* taken out of the Bible, was for the *Singing Psalms* [i.e., metrical psalms], which were translated into Verse, and much sung by all who loved the Reformation, and were in many Places used in Churches." See *The History of the Reformation of the Church of England*, 3 vols. (London: Printed by T. H. for Richard Chiswell, 1679–1715), 2:94. See also [Basil Woodd], *The Psalms of David, And other Portions of the Sacred Scriptures, Arranged according to the order of the Church of England, For every Sunday in the Year; also for the Saints' Days, Holy Communion, and other Services* (London: Watts and Bridgewater, [c. 1798]), preface, who used many of the same arguments as Tattersall, and Henry Draper, *Lectures on the Liturgy; Delivered in the Parish Church of St. Antholin, Watling Street* (London: Printed for Williams and Smith, [1806]), 202, who also held that the clause from 2 and 3 Edw. VI permitted the use of metrical versions other than Sternhold and Hopkins or Tate and Brady. Draper, like Woodd, acted upon his beliefs, publishing *A Collection of Psalms and Hymns, for Social Worship* (London: Printed for the author) in 1805. Many of the 275 hymns were taken from Watts.

34. Tattersall, *Version*, preface.

of being "translated from the inspired writings," although, in Tattersall's opinion, it did exclude all hymns. Like others, for example, De Courcy, Tattersall did not realize how thin the line could be that separated versification of scripture and verse that was freely composed. Compare, for example, the prose version of Psalm 137 in the Book of Common Prayer with the versions by Sternhold and Hopkins and Tate and Brady:

> By the waters of Babylon we sat down and wept:
> when we remembred [*sic*] thee, O sion.
> As for our harps, we hanged them up:
> upon the trees that are therein.

Sternhold and Hopkins:

> When we did sit in Babylon,
>   the rivers round about,
> Then in remembrance of Sion,
>   the tears for grief burst out.
> We hanged our harps and instruments
>   the willow trees upon,
> For in that place men for their use
>   had planted many one.

The changes are evident. Not only is "grief" given as reason for the tears and other "instruments" added to the harps, but the "willow" trees have been "planted" in anticipation of their use. Tate and Brady's metrical version goes even further:

> When we our wearied limbs to rest,
>   sat down by proud Euphrates' stream,
> We wept with doleful thoughts opprest,
>   and Zion was our mournful theme.
> Our harps, that, when with joy we sung,
>   were wont their tuneful parts to bear,
> With silent strings neglected hung,
>   on willow-trees that withered there.

The line separating versification of scripture and verse that was freely composed could be quite thin!

Taking a more common-sense approach to the issue, William Mason, rector of Aston and precentor of York Minster, added his voice to those opposed to hymnody. In his substantial *Essays, Historical and Critical, on English Church Music,* Mason treated the development of organ music, the relationship of the cathedral choir to the organ, parochial psalmody, and the relationship of text and musical setting.[35] Building on a solid historical foundation established in the second essay, Mason refuted the objections to psalmody put forth by Johnson and Warton.[36] Mason argued that at the time of the Reformation the Church of England adopted two styles of music for worship. In the cathedrals "one species of Music" was sanctioned and "in her parish Churches allowed another."[37] The cathedral style of music was the continuation of the long-established choral tradition, and the parish form was the innovative metrical psalmody. Although acknowledging Warton's argument that "they [i.e., metrical psalms] never received the Royal approbation, or obtained parliamentary sanction," Mason maintained, nonetheless, that metrical psalmody had been "adopted" in England prior to the publication of the complete version of Sternhold and Hopkins's psalter in 1562. Evidence of its adoption rested on the fact that psalmody had been publicly used in 1559 at St. Paul's without suffering interdiction from the crown. Thus, "Sternhold, or his printer, might fairly enough assert, that his Version was allowed to be sung in Churches."[38] Mason

---

35. William Mason, *Essays, Historical and Critical, on English Church Music* (York: W. Blanchard, 1795). Mason made remarkable use of the major reference works of his day but did not pursue original documents. This led him to repeat certain errors, although on at least one occasion he did correct an error in his secondary source. See John W. Draper, *William Mason: A Study in Eighteenth-Century Culture* (New York: New York University Press, 1924), 284–314.

36. Thomas Warton, poet laureate and critic, had argued against any metrical version of the Psalms, "especially if intended for the use of the Church." See his *History of English Poetry from the Twelfth to the Close of the Sixteenth Century*, ed. W. Carew Hazlitt, 4 vols. (London: Reeves and Turner, 1871), 4:137. For Warton's views on psalmody, see especially 4:124–148. D'Israeli also noted Warton's opposition to the metrical version of Sternhold and Hopkins, regarding it as a "puritanic invention." See I[saac] D'Israeli, *A Second Series of Curiosities of Literature; Consisting of Researches in Literary, Biographical, and Political History; Of Critical and Philosophical Inquiries; and of Secret History,* 2nd ed., corrected, 3 vols. (London: J. Murray, 1824), 1:194. Johnson, according to Mason, "had condemned all devotional Poetry whatever" (*Essays,* 172). Which Johnson Mason was referring to is unclear.

37. Mason, *Essays,* 168.

38. Mason based his interpretation on the account of a metrical psalm being sung publicly following the sermon on March 15, 1559. Mason mistakenly stated that this took place "ten" years before the publication of the whole psalter in 1562, when in actuality it was only three years (*Essays,* 169–170).

concluded, "Nothing more need be said historically on the subject."[39] In his opinion, the use of metrical psalms within the liturgy of the church rested upon solid ground, but there was no support for the introduction of hymns.

It is probable that Mason, a man of considerable reputation (at least in the north of England), convinced some clergy to forgo their inclinations to accept the introduction of hymns. For others, the question of the basis of authority for the incorporation of metrical psalms (or hymns) into the liturgy of the Church of England could not be decided so easily. One could appeal to 2 and 3 Edw. VI, but Sternhold and Hopkins's metrical versions had not been completed at that time. Dod's version was privileged by James I in 1603; James I's version was recommended, as well as allowed, by his successor, Charles I; and Tate and Brady's version was sanctioned by William III in council. But did such royal privileges and recommendations constitute legal authorization for inclusion in the liturgy of the church? Should not the church's song have the same authorization as the church's liturgy, that is, an act of Parliament? Or was it sufficient to have a majority of the bench of bishops concurring, as in the case of Richard Blackmore's version? Appeals were made to the Injunctions of Elizabeth I and to the statutes of Edward VI, but these were open to various interpretations. Thus, advocates and opponents of hymnody could, and did, reach opposite conclusions regarding the legality of various versions of metrical psalms and hymn collections and their use in the liturgy of the church.[40]

---

39. Mason, *Essays,* 171. Given the expansive treatment of the other topics included in his work, it is somewhat surprising that Mason devoted such a small portion of his work to the question of the legal status of metrical psalms, surveying the development of psalmody in a scant eight pages.

40. As the debate intensified during the period 1800–1820, many compilers attempted to defend their actions through either elaborate prefaces, an appeal to the Injunctions of Elizabeth I, or by securing the imprimatur of the diocesan. See, for example, Tho[mas] T. Biddulph, *Portions of the Psalms of David, Together with a Selection of Hymns, Accommodated to the Service of the Church of England, on Sundays and Other Holy Seasons of Public Worship Which She Observes* (Bristol: W. Pine and Son, 1802); James H. Stewart, *A Selection of Psalms & Hymns, Adapted to the Service of the Church of England; Revised for the use of Percy Chapel, Charlotte Street, Fitzroy Square* (London: W. M. Thiselton, 1813); and W. Hurn, *Psalms and Hymns, The Greater Part Original; and the Selected Compositions altered with a view to Purity of Doctrine and General Usefulness* (Ipswich: J. Raw, 1813).

Counterarguments

Writing in 1810, John Kempthorne indicated that a certain prejudice still existed toward hymns, although it perhaps was not as strong as it had been.[41] This prejudice continued because of the fact that "injudicious and improper Hymns" were being included in the liturgy. A supporter of metrical psalms, Kempthorne also advocated the introduction of hymns, with certain limitations.[42]

Kempthorne based his argument for the inclusion of hymns in the liturgy upon his interpretation of the rubric following the third collect in the offices: "In Quires and places where they sing, here follows the Anthem."[43] Kempthorne did not approve of choirs usurping the role of the congregation at this point in the offices, noting that they were "introduced as a temporary remedy for the irreverence and unskilfulness [*sic*] of Congregations."[44] At the time of the Reformation, Kempthorne reminded his readers, the reformers did not "prohibit" choirs in those places where they were established. Moreover, he argued, the reformers certainly did not "enjoin them in Parish Churches."[45] In fact, Kempthorne noted, the rubric only made passing reference to choirs and in no way recommended them. Further, the term *anthem* signified "any sacred song; such as may be used 'in all places where they sing,' as well as in

---

41. John Kempthorne, *Select Portions of Psalms, From Various Translations, and Hymns, From Various Authors. The Whole Arranged according to the yearly Seasons of the Church of England; with Attempts at Corrections and Improvements* (London: Printed for J. Hatchard, 1810). The title indicates clearly the character of the collection, and it is significant that his concern for the liturgical year predates Keble's work (*The Christian Year: thoughts in verse for the Sundays and Holydays throughout the year*) by seventeen years. Kempthorne, however, was not the first to organize a collection according to the liturgical year. See, for example, [Luke Booker], *Select Psalms and Hymns for the use of the Churches in Dudley, &c,* 2nd ed. (Dudley: J. Rann, 1796), which included twenty-four hymns arranged seasonally beginning with Advent. William James Porter's collection, *A Selection From the New Version of the Psalms of David* (Canterbury: J. Saffery, 1807), was organized in the same fashion, although no hymns were included. Basil Woodd's collection, discussed earlier, was perhaps the first to provide selections for every Sunday and holy day in the church year.

42. Kempthorne, ix–x. Kempthorne was concerned primarily that hymns used in the liturgy of the church reflect the subjects "brought forward by the Church of England in her Proper Lessons, Epistles, Gospels, and Collects" (v).

43. The rubric was added to the Prayer Book in 1662.

44. Kempthorne, viii.

45. Kempthorne, viii.

Choirs."[46] Thus, with this interpretation of the rubric, metrical psalms and hymns could exist side-by-side in the liturgy. Just as metrical psalms had been accepted as an alternative to the choir anthem at this point in the office, so too could hymns be used in similar fashion. Kempthorne was not alone in his views. At least one other person shared them. Writing five years later, W. M. reached this conclusion regarding the rubric after the third collect:

> [W]ho can read . . . the rubric concerning anthems after the third collect, without admitting the lawfulness of singing something distinct from the psalms? And what are meant by Anthems? Let the collections used in our cathedrals determine: there we find selections from Scripture, from the liturgy, and from modern authors, both in prose and verse constantly used. The lawfulness of other versions of the Psalms, and of Hymns, are thus, I trust, completely and fully established.[47]

Although Kempthorne's argument added additional support for the inclusion of hymns in the liturgy, it did not contribute significantly to the ongoing controversy. In fact, no one appears to have responded directly to his interpretation of the rubric. A substantial contribution in favor of the use of hymns, however, occurred a few years later as a result of William Richardson's desire to supplement the metrical psalms used in his parish.

Richardson, vicar choral of York Minster and curate of St. Michael le Belfrey, had published a collection of metrical psalms consisting of careful selections from Sternhold and Hopkins, Tate and Brady, Watts, and Merrick in 1788.[48] This served the musical needs of the parish well until it

---

46. Kempthorne, ix. As early as 1716 a certain degree of flexibility concerning what was sung at this point in the service existed. Thomas Bisse, for example, urged that by singing metrical psalms "where the Anthem is appointed, you conform to the appointment of the Church, and to the practice of Cathedral Churches; and moreover do honour to the singing Psalms themselves, by making them as Anthems, as they may not improperly be accounted" (96). See also [Thomas Collins], *The Rubrick of the Church of England, Examin'd and Consider'd; and Its Use and Observance most Earnestly recommended to all its Members, according to the Intent and Meaning of it* (London: Printed for T. Astley, 1737). This study was reprinted in *The Christian Remembrancer* 11 (1829):686–692, 749–757; 12 (1830):38–46, 111–118, 233–240, 301–307, 363–367.

47. W. M., "On the discretionary Use of Psalms and Hymns in Church," *The Christian Observer* 14 (October 1815):662. Another writer desired to learn "on what authority" the custom of singing a metrical psalm following the second lesson rather than in the appointed place rested. See Philo-Rubric, "Proper Place of the Psalm in the Church Service," *The Christian Observer* 18 (February 1819):86–87.

48. William Richardson, *A Collection of Psalms* (York: n.p., 1788).

came to be considered too limited in its contents. By 1814, or perhaps earlier, Richardson began to introduce hymns as a means of supplementing his collection of metrical psalms and received directions from his bishop to cease.[49] Seeking advice on how to respond to the bishop's request, Richardson wrote to Charles Simeon in January 1814. Simeon replied, "As to the Hymns, I would, if he insist upon it, give them up; and would select profitable portions out of the two Versions." Richardson obviously persisted in the use of hymns, for Simeon cautioned in March 1814:

> Circumstanced as you are, I feel no hesitation in saying, that you should avoid everything that can give offence, except the faithful preaching of "Christ crucified." Why should you stand out about the Hymns? You are very injudicious in this. You should consider that when a storm is raised, you are not the only sufferer. Pray study to maintain peace, though you make some sacrifices for it. . . . Put aside Hymns, which are quite unnecessary.[50]

Between 1814 and 1817 Richardson may have followed the counsel of his bishop. However, in 1817 he was ready once again to introduce a collection of hymns into his parish, selecting a collection that had been compiled by Jonathan Gray for the parish of St. Saviour.[51]

As in Richardson's previous experience (no doubt shared with Gray, a close family friend),[52] objections against admitting hymns into the church were made. As a result, Gray undertook a study of the two central questions: "what is the order of church music prescribed by our Establishment,

---

49. William Carus, ed., *Memoirs of the Life of the Rev. Charles Simeon, M.A., with a Selection from his Writings and Correspondence* (London: J. Hatchard and Son, 1847), 382–386. The bishop is not identified by Carus. If it was the archbishop, Vernon Harcourt, then sometime between 1814 and 1820 (when the Cotterill case came to his attention) he changed his opinion regarding hymnody.

50. Carus, 385–386.

51. [Jonathan Gray], *Hymns, Selected as a Supplement to a Collection of Psalms used in several Churches,* 2nd ed. (York: C. Peacock, 1817). Under the leadership of John Graham, rector, the music at St. Saviour had been steadily improving since 1798. The collection of metrical psalms referred to in the title was Richardson's. By 1817 Richardson's work was in use in "at least thirty churches, in and near York" (Gray, *Hymns,* 2nd ed., preface). See also Nicholas Temperley, *Jonathan Gray and Church Music in York, 1770–1840* (York: Borthwick Papers, 1977), 14–15.

52. For a description of the relationship between Richardson and the Gray family, see [Almyra] Gray, *Papers and Diaries of a York Family, 1764–1839* (London: Sheldon, 1927), passim.

and what is the authority of the Old and New Versions?"[53] Gray began his study by noting that the Book of Common Prayer, which contained the authorized formularies of the Church of England and was the only work prescribed by Parliament, contained no version of the Psalms except the prose version. Anthems were permitted by the rubric following the third collect in the offices, and their texts could be taken from the Prayer Book or the Bible as allowed by 2 and 3 Edw. VI. To those who held that this clause was intended to allow the Psalms to be turned into meter for the use of the church, Gray responded, "it may well be doubted whether this be not too great a latitude of interpretation."[54]

The introduction of metrical psalms into the English church, Gray argued, was largely the result of the exiles' experience on the continent during the reign of Queen Mary. Upon returning to England, they desired to replace the traditional cathedral style with the new metrical singing. In Gray's opinion, "it was no difficult task to prevail with the people to prefer the plain Psalmody, in which they found it easy to join, to that intricate music which was too refined and scientific for their taste and comprehension."[55] Elizabeth I was persuaded, "though reluctantly," to give support to the "popular feeling." Thus, the Injunctions of 1559 provided for the singing of "an hymn, or such like song." Moreover, Gray argued, since the word "Psalms is often used in a general sense as comprehending metrical Hymns, so here Hymns must be considered as comprising metrical Psalms."[56] Taken together, the Injunctions of 1559 and the general acceptance of the innovative form led Gray to conclude

[t]he practice of congregational metrical singing, therefore, though it cannot claim the authority of any positive enactment, yet is co-eval in its origin with the Reformation; and by its facility of attainment has powerfully recommended itself to popular and general use. The practice is indeed now so firmly established, that it would be vain to attempt its abolition.[57]

---

53. H. G. [Jonathan Gray], "On the Admission of Metrical Hymns into Churches," *The Christian Observer* 17 (March 1818):152. For the identification of H. G. as Gray, see *The Christian Observer* 21 (1822):421.

54. Gray, "On the Admission," 153.

55. Gray, "On the Admission," 154.

56. Gray, "On the Admission," 154.

57. Gray, "On the Admission," 155. Two years earlier, B. Richings stated that "it is fully evident, and that too on the very best and highest authorities, that there is no law to establish the use of either the Old or New Version, or to preclude a Minister from making such a selection as he may think most conducive to the benefit and instruction of his people." See his *A Selection of Psalms and Hymns, from Various Authors, Designed for the Use of Public Worship* (London: Ellerton and Henderson, 1816), vii.

The second question, the authority of the "Old Version" and the *New Version,* had been answered, in part, through Gray's examination of the origins of congregational song. Noting the work of Heylyn, Gray agreed that the "Old Version" lacked any positive enactment for use in the services of the church, having been "allowed" rather than required. Likewise, the *New Version* was merely "allowed" "to be used in such congregations as shall think fit to receive the same."[58] In Gray's opinion the "best metrical translations of the Psalms must always be greatly inferior to the authorised prose version, pointed to be sung in our churches."[59] Nonetheless, metrical forms occupied a proper place within the liturgy of the church. The authority of scripture, the practice of the primitive church, the practice of the Church of England, and the episcopal permissions given to contemporary collections vindicated the use of hymns and metrical psalms in public worship.[60]

Although an advocate of the use of metrical psalms and hymns, especially those "composed on the model and breathing the spirit of those in the Liturgy," Gray was fully aware of the use of hymns and metrical psalms that contained "expressions of familiarity and endearment" improper to the piety and dignity of the Church of England and that offended "good sense [and] correct taste."[61] Nonetheless, the church, Gray argued, should continue to seek "to have a collection of hymns, composed expressly for the use of its members." By the "united efforts of all the poets of the age," their individual work could be reduced from a hundred to ten, "tens to units, till a competent number of suitable ones was procured."[62] Interestingly, Gray does not indicate how such a collection should be authorized for use in the Church of England.

---

58. Gray expands this argument in his *An Inquiry into Historical Facts, relative to Parochial Psalmody, In reference to the Remarks of The Right Reverend Herbert, Lord Bishop of Peterborough* (York: Printed by J. Wolstenholme, 1821), 10–11.

59. Gray, "On the Admission," 156.

60. Gray, "On the Admission," 156–157. Gray noted two recent collections which had received episcopal support, those by Gardiner (*Psalms and Hymns; allowed to be sung in churches,* 1814) and [Edward Maltby, R. Tillard, and J. S. Banks, eds.], *Psalms and Hymns, Selected for the Churches of Buckden and Holveach, of Bluntisham cum Earith, and Hemingford Grey, in the Diocese of Lincoln* (London: Printed for T. Cadell and W. Davies, 1815).

61. Gray, "On the Admission," 158.

62. Gray, "On the Admission," 158–159. Gray stated in 1821 that the final two pages of this article, 158–159, contained "remarks on the composition of Metrical Hymns, added without my knowledge, and containing some opinions with which I do not accord" (*Inquiry,* 73). Unfortunately, Gray did not elaborate.

Cotterill v. Holy and Ward

Resolution to the question of the legal status of metrical psalms or hymns in the liturgy might have been long in coming if a case regarding the issue had not been brought before the Chancery Court of the diocese of York in 1820.[63] The cause for the case was the publication of the eighth edition of Thomas Cotterill's *Selection of Hymns for Public and Private Use* (Sheffield, 1819) and its introduction at St. Paul's Church, Sheffield. Before turning to the case itself, it will be helpful to chart the events that led to the incident.

Thomas Cotterill was born on December 4, 1779, at Cannock, Staffordshire. The son of a woolstapler, Cotterill graduated from St. John's College, Cambridge (B.A. 1801, M.A. 1805), of which he later became a fellow.[64] After taking Holy Orders, Cotterill became the curate at Tutbury in June 1803. From 1808 to 1817 he was the incumbent of Lane End, Staffordshire, and he held the perpetual curacy of St. Paul's, Sheffield, from 1817 to 1823. He died at Sheffield on December 29, 1823 and was buried within the walls of the church.[65]

Cotterill had been an advocate of hymns as early as 1805. In that year he contributed to a collection that contained seventy-nine hymns for public use and forty-eight hymns for private use as well as twenty-seven metrical psalms.[66] In 1810, while at Lane End, Cotterill published the first edition of his *Selection of Psalms and Hymns for Public and Private Use, adapted to the Festivals of the Church of England.* Included in that col-

---

63. In December 1819 there was a brief note in *The Christian Observer* regarding a case involving the control of singing by a warden and reference to a current case concerning church music in the Court of Arches. The first reference may have been to *Hutchins v. Denziloe and Loveland* (1792). The details of the second reference have eluded efforts to bring them to light. See "Literary and Philosophical Intelligence," *The Christian Observer* 18 (December 1819):810. Another court case revolving around who could sing, and at what point, in the service occurred in 1821. See "Right of Clergymen to controul the singing in Church; and the ringing of Church Bells," *The Christian Remembrancer* 4 (June 1822):375–377.

64. W. Odom, *Memorials of Sheffield: Its Cathedral and Parish Churches* (Sheffield: J. W. Northend, 1922), 71–72.

65. Odom, 68.

66. See [Jonathan Stubbs], *A Selection of Psalms and Hymns, for Public and Private Use* (Uttoxeter: R. Richards, 1805). There is no preface to this collection and no indication as to the intended audience. Stubbs was curate of Uttoxeter and may have intended the collection for their use. He was assisted by Cotterill, Thomas Gisborne, and Edward Cooper in compiling the work. See John Julian, *A Dictionary of Hymnology: Setting Forth the Origin and History of Christian Hymns of All Ages and Nations,* revised edition, with new supplement (London: J. Murray, 1907), 1084.

lection were at least four hymns and three metrical psalms by Cotterill.[67] Cotterill's contributions increased in the sixth edition (1815) and reached their greatest number in the eighth edition (1819).[68] No evidence appears to exist to indicate whether Cotterill introduced his work in the parish at Lane End and, if so, the kind of reception it had by the congregation. Also nothing is known about the use of hymns at St. Paul's during the early years of Cotterill's tenure.[69] What is known is that Cotterill was an active proponent of the inclusion of hymns in the service of the church and that his work enjoyed a not inconsiderable success.[70]

In the rather lengthy preface (sixteen pages) to the eighth edition of his *Selection of Psalms and Hymns,* Cotterill responded to the allegation that the "Psalms only are *authorised,* and that the introduction of Hymns *is Innovation and Irregularity.*"[71] The idea that an authority existed for the use of metrical psalms and that none existed for the use of hymns, Cotterill argued, was a "gratuitous assumption, altogether unsupported by matter of fact."[72] Cotterill dismissed all appeals to the clause in 2 and 3 Edw. VI, arguing that the clause did not refer to singing at all. If it did, Cotterill maintained, it certainly did not apply to the 1562 edition of Sternhold and Hopkins, for the clause was not law when it was introduced since Elizabeth I had "revived only that part of Edward's act, repealed by Mary, which related to the Book of Com-

---

67. Items in the collection are given without the author's name. However, working from marked copies from the collections of Brooke and Julian, scholars have been able to identify the authorship of most of the texts.

68. Four hymns were added to the sixth edition, and four additional hymns plus another metrical psalm were added to the eighth edition. James Montgomery, publisher and hymn writer, worked with Cotterill on his collection. Of the four hundred hymns Montgomery wrote during his lifetime, almost twenty-five percent remain in current use. Montgomery was also skilled as an editor, altering, rearranging, and amending a number of the items included in Cotterill's collection. The success of this work was largely because of Montgomery's abilities.

69. Cotterill's predecessor at St. Paul's was Alexander Mackenzie (1788–1816). No evidence has been found to indicate whether he introduced hymns into the parish.

70. Cotterill's work continued in use for almost forty years, especially in the north of England. The work also served as a model for later compilers, notably Edward Bickersteth's *Christian Psalmody: a collection of above 700 Psalms, hymns and spiritual songs: Selected and arranged for public, social, family and private worship* (London: L. B. Seeley and Sons, 1833), and as a source book for other collections (Cotterill and Montgomery's altered forms of the original texts usually being retained).

71. T[homas] Cotterill, *A Selection of Psalms and Hymns for Public and Private Use, Adapted to the Services of the Church of England,* 8th ed., considerably enlarged (Sheffield: Printed for the editor, by J. Montgomery, 1819), viii. Cotterill was referring to the work of Vincent and Mason.

72. Cotterill, 1819, 8th ed., viii.

mon Prayer."[73] Thus, the "Old Version" never received any authorization from Parliament. Nevertheless, Cotterill reminded his readers that this version was "set forth and allowed" to be used in the services of the church.

Although the use of metrical compositions, whether psalms or hymns, did not rest on legislative sanction (in Cotterill's estimation), there were supportive reasons for continuing their use. One reason for allowing metrical psalms to be used was their favorable reception in the 1560s. Having been introduced without legislative or royal sanction and not having received any interdictions indicated to Cotterill the positive support given by the reformers to this innovative form. A stronger reason, Cotterill maintained, was the Injunctions of 1559. Although the Injunctions were directed toward collegiate churches, Cotterill argued that the spirit of the provision entrusted the selection of any song or hymn to the discretion of the minister in charge, be it parish, cathedral, or collegiate church.[74] The course for the development of a variety of metrical and nonmetrical forms to meet the needs of the Church of England was clearly established in the sixteenth century by allowing the choral tradition to continue in cathedrals and by not preventing the development of psalmody for use in parishes. In short, the church had always allowed the use of metrical psalms and hymns.[75]

Contemporary evidence readily supported this position, Cotterill claimed. For example, if the use of hymns was an "unauthorised innovation and irregularity," then why did the clerical members of the Society for Promoting Christian Knowledge not protest their being bound with copies of the Book of Common Prayer?[76] How could the University Church at

---

73. Cotterill, 1819, 8th ed., viii.

74. Cotterill, 1819, 8th ed., x. Walker Gray, writing a few years earlier, took the opposite viewpoint, arguing that the selection was not within the discretion of the minister and that the introduction of a variety of hymns and metrical psalms had altered the "uniformity of public worship." See his *Select Portions of Psalms and Hymns, Entirely Extracted from the Prayer-Book, without alteration or addition, for the use of Cullumpton Church* (N.p.: Printed for the editor, 1815), vii. Charles Daubeny stated simply that congregational singing of hymns and metrical psalms were part of the "established order of our Church." See *A Few Plain Thoughts on the Liturgy of The Church of England: with the view of Explaining and Promoting its Rational Use, and Spiritual Design* (Bath: Printed and Sold by Meyler and Son, 1814), 27.

75. Cotterill, 1819, 8th ed., xii.

76. In this reference to the SPCK, Cotterill appears to be drawing upon an article written in 1815. In that article W. M. questioned: "Does not the same excellent and most respectable society circulate Watts's Divine Songs for Children in all our National Schools, which are taught on the principles of the Church of England? Nay further, does it not distribute even the hymns of Wesley and Doddridge in the very Common Prayer Books which it publishes? After SUCH A SANCTION, who is there to be found so captious as to object to a selection of psalms and hymns" (662)?

Oxford use a collection "to which no legal sanction has been ever given, and for which the Royal Sanction was solicited and refused," if the use of hymns was illegal? And what of the various collections that had been introduced in several dioceses with the express permission of the diocesan?[77] It was evident to Cotterill that "where there is no law there can be no transgression."[78] Thus, Cotterill concluded,

> However much it could be wished, for the sake of uniformity, that one authorised form of public Psalmody were appointed, as there is of public prayer, yet in the absence of such a desideratum, every Clergyman is necessarily left to the exercise of his own discretion, in adopting such a system of Psalmody as may appear to him best calculated to improve that important part of public worship.[79]

Although Cotterill believed firmly in his right to exercise his discretion concerning the musical portion of public worship, at least some of his parishioners believed otherwise. Sometime between the publication of the eighth edition (1819), which was a "large book issued at a high price," and March 3, 1820, when a citation was issued for Cotterill to appear before

---

77. Cotterill, 1819, 8th ed., x–xi. See, for example, Maltby, et al., which was dedicated by permission to Tomline, bishop of Lincoln. In the second edition (1820), the compilers claimed that the collection was "sanctioned by the authority of that distinguished prelate." See also Charles Daubeny, *Psalms and Hymns, Appointed to be Sung by The Congregation assembled at Christ Church, Bath* (Bath: Wood, 1816).

78. Cotterill, 1819, 8th ed., xi. Cotterill was almost certainly paraphrasing W. M., who himself was citing a source of unknown origin. W. M. affirmed the authority of the clergy in the matter of selecting material to be sung in the service based upon his interpretation of the Injunctions of Elizabeth I. He concluded, "[W]here there is no law 'against singing other versions than the old antiquated and in some respects obsolete and almost unchristian versions of Sternhold, Hopkins, Tate, and Brady, there can be no transgression in adopting a better'" (661). Robert E. Rodes Jr., in discussing the official formularies of the church (the Thirty-Nine Articles and the Book of Common Prayer) and their role in the judicial proceedings against the ritualists, commented "where they were silent, liberty prevailed." See his *Law and Modernization in the Church of England: Charles II to the Welfare State* (Notre Dame: University of Notre Dame Press, 1991), 259.

79. Cotterill, 1819, 8th ed., xi. An anonymous compiler also believed that the rector of a parish had sufficient authority to determine what was or was not used within the parish. At the request of the rector, he had collected the hymns that were in use in the parish. Numbering sixty-six, these were published in 1816. By 1828 experience had proved this collection inadequate. Thus, a new collection was completed. See *Selection of Hymns in a Great Variety of Metres, Adapted to the Use of the Established Church* (Holt, Norfolk: J. Shalders, 1828), preface. The editor of this collection was a singer in the newly formed choir (c. 1816) and represents one of the few known examples of laity involved in the development of hymnody in this period.

the court, opposition either to the use of hymns or to this particular collection emerged in the parish.[80]

On June 11, 1819, Thomas Morton, warden of St. Paul's, answered several articles during the archiepiscopal visitation held at Doncaster. Questions regarding the building and related items (books, registers, furniture, and so forth) were all answered favorably, as was the general performance of the curate, Thomas Cotterill, who was described by Morton as being "a person of pious, virtuous and exemplary Life and Conversation."[81] There was, however, one concern noted:

> The Curate for the Time being has performed the Service during my Office as Churchwarden both Forenoon and Afternoon every Sunday according to the prescribed Form of Worship and Service directed to be used in the Church of England except that he has lately introduced and caused to be given out and Sung on Sundays in the Course of such Service certain Psalms and Hymns not appointed by the Rubrick nor authorised by his Majesty according to Law and this Conduct has created much Dissatisfaction in the Minds of a Number of the Pew Owners and Persons attending divine Worship there and caused some of such Persons to absent themselves from Attendance on divine Worship on Sundays as they had heretofore done.[82]

Whether Morton made this objection on behalf of certain pew holders, by whom he was elected to office, or on his own behalf is not clear.[83] Either or both is possible.

---

80. Julian, *Dictionary,* 334. Whatever the source of the opposition, Cotterill was probably supported by the vicar of the parish, Thomas Sutton, in his use of hymns. Sutton had introduced hymns into the parish as early as 1807. See T[homas] Sutton, *Select Portions of Psalms from the New Version, Hymns and Anthems. Sung at the Parish Church in Sheffield* (Sheffield: Printed for W. Mather, 1807). A second edition was published in 1816. Hymnody was not the only controversy in which Cotterill was involved. In 1819 Cotterill refused to allow the church to be used for an oratorio performance, an action that created turmoil in the parish. See Percy M. Young, *A History of British Music* (New York: W. W. Norton, 1967), 419.

81. Thomas Morton, extract from the Registry of the Archdeaconry of York, Chanc. CP. 1820/1, The Borthwicke Institute of Historical Research, York.

82. Morton, Chanc. CP. 1820/1. Morton made one further negative comment concerning Cotterill's withholding the key to the church door on several occasions.

83. Morton became a warden in the chapel in 1818, being sworn in at the visitation on May 29. He continued in that capacity in 1819. However, in the following year, or late in 1819, George Senior became the warden. See YV/CB 19, The Borthwicke Institute of Historical Research, York. One is led to speculate that his opposition to hymns may have been part of a struggle for power. If Morton's views toward hymns reflected the views of a majority of the pew holders, then why was he not returned to office in 1820, especially since the cause had yet to be heard in court? Moreover, why did he not include his name along with that of Holy and Ward in the cause against Cotterill?

In any event, Cotterill apparently ignored the objection made by Morton, and in 1820 those opposed to the introduction of hymns sought legal recourse when Daniel Holy and Samuel Broomhead Ward made bond to prosecute in March.[84] In their statement before Granville Venables Vernon, Vicar General of the Chancery Court, Holy and Ward charged Cotterill with introducing

> of his own pretended authority into the Public performance of divine Service . . . a certain Selection of Hymns and a metrical Version of Psalms not set forth or allowed by Law to be used in Churches or Chapels of the Establishment of the Church of England or by any competent authority whatsoever.[85]

Holy, a silverplater, and Ward, esquire, and perhaps those whom they represented were certainly committed to this course of action, having paid a bond of one hundred pounds in order to instigate the action.[86] On April 13, 1820, Vernon issued the articles against Cotterill. The articles made specific reference to Cotterill's failure to adhere to the prescribed form of worship in the Church of England by introducing an unauthorized selection of hymns and metrical psalms in the services of St. Paul's and stated that Cotterill was "compelled to desist from using or causing the aforesaid Selection of Psalms and Hymns to be used or sung."[87]

The cause was heard on July 6, 1820. According to Gray, Cotterill ad-

---

84. The exact date is difficult to determine since the record of the action in the Court Act Book lacks specific details regarding what occurred at each appearance before the court. We know that the citation was issued on March 3, 1820, and that counsel appeared before the court on March 16 and 23. Since the Articles are dated April 13, 1820, and there is no record of a court appearance between March 23 and April 13, the bond to prosecute must have been filed on one of the dates in March. It is possible that Cotterill never appeared personally before the court, having appointed James Robert Fryer as his Proctor on March 21. Holy and Ward appointed Frederick William Storry to represent them on March 29. See Chanc. AB. 51, The Borthwicke Institute of Historical Research, York.

85. Bond to Prosecute, Chanc. CP. 1820/1.

86. The opposition to hymns may not have been restricted to members of the parish. Julian stated that opposition was "strengthened by outside feeling," although exactly what he meant by this is unclear (*Dictionary,* 334). In similar fashion, Benson noted that "some outside opponents of hymns took advantage" of the situation (*English Hymn,* 355). Evidence to support their statements has not been found, although it is entirely possible that such was the case.

87. Chanc. CP. 1820/1.

mitted introducing his *Selection* into the church.[88] Counsel then proceeded to argue the legality or illegality of his actions. Vernon, recognizing the importance of the issue, took the matter under advisement, noting before adjourning the court that "there was, perhaps, not a Clergyman in the kingdom who had not violated the law, if Mr. Cotterill had done so." He also noted that the archbishop had indicated his willingness to be a mediator and that he "thought it much for the interest of religion that a compromise should take place."[89]

On July 28, Vernon rendered his decision. In his opinion, the case was important for two reasons: first, the legal issue of the introduction of hymns and metrical psalms into the liturgy, and second, the fact that this practice, that is, the use of metrical forms, had been "adopted by a majority of the Established Clergy."[90] On the second point, Vernon believed that the church had benefited from the inclusion of metrical forms in the liturgy, intimating that even if not legally sanctioned their positive contributions outweighed any negative considerations. He noted,

---

88. Jonathan Gray's *An Inquiry* (1821) is the primary source for this and following paragraphs. The work was written in response to the bishop of Peterborough's *Charge* of 1820. Unlike modern law courts, much of what passed before an ecclesiastical court was not recorded. See B. D. Till, "The Administrative System of the Ecclesiastical Courts in the Diocese and Province of York, Part III: 1660–1883" (Thesis, University of York: Borthwicke Institute of Historical Research, 1963), 132. For an assessment of Gray's contributions to church music, see Temperley, *Jonathan Gray*. For an overview of Gray's life, see Almyra Gray, 106–117.

89. Gray, *Inquiry,* 47. The archbishop, Vernon Harcourt, had approached Cotterill prior to the hearing, suggesting that he compile a new edition: "Send it to me and undertake to cut out every hymn which I do not sanction. Dedicate the book to me. Then we have them." See *Harcourt Papers,* XII, 248, cited by A. M. G. Stephenson, "Archbishop Vernon Harcourt," *Studies in Church History* 4 (1967):150. Although volume twelve of the *Harcourt Papers* has been examined, the citation has eluded confirmation. Harcourt's positive views of hymnody may have been, in part, because of the fact that in his son's parish, Bishopthorpe, a selection of metrical psalms and a supplement containing more than one hundred hymns were in use. See Cotterill, 1819, 8th ed., xi. In Stephenson's estimation, Harcourt's support of Cotterill was one of only two positive actions in his forty-year archiepiscopate (1807–1847).

90. Gray, *Inquiry,* 48. The editors of the Buckden collection had observed "that there are perhaps not many large congregations in the national Church, where some version of the Psalms, different from the old and new versions, and some Hymns, founded upon the history and doctrines of the gospel, have not been admitted" (Maltby, et al., vi). Writing two years earlier, C. H. Wollaston had denounced the "too prevalent [introduction of] unauthorized hymns." See *A Selection of Psalms, From the New Version, with the Morning and Evening Hymns; For the Use of Parish Churches,* 2nd ed. (East Dereham: W. Barker, 1813), iv.

So much advantage accrues from the prevalent usage of introducing into the church service Hymns and versions of Psalms, more edifying and acceptable to the congregations than any compositions which have obtained the sanction of competent authority, that I should have gladly evaded the necessity of deciding the legality of this usage.[91]

Vernon could not, however, dismiss the legal question, and "in this view I am bound to say that this Article is admissible."[92]

The legal issue, in the court's opinion, rested on two points: first, the effect of the prohibition under the Statutes of Uniformity, and second, the restrictive operation of ecclesiastical supremacy. Under the statutes 12 Car. II and 1 Eliz., all metrical versions of the Psalms, including the "Old Version" and the *New Version,* as well as all hymn collections, were excluded from use. Moreover, if strictly interpreted, they prohibited the sovereign from permitting any variation to the liturgy, including occasional prayers and thanksgivings. Vernon also considered the clause in 2 and 3 Edw. VI as being still in force because of the statute 1 Eliz. This too did not allow any version of the Psalms except the prose version contained in the Book of Common Prayer, and it certainly did not support the use of hymns. Finally, in his opinion, the rubric referring to anthems following the third collect in the offices could not be construed in a liberal manner: "the construction of this word [i.e., anthem] must be limited to literal extracts from the Bible or Liturgy."[93]

Having cited the relevant statutes, Vernon stated, however, that it was clear that these statutes "are not to be construed so rigidly, as to exclude from divine service all intervention of musical performances, nor would such performances subject the Clergy to penalties in the temporal Courts." [94] Moreover, the fact that various metrical versions of the Psalms had from time to time been permitted for use in the liturgy without being contested supported the presumption "that their performance was not restrained by any Statute." [95] Such permissions became more important with reference to the second point to be considered: the restrictive operation of ecclesiastical supremacy.

Vernon held that if all permissions for the use of various metrical versions of the Psalms were not purely gratuitous, or an arbitrary assumption of controlling jurisdiction, then we must infer from them that all versions of the Psalms destitute of similar sanction are illegal. The fact that a number of versions had been "allowed and permitted to be used in all such

---

91. Gray, *Inquiry,* 48.
92. Gray, *Inquiry,* 48.
93. Gray, *Inquiry,* 49.
94. Gray, *Inquiry,* 49–50.
95. Gray, *Inquiry,* 50.

churches, chapels, and congregations, as shall think fit to receive the same" was a decisive indication that, at least in the minds of the versifiers and compilers, such permission was required.[96] Moreover, one could infer that the episcopal bench also believed that even "their approbation would not suffice, to authorise their introduction in their respective Dioceses." Thus, Vernon concluded: "It seems then, on the whole, that for whatever may be supplementary to the Liturgy established by Statute, and not repugnant thereto, authority must emanate from the head of the Church."[97] In earlier times that had been "in practice, as well as in right," the crown and Convocation. Since the latter had ceased to function, such jurisdiction was now exercised by the king in council, and "nothing can be permitted to intervene in the service of the church without that, or legislative authority."[98]

The decision that, strictly speaking, no legislative enactment enjoined the use of any metrical version of the Psalms or any collection of metrical hymns in the liturgy of the Church of England did not mean that those opposed to their use could successfully prosecute in the courts. The fact that several metrical versions had been permitted and used without being contested led Vernon to conclude that as long as their use did not interfere with the proper order of the liturgy they could not be excluded. The same, Vernon argued, applied to the use of hymns.[99] In short, Vernon gave greater weight to "unquestioned usage" than to the official formularies of the church—the Thirty-Nine Articles and the Book of Common Prayer.[100]

Having presented the legal issues, Vernon admonished the parties involved:

It is however fit that it should be understood, that no advantage can be taken for the purposes of vexation, of this construction of the law. The Court may be

96. For example, Dod, James I, Tate and Brady, and Blackmore.

97. Gray, *Inquiry,* 51.

98. Gray, *Inquiry,* 51–52.

99. Vernon was essentially repeating the opinions of Gray, which had been published in the March 1818 issue of *The Christian Observer.* Those opinions were supported by C. C. in the August issue of the same year. See "Remarks on Metrical Translations of the Psalms," *The Christian Observer* 17 (August 1818):510–513. Vernon's judgment was reflected in the title of Anthony Sillery's collection, *The Christian Choir, or a system of Christian Psalmody, for Public and Private Worship; Comprising 1. Liturgic [sic] Hymns, in an easy method for Chanting—with Music of Chants and Sanctusses [sic]—some of these original. 2. Selections of Psalms, Anthems, and Hymns, with Arguments and Annotations, practical and devotional. Also, Some account of Psalmody in Public Worship, especially in the Established Church, since the Reformation, with evidence that the Psalms in metre, and Hymns, are in the same position with respect to the laws of the Church* (Dublin: W. Curry Jr., 1835).

100. Gray, *Inquiry,* 50.

called upon to exercise its controlling jurisdiction, and to admonish the party who may deviate from the limits which I have traced out; but it will never condemn in costs in such cases, except where very peculiar circumstances shall aggravate the technical irregularity into an offence — and I think it my duty to state, even in the present state of these proceedings, that no such circumstances exist here. I feel that the promoters of these articles were fairly entitled to a decision of the legal question to the best of my judgment, but if they proceed to call for sentence in this cause, and decline the mediation which I before suggested, I shall consider them as wanting not only in a sense of their own interest, but in a regard to Christian charity and practical religion.[101]

Both parties agreed to accept the suggested mediation of the archbishop.[102] Cotterill withdrew the eighth edition of his work and, after considerable revision, submitted a new selection to the archbishop for his imprimatur. The revised collection was dedicated to the archbishop and was published in 1820, the archbishop graciously providing copies to St. Paul's.[103]

It is difficult to state with any certainty what immediate effect this decision of the court had on the development of hymnody in the Church of England.[104]

---

101. Gray, *Inquiry,* 52.

102. Although both parties appeared to have agreed publicly to the compromise, based upon Gray's account, court records indicate that on November 2, 1820, Fryer was assigned to contest the ruling. There are no further entries in the court records after that date concerning either party. Apparently, any further proceedings were dropped.

103. *A Selection of Psalms and Hymns, for Public Worship* (London: Printed for T. Cadell, in the Strand, 1820). The dedication read: "To The Most Reverend Edward, Lord Archbishop of York, This Collection of Psalms and Hymns is, with His Grace's Permission, Inscribed, by His Most Faithful and Obliged Servant, The Editor." The copies presented to St. Paul's were inscribed: "The gift of his Grace the Lord Archbishop of York." In an account of the case published in 1821, it was noted that the number of copies presented was one thousand. Moreover, it was reported that two other ministers were threatened with legal action if they too did not withdraw Cotterill's earlier collection and replace it with the new. The archbishop presented copies to those parishes as well in order to avoid the "possibility of dissatisfaction." See "Literary and Philosophical Intelligence," *The Christian Observer* 20 (April 1821):258–259. This collection was used widely in the north of England for the next forty years. The success of the collection was primarily because of the editorial skills of James Montgomery, who assisted Cotterill in this edition and the eighth.

104. Lionel Adey implies that as a result of this case Anglican clergy could now legally use hymns during services. See his *Class and Idol in the English Hymn* (Vancouver: University of British Columbia Press, 1988), 34. Such was not the case. In fact, it was only in 1980 that rubrical directions for the use of hymns were included in a Prayer Book (*The Alternative Prayer Book*), making them legal. There is still no official hymnal for the Church of England, however.

One immediate effect was the removal of any opposition at St. Paul's. It is also clear that in the years following this event the number of collections of hymns available for parish use increased dramatically. Between 1821 and 1850 at least seventy-eight hymnals were published, and in the next ten years an additional forty-three collections appeared. In comparison with the number of collections available between 1760 and 1800, the increase can only be described as monumental. Although it is difficult to establish direct lines of causation, it is evident that a pronounced shift in attitude toward the inclusion of hymns in the liturgy of the Church of England occurred in the years following the Cotterill case. This shift can be seen, in part, explicitly and implicitly in the responses of certain bishops to the increasing use of hymns.

Episcopal Opposition

Although the archbishop of York's intervention in Cotterill's case enabled a compromise to be reached, other bishops were not as favorably disposed toward the inclusion of hymns in the liturgy. Herbert Marsh, bishop of Peterborough, objected strongly to the introduction of unauthorized hymns. In a *Charge* to the clergy of his diocese, Marsh disputed the claim that although the Acts of Uniformity restricted a clergyman's freedom to change in any respect the rites of the church, they did not apply to the use of metrical psalms or hymns, thus giving discretionary authority for their use.[105] Marsh acknowledged that those who accepted this interpretation were correct in believing that Sternhold and Hopkins's metrical psalms, and those of others, were not within the scope of any Act of Uniformity strictly interpreted. But, Marsh maintained, "a *freedom from obligation* to the performance of one thing does not imply a *freedom from restraint* as to the performance of any other."[106] No one was required to use either the "Old Version" or the *New Version*. Yet, no one was free to use any other ver-

---

105. [Herbert Marsh], *A Charge, Delivered at the Primary Visitation of Herbert Lord Bishop of Peterborough, In July, 1820. With an Appendix, containing some remarks on the modern custom of Singing in Our Churches Unauthorized Psalms and Hymns* (London: F. C. and J. Rivington, 1820), 31. Marsh's negative views of hymnody may have been, at least in part, because of his views toward Methodism and Evangelicalism. According to Soloway, Marsh believed that both were "dedicated to the abolition of distinctive church doctrine and the encouragement of generalized fanaticism." See Richard Soloway, "Episcopal Perspectives and Religious Revivalism in England 1784–1851," *Historical Magazine of the Protestant Episcopal Church* 40 (March 1971), 41.

106. Marsh, *Charge*, 32.

sion at their own discretion. The various Acts of Uniformity, Marsh argued, had "no less for their object a uniformity of *doctrine,* than a uniformity in *external worship.*"[107] To introduce hymns or metrical psalms containing doctrine inconsistent with the doctrine contained in the Book of Common Prayer was to negate the purpose of the Acts of Uniformity.[108]

Marsh did not fear "gross and glaring" violations as much as he did "gradual encroachments:"

> [They] are so much the more to be dreaded, because on the one hand they are less open to detection, and on the other hand more open to evasion, when they *are* detected. In this manner a Hymn Book, without impugning the doctrines of our Church in such a manner, as to expose the Clergyman who uses it, to Ecclesiastical censures, may tend to *undermine* those doctrines, and prepare the persons who are accustomed to sing from it, for the reception of doctrines, which are entirely adverse to those of the Established Church.[109]

Proper authority existed for determining what could and could not be used

---

107. Marsh, *Charge,* 32. Richard Mant, bishop of Down and Connor, agreed with Marsh on the need for uniformity in all aspects of the church's worship, including singing. See *Thoughts on the Singing of Unauthorised Hymns, in Publick Worship; Respectfully Submitted to the Consideration of the Archbishops and Bishops of the United Church of England and Ireland* (London: Printed for J. G. and F. Rivington, 1835). Rann Kennedy contended there was no need for such a "strict uniformity" in psalmody that "every congregation must be using the same words at the same time." He did, however, agree with Marsh that only those hymns that had received the same legal sanction as the Book of Common Prayer should be used in church. See Kennedy's *Thoughts on the Music and Words of Psalmody, As At Present in Use Among the Members of the Church of England* (London: Longman, Hurst, Rees, Orme, and Brown, 1821), 94.

108. The same objection was voiced by the bishop of Killaloe, Ludlow Tonson (Baron Riversdale) in 1845: "The Prayer Book was prescribed—how could it be right to introduce hymns giving unauthorised and perhaps heretical teaching." Cited by W. K. Lowther Clarke, *A Hundred Years of Hymns Ancient and Modern* (London: W. Clowes and Sons, 1960), 15. Unfortunately, Clarke does not indicate the source of this quotation.

109. Marsh, *Charge,* 33. Earlier, Marsh had indicated his concern over liturgical indifference. He believed that the Evangelicals were dedicated to the destruction of the doctrines of the Church of England, and their disregard for its formularies was a step toward achieving their goal. See Herbert Marsh, *A Reply to the Strictures of Isaac Milner, D.D., Dean of Carlisle, etc.* (Cambridge: J. Hodson, 1813), 136–137, and the anonymous *A letter to the Rev. H. Marsh . . . in confutation of his opinion, that the Dissenters are aiming at the subversions of the Religious Establishment of this country . . . by a Protestant Dissenter and a Layman* (London: n.p., 1813).

in the service, namely, the authority of the king in council. Such authority, Marsh believed, had clearly been given to the metrical versions of the Psalms by Sternhold and Hopkins and to those by Tate and Brady. In his judgment then, no clergyman officiating as a minister of the church had the right to "oppose his private opinion to public authority."[110] Until such time when a new collection obtained the royal permission, Marsh concluded, "the two authorised Versions, which are printed at the end of our Prayer Books, are the only collections of psalms and hymns, which we can legally sing in the public service of the Church."[111]

Marsh was not the only bishop to express his opposition to the introduction of unauthorized hymns. The bishop of Killaloe, Ludlow Tonson (Baron Riversdale), queried the rural deans of his diocese whether "any thing [was] sung in the Church besides the authorized Versions of the Psalms."[112] Contending, like Marsh, that only two versions were authorized, Tonson argued that the principle that should guide all clergy with re-

---

110. Marsh, *Charge,* 36. Richard Mant echoed Marsh's views in 1845. See *Horae Liturgicae* (London: J. W. Parker, 1845), 28.

111. Marsh, *Charge,* 38. The editor of *The Christian Remembrancer* clearly supported Marsh's position on hymnody, commenting in an introduction to extracts from the *Charge* that hymnody was "a subject which is but ill understood, and which his Lordship appears to have placed in its proper light." See "Bishop of Peterborough on unauthorized Psalms and Hymns," *The Christian Remembrancer* 3 (April 1821):209. Although Jonathan Gray disagreed with Marsh concerning the authorization of the "Old Version" and the *New Version,* he supported the need for an authorized version(s) for use in the church: "As a friend to uniformity of worship, I wish that such a work as this [i.e., Cotterill's *Selections*] were set forth by LEGISLATIVE ENACTMENT. Not that all other *existing* Selections should at once be banished from the Churches in which they are used; for a measure so compulsory would excite opposition, and lead to schism, instead of inducing conformity. But if it were merely enacted, that no Selection or Version should *in future* be introduced into any Church, except the prescribed Selection, further innovation would be prevented." Cited by A. Gray, 75. Others also disagreed with Marsh's views. See, for example, *A Collection of Hymns, Selected for the use of Congregations and Families* (Boyle: J. Bromell, 1822), preface.

112. [Ludlow Tonson], *A Charge delivered to the Clergy of the Diocese of Killaloe, July 25, 1821* (1821), 38ff, cited by Henry John Todd, *Observations upon the Metrical Version of the Psalms, Made by Sternhold, Hopkins, and Others: With a View to Illustrate the Authority with Which this Collection was at First Admitted, and how that Authority has been since regarded, in the Public Service of the Established Church of England: and Thence to Maintain, in This Venerable Service, the Usage of Such Metrical Psalmody Only as is Duly Authorized. With Notices of Other English Metrical Versions of the Psalms* (London: Printed for F. C. And J. Rivington, 1822), 22.

gard to matters of liturgy was "uniformity, regulated by the competent authority." Therefore,

> if there be any part of the public worship proposed for the use of a congregation, which cannot be brought within the rule of this principle, *it cannot be justified, and ought not to be admitted.* Now this will at once banish from the worship of the Church all that variety of modern compositions under the name of Hymns, *which without any shadow or semblance of authority, have been introduced in many places into our national service.*[113]

Tonson held firmly that the only authorized version of metrical psalms was that of Tate and Brady, standing upon "plain and express authority" of king and council. Because the use of that version was "allowed and permitted," rather than required, the bishop also held that a parish could use the "Old Version." If a congregation did not think it "fit to receive the same" [i.e., the *New Version*], then the only other version "allowed and permitted" was the "Old Version." Thus, these two versions "both profess to have, and one of them directly and expressly has, and by inference and implication the other has also, authority to be used in all such Churches as shall think fit to receive them."[114] Although both versions were permitted and allowed, all clergy, Tonson noted, were free at their discretion not to use either one, for neither was required. Nonetheless, he stated,

> no Clergyman whatever is at liberty to introduce such compositions, as I have before spoken of, into his Church, in preference or in addition to the Psalms; or to introduce any other Version of the Psalms in preference, or in addition to those which we have been now considering; because he cannot plead for their introduction that they are permitted and allowed by any authority at all.[115]

Tonson, like Marsh, publicly voiced his opposition to the introduction of hymns into the services of the church, offering little hope to those who desired to expand the musical options for congregational singing.

It is difficult to know with any degree of certainty how many clergy followed their admonitions regarding the use of hymns. Undoubtedly, some clergy heeded the advice of their bishop, and some pressed on in their use of hymns. In at least one instance, one bishop, who stated his opposition privately, was successful in preventing the publication of a collection of hymns.

Reginald Heber, before presuming to publish his collection of hymns (which had been prepared for the use of his parish), sought the advice of

---

113. Tonson, *Charge,* 1821, 38ff, cited by Todd, 22–23.
114. Tonson, *Charge,* 1821, 38ff, cited by Todd, 26.
115. Tonson, *Charge,* 1821, 38ff, cited by Todd, 27.

the bishop of London rather than his diocesan (Lichfield), for reasons of "age and infirmity."[116] In a letter to the bishop, Heber commented that since so many clergy had for "many years back" taken the "liberty" of providing collections for their congregations it would appear that such, "if custom alone were to be our guide, would seem already sufficiently authorized."[117] Admitting that hymnody was not "regularly authorized by the rubric," Heber, nonetheless, believed that

> any attempt to suppress it entirely would be so unpopular, and attended with so much difficulty, that I cannot help thinking it would be wiser, as well as more practicable, to *regulate* the liberty thus assumed, instead of authoritatively taking it away.[118]

The evil that so many attached to the use of hymns, Heber argued, was because of the presence of objectionable expressions and improper diction or sentiment in so many texts presently in use. A collection that avoided such faults, and one based upon the "history or doctrine contained in the Gospel [appointed] for each" Sunday, would do much to remedy the present abuse of hymns, satisfy the "love of devotional poetry" of the "lower orders," and provide a means for "attracting the multitude."[119] To that end, Heber sought the advice of the bishop. "I feel I am taking a great liberty, but one for which I hope I shall be pardoned, in requesting to know whether you think it possible or advisable for me to obtain the same kind of permission for the use of my hymns in churches which was given to Tate? and if so, what is the channel through which I should apply?"[120] The bishop, unfortunately, counseled Heber not to proceed, the time not being ripe for hymns. Thus, Heber's work was not published until after his death in 1827.[121]

---

116. Reginald Heber, "Bishop Heber's Letter," *The Christian Remembrancer* 17 (1835):622. The letter is dated October 4, 1820. It is possible that Heber's letter was prompted by the favorable decision reached in the Cotterill case (July 28, 1820). Four hymns for the four Sundays of Advent had been published in 1811. See D. R. [Reginald Heber], "Hymns appropriate to the Sundays and principal Holidays," *The Christian Observer* 10 (October 1811):630–631.

117. Heber, "Bishop Heber's Letter," 622.

118. Heber, "Bishop Heber's Letter," 625.

119. Heber, "Bishop Heber's Letter," 622–623.

120. Heber, "Bishop Heber's Letter," 625.

121. Reginald Heber, *Hymns, Written and Adapted to the Weekly Church Service of the Year* (London: J. Murray, 1827). In addition to Heber's compositions (more than half of the collection), the collection included items by H. H. Milman, Sir Walter Scott, Jeremy Taylor, and Joseph Addison, to name a few. The collection was dedicated, "with permission," to the archbishop of Canterbury. One cannot help but wonder if the collection would have been published sooner if Heber had sought the advice of his own diocesan rather than the bishop of London.

It is difficult to determine completely why these bishops opposed the use of hymns. The legal question was sufficient ground in their opinion for denying the introduction of this innovation. Nonetheless, these bishops apparently did not take any legal steps to prevent their use. They may not have been inclined to prosecute perceived offenses because of the difficulties of pursuing cases in the courts. Eighteenth-century courts were "so mysterious and frightening" that most bishops were reluctant to use them.[122] Matters did not improve significantly in the opening decades of the nineteenth century. Even in conflicts more easily defined than the issues surrounding hymns, for example, drunken incumbents or an incestuous parishioner, to pursue remedy in the courts was viewed as much as an ordeal for the plaintiff as for the defendant. In some instances, clergy who proceeded to court felt that they "owed the bishop an explanation" for doing so.[123] The reverse may have been equally true.[124]

The events in France had brought to the fore what an unbridled populace could do.[125] To the extent that those who advocated hymns were seen as threats to the status quo, opposition was perhaps inevitable. In fact, those who advocated any innovation may have provoked negative reactions from the episcopal bench.[126] As the threat of revolution diminished with the passing of time, certain bishops may have relaxed their opposition to

---

122. Robert E. Rodes Jr., *Law and Modernization in the Church of England: Charles II to the Welfare State* (Notre Dame: University of Notre Dame Press, 1991), 14.

123. Rodes Jr., 14.

124. One person observed in 1831 that although it was doubtful that a bishop could interfere effectively to prevent the introduction of hymns, it was also doubtful that the clergy could maintain their position against a bishop. He observed further, "Much to the honour of our prelates and clergy, such a collision has never yet taken place: for, as often as the point has been agitated, one party or the other has usually relaxed, so as to prevent the disgraceful spectacle of a bishop and his clergy conflicting in a court of law." See T., "On the Neglect of Congregational Singing," *The Christian Observer* 31 (June 1831):339. This implies that a fairly substantial number of conflicts occurred between bishops and clergy over the introduction of hymns prior to this date.

125. Eugene Stock believed that the "French Revolution had filled the British mind with terror and dismay." See his *The English Church in the Nineteenth Century* (London: Longmans and Green, 1910), 11.

126. [George Henry] Law assured his clergy that "no one can view with juster abhorrence than myself the rash and uplifted hand of innovation." See *A Charge Delivered to the Clergy of the Diocese of Chester . . . in July and August, 1820* (London: n.p., 1820), 8. Compare F. C. Mather's view that "conservative feeling reinforced traditional practice." See his "Georgian Churchmanship Reconsidered: Some Variations in Anglican Public Worship 1714–1830," *Journal of Ecclesiastical History* 36 (April 1985):276.

hymns (and other innovations), seeing the development in a more positive light and as less of a threat.

It has been argued that episcopal attitudes toward revivalism changed in the early decades of the nineteenth century.[127] To the extent that hymnody was linked with revivalism, it is not impossible that attitudes toward hymnody shifted also. For example, John Randolph, bishop of Oxford, viewed Evangelicals as a greater danger than any external enemies.[128] The link between Evangelicals and hymnody in Randolph's mind was perhaps unavoidable. Certainly, more than one person had noted with relish or disdain Evangelical involvement with the development of hymnody. Edward Maltby, bishop of Durham (and perhaps the most conservative of the Whig appointments), also viewed Evangelicals as a threat.[129] Yet he clearly was favorably inclined toward hymnody, having produced a collection of hymns in 1815.

Although clearly opposed to this development, these bishops represented the minority opinion. Writing in 1829, one reviewer commented,

> Many of the Bishops, very wisely, do not interfere with the selections of Psalms or Hymns which their clergy may think fit to introduce for the spiritual edification of the flocks committed to their care; others, however, a little more busy and pertinacious, would not for a world have any thing but Tate and Brady within the limits of their Episcopal jurisdiction.[130]

Although powerful voices raised in opposition to hymns, they did not prevail. The tide had turned. As early as 1821 one participant in the controversy acknowledged that "it is now wholly unnecessary to enter into a discussion of their legality." The question to be addressed was the "*inexpediency* of their being used without *authority*."[131]

---

127. Soloway, "Episcopal Perspectives," 36.

128. John Randolph, *A Charge Delivered to the Clergy of the Diocese of Oxford, by John, Lord Bishop of that Diocese at His Triennial Visitation in MDCCCV* (Oxford: W. Hanwell and J. Parker, 1805), 6–7. Another bishop who shared Randolph's views was John Fisher (Exeter). See *A Charge Delivered to the Clergy of the Diocese of Exeter, at the Primary Visitation of John, Lord Bishop of Exeter, 1804 and 1805* (Exeter: n.p., 1805), 22–24.

129. Soloway, "Episcopal Perspectives," 58.

130. "Review of Religious Publications," *The Evangelical Magazine* 7, n.s. (February 1829):64.

131. Kennedy, *Thoughts,* 92. Owen Chadwick held that "[i]n 1827 nearly all high churchmen still refused to allow hymns in their churches." See his *The Victorian Church,* 2 vols. (London: A. and C. Black, 1966, 1970), 1:67. Such may indeed have been the case. Nonetheless, evidence indicates that at least some high churchmen, e.g., Keble and Heber, viewed the introduction of hymns favorably. Only a more thorough study can ascertain the number of those opposed to and those who supported hymnody.

Summary

Throughout the 1820s a number of advocates of hymnody maintained "the propriety of metrical additions being made to our church singing beyond the authorized versions of the Book of Psalms."[132] Even so, a certain degree of hesitancy remained. J. Bull, for example, acknowledged that although his collection of hymns "may be suitable for general use, are we authorized to adopt them?"[133] Bull admitted that in offering his work for use in the church he was treading "on tender ground." Yet he firmly believed that the use of hymns was not "forbidden." Like Marsh he desired that collections have "the public sanction of those who are placed in authority," but until that occurred he was prepared to use hymns nonetheless.[134]

The attitude expressed by Bull is an accurate reflection of the mood of the majority of worshippers toward the use of hymns in the liturgy in the 1820s.[135] Opposition to their use based upon the question of authorization

---

132. See, for example, Pastor, "Sternhold's Psalms," *The Christian Observer* 26 (October 1826):600–601.

133. J. Bull, *Devotional Hymns, Designed Especially for Public Worship Founded Chiefly on the Collects, Epistles, and Gospel, for Each Sunday in the Year, and for the Fasts, Festivals, and Public Offices of the United Church of England and Ireland. With an Appendix, Containing Some Hymns for General Use, and Also for the Anniversaries of Sunday Schools and Other Public Charities* (London: C. and J. Rivington, 1827), x. See also *A Selection of Psalms and Hymns, for the use of Handsworth Church, in Staffordshire* (Birmingham: M. M. Chapman, 1826).

134. Bull, x–xi. Many, however, continued to maintain the position that only those versions "at present authorized" could be used in the service of the Church of England. See, for example, C., "Observations on a New Version of the Psalms," *The Christian Remembrancer* 3 (July 1821):397. The curate of Wateringbury (Kent) noted in 1826: "I conceive I might as well read a psalm not in the Prayer Book, as . . . sing one not authorized by the Head of our Church." Cited by Nigel Yates, *Buildings, Faith, and Worship: The Liturgical Arrangement of Anglican Churches 1600–1900* (Oxford: Clarendon, 1991), 65. As late as 1831, some clergy continued to use exclusively either the "Old Version" or the *New Version* because of their concern over the legality of other versions. See J. A. Latrobe, *The Music of the Church Considered in its Various Branches, Congregational and Choral* (London: R. B. Seeley and W. Burnside, 1831), 191–192.

135. Kennedy commented that "the people in general have undeniably a strong partiality for hymns" (*Thoughts,* 106).

would continue for several decades.[136] The central issue, however, had been decided in *Cotterill v. Holy and Ward*. The decision by the court that although no legal support could be found for their use, the historical evidence indicated that metrical psalms had achieved a place in the liturgy nonetheless, and by extension hymns had as well. Moreover, because the court made it very clear that prosecuting this particular breach of the rubrics of the Book of Common Prayer and the Acts of Uniformity would not lead the court to "condemn in costs," it meant that no effective means for preventing the use of metrical psalms or hymns existed.[137] Thus, one effect of this case was to open the floodgates for hymns to be introduced into the liturgy of the church.[138] Another effect was to provide an option where none existed rubrically because of the vicissitudes of enforcement.

Clearly, the church was not yet of one mind regarding the inclusion of

---

136. See, for example, the following series of exchanges: Richard [Mant, bishop of] Down and Connor, "On the Use of Psalms and Hymns in the Public Service of the Church," *The Christian Remembrancer* 20 (February 1838):85–88; [Editor], "On the Use of Psalms and Hymns," *The Christian Remembrancer* 20 (February 1838):85–91; R[ichard] D[own] and C[onnor], "On the Use of Psalms and Hymns in the Public Service of the Church," *The Christian Remembrancer* 20 (March 1838):159–164; [Editor], "On the Use of Psalms and Hymns," *The Christian Remembrancer* 20 (April 1838):233–236. Even massive treatises on the subject (105 pages), such as that of Henry Todd, failed to stem the tide. Jonathan Gray, after reviewing Todd's work, observed that "he had left the question as he found it," i.e., unanswered. See his "Reply to Mr. Todd's Argument on Sternhold's Psalms," *The Christian Observer* 26 (December 1826):736–739. By 1860 the question had ceased to be of concern. In an article on the subject of hymnody, R. L. noted that "it may seem to be unnecessary at this time to discuss the ... question; for, legally or illegally, there are few clergymen now who stand so steadfastly on the old ways as to confine themselves to the metrical versions of the psalms." See "Hymns and Hymn-Tunes for Congregational Worship," *Fraser's Magazine* 62 (September 1860):305.

137. Gray, *Inquiry,* 52.

138. In Frost's estimation, the result of this case was the winning of the battle for hymnody. See Maurice Frost, ed., *Historical Companion to Hymns Ancient and Modern* (London: W. Clowes and Sons, 1962), 108. In similar fashion, Temperley described it as "a decisive victory for the Evangelical party, supporting both of their main principles in the reform of church music: the equal validity of hymns and metrical psalms, and the inferiority of both to the liturgy. It led to the virtual disappearance, within a generation or so, of both the 'Old' and the 'New' Versions of the metrical psalms, and paved the way for the development of the Victorian hymn book" (*Jonathan Gray,* 18). It should be noted, however, that this was not exclusively an Evangelical victory. A significant number of non-Evangelicals, as we have seen, also supported the inclusion of hymns in the liturgy. It should also be noted that some Evangelicals opposed this innovation.

hymns in the liturgy. Writing in 1831, one person commented, "[w]hether a clergyman may of his own accord introduce hymns, is one of those ecclesiastical questions which does not to this moment appear to be authoritatively settled."[139] And the Church of England would not come near to being of one mind until after the publication of *Hymns Ancient and Modern* in 1861. In the intervening years the controversy over the inclusion of hymns in the liturgy would undergo a transformation. From 1830 until the opening years of the twentieth century, the debate was not on the question of whether to sing hymns, but what hymns to sing.[140] That debate, however, lies outside the limitations of this book.

---

139. T., 338.

140. Robert Druitt, for example, made it clear that although hymns could be used (Druitt preferred the canticles of the Prayer Book), care had to be exercised that they were "worthy of admission into the church." "Unfortunately," he noted, "there are many collections of modern hymns, which are as mean and commonplace in their diction, as they are irreverent and audacious in their sentiments; whilst as for the music they are sung to, it is impossible to find words degrading enough to express its most unredeemable meanness and vulgarity." See his *A Popular Tract on Church Music, with remarks on Its Moral and Political Importance, and a practical Scheme for its Reformation* (London: F. and J. Rivington, 1845), 42. A. J. B. Beresford-Hope observed, "Once a set of words, however mean or fanatical, and once the voice of melody, however vulgar or boisterous the tune may be, are admitted into the congregation assembled for worship, the fierce dispute about the lawfulness of a liturgical and musical service has been settled in the affirmative, and all that remains is question of degree." See his *The English Cathedral of the Nineteenth Century* (London: J. Murray, 1861), 117. See also John Mason Neale, "English Hymnology: its History and Prospects," *The Christian Remembrancer* 18, n.s. (October 1849):302–343; John Jebb, *The Choral Service of the United Church of England and Ireland: Being an Enquiry into The Liturgical System of the Cathedral and Collegiate Foundations of the Anglican Communion* (London: J. W. Parker, 1843), 393–394; and the anonymous "Psalms and Hymns," *The British Critic, and Quarterly Theological Review* 63 (July 1842):1–33.

Conclusion

This book has examined the shift from metrical psalmody to hymnody in the Church of England. Although many aspects of this topic remain obscure and much simply may never be known, a great deal can be surmised or constructed based upon the material examined, and, on some points, certain judgments appear to be beyond question.

It seems clear that the introduction of hymnody into the liturgy of the Church of England was almost solely because of the initiative of the clergy. Almost every collection noted in this study was compiled by a member of the clergy. Although there are a few examples of collections made by laity, they are decidedly in the minority. Moreover, in only one instance can it be said with certainty that the demand for a change in congregational song was because of the laity.[1] Further, and not surprisingly, the participants at every level of the development of hymnody were almost exclusively male. Only one collection by a woman has been identified (*Original Hymns for Village Worship,* c. 1824), and there is no indication whether or not she was an Anglican.[2]

Also within the realm of certainty is that the introduction of hymns was widespread throughout England. Although London enjoys the distinction of being the earliest center (as a result of the introduction of hymns in the 1760s in the various charitable institutions there), hymns were also being introduced at the same time in a number of geographical locations. As the use of hymnody increased during the eighteenth century, other centers

---

1. Thomas Cannon's collection was made specifically at the request of his congregation.

2. The reviewer of her work made the disparaging remark, "'She hath done what she could,' and her offering will doubtless be accepted by the Great Master." See "Review of Religious Publications," *The Evangelical Magazine* 2, n.s. (Supplement 1824):580.

emerged, most notably York. Only exhaustive research will reveal if there are areas that escaped this development for any significant period of time.

This study supports Norman Sykes's reassessment of the eighteenth-century church. Contrary to the long-accepted interpretation, the eighteenth-century church, at least with regard to congregational song, was not as lethargic, not as worldly, not as self-seeking as has been thought.[3] The evidence clearly indicates that the church was passionately concerned about the performance standards and content of congregational song, be it metrical psalms or hymns. It also indicates that the character and implementation of worship, in general, was of great concern. Moreover, these concerns were not restricted to certain segments within the Church of England. No rigid party lines denoting supporters or opponents of hymnody can be drawn. There were Evangelicals who opposed hymnody and Evangelicals who advocated hymnody; there were non-Evangelicals who advocated hymnody and non-Evangelicals who opposed hymnody.

The majority of those who advocated hymnody, however, were Evangelical clergy. This study calls for a more nuanced description of their involvement in the development of hymnody and their attitude toward the Book of Common Prayer. It has become commonplace to describe Evangelicals as "strict churchmen."[4] In many respects, such a description is accurate. Evangelicals, for example, generally regarded cooperation with Dissenters with distrust, if not distaste,[5] and they attempted, with varying

---

3. This view of the eighteenth-century Church of England found full expression in the work of John H. Overton and Frederic Relton, *The English Church from the Accession of George I to the End of the Eighteenth Century, 1714–1800* (London: Macmillan, 1906); C. J. Abbey and J. H. Overton, *The English Church in the Eighteenth Century* (1878); and C. J. Abbey, *The English Church and its Bishops, 1700–1800* (1887). A reassessment was done by Norman Sykes, *Church and State in England in the Eighteenth Century* (1934). Likewise W. K. Lowther Clarke challenged the portrayal of the eighteenth-century church as having a "spirit of complacency." See his *Eighteenth Century Piety* (London: SPCK, 1944), 1. Although Sykes and Clarke argue persuasively for a new understanding, especially Sykes, the older perspective continues to be found. See, for example, J. H. Plumb, *England in the Eighteenth Century* (Harmondsworth: Penguin, 1950); Horton Davies, *Worship and Theology in England: From Watts and Wesley to Maurice, 1690–1850* (1961); Alan Gilbert, *Religion and Society in Industrial England: Church, Chapel and Social Change, 1740–1914* (London: Longmans, 1976); Roy Porter, *English Society in the Eighteenth Century* (Harmondsworth: Penguin, 1982).

4. See, for example, Kenneth Hylson-Smith, *Evangelicals in the Church of England, 1734–1984* (Edinburgh: T. And T. Clark, 1989), 12. Bebbington argued that as criticism of Evangelicals increased, it became important to "stress loyalty to the forms of the Church of England." See D. W. Bebbington, *Evangelicalism in Modern Britain: A History from the 1730s to the 1980s* (London: Unwin Hyman, 1989), 31.

5. Haweis, apparently, was an exception, cooperating with Dissenters in missionary endeavors. See Hylson-Smith, 48.

degrees of success, to push forward their cause within the existing structures and limitations of the Church of England.[6] Included in those structures was the Book of Common Prayer, with all of its legally binding rubrics. A number of scholars have characterized the Evangelicals as being strong advocates of the Prayer Book and resistant to any alterations.[7] Yet, with regard to hymns, they were boldly innovative.

The irony of the contradictory positions must not be overlooked. On one hand, a significant number of Evangelical clergy were more than willing to introduce the innovative hymnody into the liturgy of the Church of England—which clearly was not provided for in the rubrics of the Prayer Book.[8] On the other hand, they were opposed to other innovations that had been proposed. Partly this was because of their concern that such revisions would be

---

6. Hylson-Smith argued that "[a]s the [eighteenth] century wore on irregularity among Evangelicals diminished and, as a body, their conformity to Church order became more definite" (37).

7. Hylson-Smith used the word *enthusiastic* to describe Evangelical support of the prayer book (107). Nicholas Temperley portrayed the Evangelicals as differing from the Methodists in "their strict adherence to church law and discipline, including the requirement of the Act of Uniformity that all public worship be conducted according to the Book of Common Prayer." See his *Jonathan Gray and Church Music in York, 1770–1840* (York: Borthwick Papers, 1977), 9. Clearly, the introduction of hymns was not in accordance with the rubrics of the Prayer Book. At best, one can support such descriptions by arguing that if hymns or metrical psalms were used on either side of the liturgy, i.e., before or after the office (according to the Injunctions of 1559), then strictly speaking they were not part of the liturgy. Evidence, however, exists that indicates that hymns and/or metrical psalms were used following the lessons and before and/or after the sermon, thus within the liturgy itself.

8. A proposed revised liturgy was published in 1791 that altered the rubric in the offices to read: "After these [i.e., the lessons] a hymn may be sung." See *A Liturgy compiled from The Book of Common Prayer reformed, according to the plan of The Late Dr. Samuel Clarke; together with a Collection of Psalms and Hymns, for Public Worship* (Plymouth: M. Haydon and Son, 1791). A manuscript note indicates that the hymns were compiled by the Rev. W. Porter of Plymouth. It appears that this collection of hymns had been previously published separately. See *A Collection of Hymns and Psalms for Public Worship, from Different Authors* (Plymouth: B. Haydon, 1790). Another proposal would have shortened the service by approximately one-half, "without the omission of what is essentially necessary." Bound with the proposal were extracts from the *New Version.* See *Abridgement of the Book of Common Prayer, And Administration of the Sacraments, and other Rites and Ceremonies of The Church, According to the Use of The Church of England: Together with the Psalter, or Psalms of David, Pointed as they are to be sung or said in Churches* (London: n.p., 1773), iv. Interestingly, no rubric in the proposal mentions the inclusion of hymns or metrical psalms in the liturgy. Gordon Rupp indicated that proposed changes to the Book of Common Prayer were advocated in a number of "contemporary pamphlets." See his *Religion in England 1688–1791* (Oxford: Clarendon, 1986), 506.

along lines that further restricted their desire for a more "vital Christianity" and partly because of their opposition to the developing Unitarian theology.[9]

Further, the portrayal of Evangelicals as strict observers of the rubrical directions of the Book of Common Prayer is simply not accurate. Some scholars have argued that the eighteenth-century church had no desire to improve the Book of Common Prayer, although proposals for reform were published during the course of the century.[10] The inclusion of hymns as well as metrical psalms, however, in the liturgy must be regarded as evidence of a desire to improve the services of the church. This seems even more apparent when it is noted that the 1662 Book of Common Prayer made no provision for either metrical psalms or hymns. Contrary to the interpretation that the inadequacies of the 1662 Book of Common Prayer were not perceived until the end of the nineteenth century, it is clear that with regard to congregational singing its limitations were felt strongly by 1760.[11]

If more nuanced descriptions are needed concerning the role of Evangelicals in the development of hymnody, they are also necessary to indicate accurately the involvement of other groups. Hylson-Smith, for example, reached this oversimplified conclusion: "Non-Evangelical clergy rigidly adhered to the two old versions, Sternhold and Hopkins's collection of metrical psalms and the more recent version by Tate and Brady. They denounced hymns as a deplorable and disloyal innovation."[12] As the evidence indicates, the history of this development cannot be painted in such black and white contrasts.

As with any unexplored topic, conclusions based upon surmise and construction must, by nature, be more tentative. It has been argued that the Church of England in the nineteenth century "successfully combined the preservation of the historic traditions and continuities of Anglicanism with an infusion of new inspiration from a rediscovered Catholic-

---

9. T[homas] Haweis, *Carmina Christo; or, Hymns to the Saviour: Designed for the Use and Comfort of those who Worship the Lamb that was Slain* (Bath: S. Hazard, 1792), preface. In his words, "There is one book which next to the blessed Book of God I venerate, the *Book of Common Prayer*. Many attempts have of late been formed by some who plead peculiar tenderness of conscience, to introduce a *new liturgy* more conformed to the rational, philosophical, enlightened opinions of modern divinity, and to expunge our antiquated creeds. Hitherto indeed their efforts have been abortive, and I cannot for Zion's sake but hope and pray, that the day of such innovations may be far distant. Procul! O procul absit!"

10. See, for example, W. K. Lowther Clarke, *Eighteenth Century Piety* (London: Methuen, 1962), 28.

11. See, for example, Donald Gray, "The Revision of Canon Law and Its Application to Liturgical Revision in the Recent History of the Church of England," *The Jurist* 48 (1988):638–652.

12. Hylson-Smith, 55.

ity."[13] It has also been argued, against this view, that the parochial structure of Anglicanism prevented certain developments in the Church of England and was "one to which churchmen clung obstinately."[14] The truth lies somewhere in between:

> At the local level the Church of England could be much more flexible and innovative than these arguments suggest; parish life was marked by more intense doctrinal conflict than Anglican historians have tended to note, but at the same time the parochial system proved to be much less of an impediment to the activities of churchmen—and to the growth of different religious traditions within Anglicanism—than their critics have sometimes supposed.[15]

Although the preceding observation concerns the Victorian church, the same seems to apply, at least with regard to hymnody, to the eighteenth-century church and the church in the early nineteenth century.

The evidence presented in this study suggests that the eighteenth-century Church of England was more flexible and innovative than has previously been assumed. The blatant disregard of the rubrics of the Book of Common Prayer and the Injunctions of 1559, with regard to the use of hymns within the liturgy of the church, by a considerable number of clergy indicates that the needs of the congregation exceeded the legal demands for conformity to the established formularies of the church and that the clergy willingly attempted to meet those needs rather than blindly obeying the formularies. This willingness to consider first the needs of the people rather than the restrictions of the Prayer Book raises the question of the relationship of this development with that surrounding the introduction of a more elaborate ceremonial in the latter half of the nineteenth century. This study suggests that the revival of ceremonial in the nineteenth century, which contributed to the eclecticism so characteristic of the modern Anglican church, has earlier origins than the second generation of the Tractarians. The judgment made by the commission appointed in 1904 to investigate the ritualist movement must be extended to include the introduction of hymnody in the eighteenth century:

---

13. J. N. Morris, *Religion and Urban Change: Croydon: 1840–1914* (Woodbridge, Engl.: Boydell, 1992), 49.

14. Morris, 49. Morris is referring to John Kent, who noted that "Anglican history has been written on the principle—it is far more than an assumption—that the parochial system is the ideal type of the ecclesia; this belief is deeply rooted in the institutions as they are, and has been transmitted to generation after generation of priests." See Kent's *The Unacceptable Face: The Modern Church in the Eyes of the Historian* (London: SCM, 1987), 95.

15. Morris, 50.

The law of public worship in the Church of England is too narrow for the religious life of the present generation. It needlessly condemns much which a great section of church people, including many of her most devoted members, value.[16]

In both liturgical developments, the introduction of hymnody and the introduction of ceremonial, the law was too narrow to meet the needs of the church. Since it was apparent to all that the law would not be changed, the law had to be disregarded. Thus, every parish was free to determine its own style of worship within the remaining strictures of the Book of Common Prayer. This attitude toward worship found expression first in the introduction of hymns and later in the addition of ceremonial. Thus, the liturgical revival of the latter half of the nineteenth century was actually a continuation of an eighteenth-century development.

This study has explored the history of the introduction of hymnody into the liturgy of the Church of England from 1760 to the 1820s. It is hoped that it has demonstrated the contributions that the study of church music can make to one's understanding of church history. This study has challenged those scholars who have tended to paint the history of hymnody in sharp contrasts of black and white. It has also challenged the belief that the eighteenth-century church was without vigor or life and that the liturgical revival in the Church of England in the nineteenth century was solely because of the disciples of the Tractarians.[17]

Although this subject has been largely unknown and unstudied, it must step out of the shadows of history and into the light of academic study. Through the study of congregational music, be it metrical psalms or hymns, possibilities are opened to the church historian for gaining new insights into and a deeper understanding of the religious affections of a particular period in church history. Moreover, it can provide the historian with a wealth of information that is otherwise inaccessible. Although much has been accomplished in this study, much remains to be done. Nonetheless, the task, once undertaken, will further our understanding of an important and complex period of English church history.

---

16. *Report of the Royal Commission on Ecclesiastical Discipline*, 1:75–76.

17. Nigel Yates, in his recent study, also argues that surviving evidence indicates a vigorous eighteenth-century church. See his *Buildings, Faith, and Worship: The Liturgical Arrangement of Anglican Churches 1600–1900* (Oxford: Clarendon, 1991). See also J[ohn] Wickham Legg, *English Church Life from the Restoration to the Tractarian Movement, Considered in Some of its Neglected or Forgotten Features* (London: Longmans and Green, 1914); and F. C. Mather, "Georgian Churchmanship Reconsidered: Some Variations in Anglican Public Worship 1714–1830," *Journal of Ecclesiastical History* 36 (April 1985):255–283.

Bibliography

Primary Sources

A. Manuscripts

The Borthwicke Institute of Historical Research, York.
  Chanc. AB. 51.
  Chanc. CP. 1820/1.
  YV/CB 19.
Lambeth Palace Library, London.
  MS 2103.

B. Articles, Books, Collected Writings, Hymnals, Psalters

Abbot, Charles. *Hymns Composed for the Use of St. Mary's Church, in the Town of Bedford*. Bedford: W. Smith, 1791.

Abbot, Henry. *The Use and Benefit of Church-Musick, towards quickning [sic] our Devotion. A Sermon Preach'd in the Cathedral-Church of Gloucester, At the Anniversary Meeting of the Three Choirs, Gloucester, Worcester, and Hereford. September 9, 1724*. London: Printed for Jonah Bowyer, 1724.

Abridgement of the Book of Common Prayer, And Administration of the Sacraments, and other Rites and Ceremonies of The Church, According to the Use of The Church of England: Together with the Psalter, or Psalms of David, Pointed as they are to be sung or said in Churches. London: n.p., 1773.

Arber, Edward, ed. *A brief discourse of the troubles at Frankfort [sic] 1554–1558 A.D. Attributed to William Whittingham, dean of Durham*. London: E. Stock, 1908.

Arnold, John. *The compleat psalmodist: or, The organist's, parish-clerk's and psalm-singer's companion*. London: Printed by R. Brown, 1739.

B., H. F. "On Congregational Singing." *The Evangelical Magazine* 12, n.s. (December 1834):545–546.

B., J. *A Collection of Hymns, for the use of all Christians*. Hereford: W. H. Parker, 1787.

B., R. P. "Practical Plan for improving Village Psalmody." *The Christian Observer* 26 (June 1826):339–341.

Banister, Robert. *Scriptural Hymns, Selected for the Congregation of All Saints' Church, Liverpool.* Liverpool: H. Forshaw, 1801.

[Barbauld, A. L.]. *Hymns in Prose for Children.* London: n.p., 1781.

Barrett, J. T. *Select Portions of the New Version of the Psalms of David, adapted to the services of the United Church of England and Ireland for the Sundays and Principal Fasts and Festivals Throughout the Year, to which are added Psalms and Hymns for Particular Occasions.* London: J. Burslem, 1816.

B[arton], W[illiam]. *The Book of Psalms in metre.* London: M. Simmons, for the Companie of Stationers, 1644.

————. *The Book of Psalms in metre, lately translated, with many whole ones, and choice collections of the Old Psalms added to the first impression . . . now much augmented.* London: Printed by G. M., 1645.

Bennett, T. *Sacred Melodies. A Collection of Psalms and Hymns as sung at the Cathedral Church, and the Chapel of St. John the Evangelist, Chichester, composed, selected, and adapted By T. Bennett, Organist.* N.p.: n.p., [c. 1815?].

Bennett, William J. E. *The Principles of the Book of Common Prayer Considered.* London: W. J. Cleaver, 1845.

Benson, Christopher. *Rubrics and Canons of the Church of England Considered.* London: John W. Parker, 1845.

Berridge, John. *A Collection of Divine Songs, Designed chiefly for the Religious Societies of Churchmen, In the Neighbourhood of Everton, Bedfordshire.* London: n.p., 1760.

————. *Sion's Songs, or Hymns: Composed For the Use of them that love and follow the Lord Jesus Christ in Sincerity.* London: Printed for Vallance and Conder, 1785.

Beveridge, William. *Defence of the Book of Psalms, Collected into English Metre, by Thomas Sternhold, John Hopkins and others. With Critical Observations on the late New Version and the Old.* London: n.p., 1710.

[Bewsher, John]. *A Selection of Hymns for the use of the Parish Church, St. Neots (Hunts).* N.p.: J. C. Sharp, 1792.

Bickersteth, Edward. *Christian Psalmody: a collection of above 700 Psalms, hymns and spiritual songs: Selected and arranged for public, social, family and private worship.* London: L. B. Seeley and Sons, 1833.

Biddulph, Tho[mas] T. *Portions of the Psalms of David, Together with a Selection of Hymns, Accommodated to the Service of the Church of England, on Sundays and Other Holy Seasons of Public Worship Which She Observes.* Bristol: W. Pine and Son, 1802.

"Bishop of Peterborough on unauthorised Psalms and Hymns." *The Christian Remembrancer* 3 (April 1821):209–213.

Bisse, Tho[mas]. *The Beauty of Holiness in the Common-Prayer: As set forth in Four Sermons Preach'd at the Rolls Chapel.* London: Printed by W. B. for H. Clements, 1716.

————. *A Rationale on Cathedral Worship or Choir-Service. A Sermon Preach'd in the Cathedral Church of Hereford, At the Anniversary Meeting of the Choirs of Worcester, Gloucester, and Hereford, Sept. 7. 1720.* London: Printed for W. and J. Innys, 1720.

Blackmore, Richard. *A New Version of the Psalms of David, Fitted to the Tunes used in Churches.* London: Printed by John March, 1721.

The Book of Psalms, in metre: Fitted to the Various Tunes in Common Use: Wherein Closeness to the Text and Smoothness of the Verse are Preferred to Rhyme. London: Printed for G. Leighton, 1819.

[Booker, Luke]. *Select Psalms and Hymns for the use of the Churches in Dudley, &c.* 2nd ed., to which is added a supplement. Dudley: J. Rann, 1796.

———. *Select Psalms and Hymns, for the use of the Churches in Dudley, &c.* 3rd ed., with supplement. Dudley: J. Rann, 1813.

B[oteler], W[illiam]. *Some Select and more Practical Psalms, Serving for all occasions. Turned into Double Metre. Intended for the use of Private Families or Persons.* London: n.p., 1666.

Bowles, W. L. *The Parochial History of Bremhill.* London: J. Murray, 1828.

[Breckell, John, and W. Enfield?]. *A Collection of Psalms Proper for Christian Worship; with Additions.* Liverpool: Printed for J. Gore, 1787.

A Brieff discours off the troubles begonne at Franckford in Germany Anno Domini 1554. Abowte the Booke off common prayer and Ceremonies, and continued by the Englishe men theyre, to thende off Q. maries Raigne, in the which discours, the gentle reader shall see the very originall and beginninge off all the contention that hath byn, and what was the cause of the same. London: n.p., 1575.

Brown, [John]. *A Dissertation on the Rise, Union, and Power, The Progressions, Separations, and Corruptions, of Poetry and Music.* London: Printed for L. Davis and C. Reymers, 1763.

Bull, J. *Devotional Hymns, Designed Especially for Public Worship Founded Chiefly on the Collects, Epistles, and Gospel, for Each Sunday in the Year, and for the Fasts, Festivals, and Public Offices of the United Church of England and Ireland. With an Appendix, Containing Some Hymns for General Use, and Also for the Anniversaries of Sunday Schools and Other Public Charities.* London: C. and J. Rivington, 1827.

Burnet, Gilbert. *The History of the Reformation of the Church of England.* 3 vols. London: Printed by T. H. for Richard Chiswell, 1679–1715.

Burroughs, John. *The Devout Psalmodist. II Sermons. I. Concerning singing Psalms with Devotion and Melody. II. Shewing the Indecency and Irreverence of Sitting at the singing of solemn Praises to God.* London: J. Downing, 1712.

Burton, Charles. *Psalms and Hymns, Selected and Arranged for the Use of All-Saints' Church, Grosvenor Square, Manchester.* Manchester: J. Gleave, 1820.

C. "Observations on a New Version of the Psalms." *The Christian Remembrancer* 3 (July 1821):397–399.

———. "On Psalmody." *The Christian Remembrancer* 3 (August 1821):466–469.

C., C. "Remarks on Metrical Translations of the Psalms." *The Christian Observer* 17 (August 1818):510–513.

Cadogan, William Bromley. *Psalms and Hymns.* 2nd ed. London: W. Justins, 1787.

[Cameron, Lucy]. *The Singing Gallery.* London: Printed for William Whittlemore, 1823.

Cannon, T[homas]. *Select Psalms and Hymns, for the use of St. John's Chapel, West-Lane, Walworth, and the City Chapel, London.* 2nd ed., revised and corrected. London: Minerva, [1793?].

[Case, John]. *The Praise of Musicke: Wherein besides the antiquitie, dignitie, delectation, & use thereof in ciuill matters, is also declared the sober and lawfull use of the same in the congregation and Church of God.* Oxford: I. Barnes, 1586.

[Cecil, Richard]. *The Psalms of David Selected from Various Versions, and adapted to Public Worship.* London: Sold by J. Mathews, 1785.

———. *The Psalms of David Selected from Various Versions, and adapted to Public Worship.* A new edition, with appendix. London: n.p., 1806.

Chandler, C. *A Handful of Flowers for a Christian: A Collection of Hymns, Extracted from the most Evangelical Authors.* [London]: Printed for the author, by Axtell and Purdon, 1786.

Chetham, John. *A book of psalmody, containing variety of tunes for all the common metres of the Psalms in the old and new versions and others for particular measures.* London: Printed by W. Pearson, 1718.

Clarke, Thomas. *Psalm-Singing. A Village Sermon, on the Usefulness and Delight of Psalm-Singing, Preached in the parish Church of St. Stephen, Herts.* London: Printed for C. and J. Rivington, 1824.

C[ole], W. *A Key to the Psalms, Being an Easy, Concise, and Familiar Explanation of Words, Allusions, and Sentences in Them, Selected from Substantial Authorities, Tending to Promote Expeditiously the Better Understanding of Them Among the Ignorant in General, and for the Information of the Lower Class of People in Particular.* Cambridge: F. Hodson, 1788.

Cole, William. *A View of Modern Psalmody, Being an Attempt to Reform the Practice of Singing in the Worship of God.* Colchester: J. Chaplin, 1819.

A Collection of Hymns and Psalms for Public Worship. London: Printed for J. Johnson, 1775.

A Collection of Hymns and Psalms for Public Worship. 2nd ed. London: Printed for J. Johnson, 1784.

A Collection of Hymns and Psalms for Public Worship. 3rd ed., improved. London: Printed for J. Johnson, 1793.

A Collection of Hymns and Psalms for Public Worship, from Different Authors. Plymouth: B. Haydon, 1790.

A Collection of Hymns, for Public Worship. Totnes: Cleave and Fisher, 1797.

A Collection of Hymns for Public Worship: On the General Principles of Natural and Revealed Religion. Salisbury: n.p., 1778.

A Collection of Hymns, Selected for the use of Congregations and Families. Boyle: J. Bromell, 1822.

A Collection of Psalms and Hymns, Chiefly intended for Public Worship. Cheltenham: H. Ruff, 1809.

[A] *Collection of Psalms and Hymns for Christian Worship.* Newry: J. Gordon, 1783.

A Collection of Psalms and Hymns for Divine Worship. 2nd ed., with considerable additions. Exeter: W. Grigg, 1779.

A Collection of Psalms and Hymns for Public and Private Worship; more partic-

ularly Designed for the Use of the Congregation at Woolwich-Chapel. London: Minerva, 1791.

A Collection of Psalms & Hymns, from various authors; adapted chiefly to Public Worship. Lancaster: H. Walmsley, 1780.

A Collection of Psalms and Hymns Proper for Christian Worship. Londonderry: S. Boyd, 1808.

A Collection of Psalms and Hymns, Selected for Divine Worship. Chichester: W. Mason, n.d.

A Collection of Psalms, Hymns, and Spiritual Songs, fitted for Morning an[d] Evening Worshi[p] in a Private Family. London: Printed for T. Parkhurst, 1701.

A Collection of Psalms, taken from the two versions, appointed, by Authority, to be used in the Church of England. Cambridge: n.p., 1784.

A Collection out of the Book of Psalms, extracted from various versions, with an Original Version of Several Psalms: Adapted to each Sunday in the Year, according to the order of The Church of England: to which are added, Select Hymns for the Principal Festivals, &c. London: Printed for the editor, by W. Wilson, 1806.

[Collins, Thomas]. *The Rubrick of the Church of England, Examin'd and Consider'd; and Its Use and Observance most Earnestly recommended to all its Members, according to the Intent and Meaning of it.* London: Printed for T. Astley, 1737.

Coningesby, George. *Church-Musick Vindicated; And the Causes of its Dislike Enquired into.* Oxford: L. Lichfield, 1733.

Considerations on the Expediency of Revising the Liturgy and Articles of the Church of England: in which Notice is taken of the Objections to that Measure, urged in Two late Pamphlets. London: Printed for T. Cadell, 1790.

Conyers, Richard. *A Collection of Psalms and Hymns, From Various Authors: For the Use of Serious and Devout Christians of Every Denomination.* London: n.p., 1767.

————. *A Collection of Psalms and Hymns, From Various Authors: For the Use of Serious and Devout Christians of Every Denomination.* A new edition, with additions. London: J. and W. Oliver, 1774.

Cotterill, T[homas]. *A Selection of Psalms and Hymns, for Public and Private Use, Adapted to the Festivals of the Church of England; and to some portions of the Epistles, Gospels, or Lessons, appointed For every Sunday throughout the Year.* 7th ed. Staffordshire: C. Chester, 1815.

————. *A Selection of Psalms and Hymns for Public and Private Use, Adapted to the Services of the Church of England.* 8th ed., considerably enlarged. Sheffield: Printed for the editor, by J. Montgomery, 1819.

————. *A Selection of Psalms and Hymns, for Public Worship.* London: Printed for T. Cadell, in the Strand, 1820.

————. *A Selection of Psalms and Hymns for the Use of St.Paul's and St. James's Churches, Sheffield; Adapted to the Services of the Church of England.* Sheffield: J. Montgomery, 1819.

————. *A Selection of Psalms and Hymns: For the Use of St.Paul's Church, in Sheffield.* London: T. Cadell, 1820.

Cottle, Joseph. *A New Version of the Psalms of David.* London: Printed for Longman and Co., 1801.

————. *A Version of the Psalms of David, attempted in metre.* 2nd ed. London: Printed for Longman and Co., 1805.

Cotton, H. "On Psalmody." *The Christian Remembrancer* 3 (June 1821):327–331.

A Course of Singing Psalms, Beginning On the First Sunday in January, And again On the First Sunday in July: And also proper Psalms for particular Days and Occasions. Agreeable To the Directions given by the late Lord Bishop of London to the Clergy of his Diocese, in the Year 1724. Together With the Tunes adapted to each Psalm. London: n.p., 1767.

Crowley, Robert. *The psalter of David newely translated into Englysh metre in such sort that it maye the more decently, and wyth more delyte of the mynde, be read and songe of al men.* London: n.p., 1549.

[Cunningham, John W.] *Select Portions of Psalms, Extracted from Various Versions, and adapted to Public Worship. With an Appendix, containing Hymns for the Principal Festivals of the Church of England.* London: Ellerton and Henderson, 1811.

D., D. "On Strict Adherence to the Rubric." *The Christian Remembrancer* 20 (November 1838):681–682.

Dallas, Alexander. *What says the Rubric? The Present Truth.* London: J. Nisbet, 1843.

Daubeny, C[harles]. *A Few Plain Thoughts on the Liturgy of The Church of England: with the view of Explaining and Promoting its Rational Use, and Spiritual Design.* Bath: Printed and Sold by Meyler and Son, 1814.

————. *Psalms and Hymns, Appointed to be Sung by The Congregation assembled at Christ Church, Bath.* Bath: Wood, 1816.

[Day, W.] *A Collection of Psalms and Hymns, for Public Worship.* Evesham: J. Agg, 1795.

Dealtry, William. *The Excellence of the Liturgy. A Sermon, Preached at All Saints' Church, Southampton, on Wednesday, April 22, 1829.* London: J. Hatchard and Son, 1829.

De Courcy, [Richard]. *A Collection of Psalms and Hymns, Extracted from different Authors, With a Preface.* Shrewsbury: T. Wood, 1775.

————. *A Collection of Psalms and Hymns, Extracted from different Authors.* 2nd ed. Shrewsbury: T. Wood, 1782.

Denham, John. *A Version of the Psalms of David, Fitted to the Tunes Used in Churches.* London: Printed for J. Bowyer, 1714.

A Directory for the Publique Worship of God, Throughout the Three Kingdoms of England, Scotland, and Ireland. London: Printed for E. Tyler, A. Fifield, R. Smith, and J. Field, 1644.

D'Israeli, I[saac]. *A Second Series of Curiosities of Literature; Consisting of Researches in Literary, Biographical, and Political History; Of Critical and Philosophical Inquiries; and of Secret History.* 2nd ed., corrected. 3 vols. London: J. Murray, 1824.

The Divine Musical Miscellany. N.p.: n.p., [c. 1755?].

D[od], H[enry]. *Al the Psalmes of Dauid: with certeine songes & Canticles of Moses, Debora, Isaiah, Hezekiah & others . . . Nowe faithfully reduced into easie meeter, fitting our common tunes.* [London]: n.p., 1620.

Doddridge, Philip. *Hymns founded on Various Texts in the Holy Scriptures. Published from the Author's Manuscript by Job Orton.* Salop: J. Orton, 1755.

Draper, H[enry]. *A Collection of Psalms and Hymns, for Social Worship.* London: Printed for the author, 1805.

———. *Lectures on the Liturgy; Delivered in the Parish Church of St. Antholin, Watling Street.* London: Printed for Williams and Smith, [1806].

[Druitt, Robert]. *Conversations on the Choral Service; Being an Examination of Popular Prejudices Against Church Music.* London: T. Harrison, 1853.

———. *A Popular Tract on Church Music, with remarks on Its Moral and Political Importance, and a practical Scheme for its Reformation.* London: F. and J. Rivington, 1845.

Drummond, George, and Edward Miller. *Select Portions of the New Version of Psalms, For every Sunday throughout the year; with the Principal Festivals and Fasts for the use of Parish Churches. The words selected by the Rev. George Hay Drummond; the music selected, adapted, and composed by Edward Miller.* London: W. Miller, 1790.

———. *Select Portions of the New Version of Psalms, For every Sunday throughout the Year; with the Principal Festivals and Fasts. For the Use of Parish Churches.* 7th ed. London: n.p., 1791.

Dunderdale, J. *A Selection of Psalms and Hymns, Adapted to the Principal Fasts and Festivals of the Church of England.* Burslem: J. Tregortha, 1817.

Edwards, John. *A Collection of Hymns and Spiritual Songs, For the Use of Serious and Devout Christians, of All Denominations.* 2nd ed., With additions and alterations. Leeds: G. Wright, 1769.

Elliot, R. *Psalms and Hymns and Spiritual Songs: in Two Parts. The First being a Collection from Various Authors. The Second Part, Together with a Preface on the Nature, Use and Benefit of Divine Psalmody.* London: Printed for the author, 1769.

Engel, Carl. *Reflections on Church Music, For the Consideration of Churchgoers in General.* London: G. Scheurmann, 1856.

Evans, Robert Wilson. *A Day in the Sanctuary: with an Introductory Treatise on Hymnology.* London: J. G. F. and J. Rivington, 1843.

Extracts from the Two Versions of the Psalms, Now Generally in Use; to be occasionally sung in St. John's Church, Wakefield, To the best and most familiar Old Tunes. Wakefield: E. Waller, 1799.

Family-Hymns. Gather'd (mostly) out of the best Translations of David's Psalms. 2nd ed., corrected. London: Printed for T. Parkhurst, 1702.

Fawcett, John. *Hymns: Adapted to the Circumstances of Public Worship, and Private Devotion.* Leeds: G. Wright and Son, 1782.

Fisher, John. *A Charge Delivered to the Clergy of the Diocese of Exeter, at the Primary Visitation of John, Lord Bishop of Exeter, 1804 and 1805.* Exeter: n.p., 1805.

[Ford, D. E.]. *Observations on Psalmody.* London: Westley and Davis, 1827.

[Formby, Henry]. *Parochial Psalmody Considered.* London: E. Mackenzie, 1845.

Foxe, John. *Acts and Monuments.* London: n.p., 1563.

Fuller, Thomas. *The Church-History of Britain: From the Birth of Jesus Christ, Until the Year M.DC.XLVIII.* London: Printed for J. Williams, 1655.

Gibson, Charles Reginald. *A Dispassionate Enquiry into the Causes and Effect of the 'Hymn Book Controversy,' At Darford: In a Letter Addressed to the Reverend C. Gillmore, Vicar.* Dartford: Printed for the author, by Dunkin, 1848.

[Gibson], Edmund. *The Excellent Use of Psalmody, with a Course of Singing-Psalms for half a year.* 1724. Reprinted in vol. 1, *Religious Tracts, Dispersed by the Society for Promoting Christian Knowledge.* London: F. and C. Rivington, 1800.

Goode, William. *An Entire New Version of the Book of Psalms; in which an attempt is made to accommodate them to the Worship of the Christian Church, in a variety of measures now in general use: with Original Preface and Notes, critical and explanatory.* 2 vols. London: W. Wilson, 1811.

Goodridge, Richard. *The Psalter or Psalms of David set to New Tunes.* 2nd ed. Oxford: n.p., 1684.

The Gospel Magazine 3 (March 1768):140–142; (April 1768):188ff; (May 1768):233–237; (June 1768):278ff; (July 1768):324ff; 4 (March 1769):128ff.

[Gray, Jonathan]. *Hymns, Selected as a Supplement to a Collection of Psalms Used in Several Churches.* York: C. Peacock, for J. Wolstenholme, 1817.

———. *Hymns, Selected as a Supplement to a Collection of Psalms used in several Churches.* 2nd ed. York: C. Peacock, 1817.

———. *Hymns Selected as a Supplement to a Collection of Psalms Used in several Churches.* 5th ed. York: J. Wolstenholme, 1820.

———. *Hymns, Selected as a Supplement to a Collection of Psalms, used in several Churches.* A new edition, improved. York: T. Marsh, 1839.

———. *An Inquiry into Historical Facts, relative to Parochial Psalmody, In reference to the Remarks of The Right Reverend Herbert, Lord Bishop of Peterborough.* York: Printed by J. Wolstenholme, 1821.

———. "On the Admission of Metrical Hymns into Churches." By H. G. *The Christian Observer* 17 (March 1818):152–159.

———. *Psalms and Hymns for Parish Churches; with A Preface to the Hymns, containing An Inquiry into the Origin of Metrical Psalmody, and a Vindication of the Use of Metrical Hymns in Parochial Worship.* York: J. Wolstenholme, 1826.

———. "Reply to Mr. Todd's Argument on Sternhold's Psalms." *The Christian Observer* 26 (December 1826): 736–739.

Gray, Walker. *Select Portions of Psalms and Hymns, Entirely Extracted from the Prayer-Book, without alteration or addition, for the use of Cullumpton Church.* N.p.: Printed for the editor, 1815.

H., E. *Scripture Proof for Singing of Scripture Psalms, Hymns and Spiritual Songs: or, An Answer to several Queries and Objections frequently made use of to stumble and turn aside young Christians from their Duty to God in Singing of Psalms, Gathered out of the Scriptures of Truth. To which is added The Testimony of some Learned Men, to prove that Scripture Psalms are intended by all those three words, Psalms, Hymns and Songs, used by the Apostle.* London: Printed for J. Astwood, 1696.

H., M. T. "Letter to the Editor." *The Christian Observer* 3 (January 1804):17–18.

Haweis, T[homas]. *Carmina Christo; or, Hymns to the Saviour: Designed for the*

Use and Comfort of those who Worship the Lamb that was Slain. Bath: S. Hazard, 1792.

————. *Carmina Christo; or, Hymns to the Saviour: Designed for the Use and Comfort of those who Worship the Lamb that was Slain.* 2nd ed. London: T. Chapman, 1795.

————. *Carmina Christo; or, Hymns to the Saviour: Designed for the Use and Comfort of those who Worship the Lamb that was Slain.* A new edition, very considerably enlarged. London: S. and C. McDowall, 1808.

[Hawker, Robert]. *Psalms and Hymns sung by the Children of the Sunday School, in the Parish Church of Charles, Plymouth, at the Sabbath Evening Lecture.* 9th ed. Plymouth: P. Nettleton, [c. 1805?].

————. *Psalms and Hymns sung by the Children of the Sunday School, in the Parish Church of Charles, Plymouth, at the Sabbath Evening Lecture.* 13th ed. Plymouth: P. Nettleton, [1807].

Hawkins, William Bentinck. *A Few Plain Words, suggested by some Recent Proceedings in the Diocese of Exeter, addressed to Members of the Church of England.* London: F. and J. Rivington, 1845.

Heber, Reginald. "Bishop Heber's Letter." *The Christian Remembrancer* 17 (1835):622–626.

————. "Hymns appropriate to the Sundays and principal Holidays." By D. R. *The Christian Observer* 10 (October 1811):630–631.

————. *Hymns, Written and Adapted to the Weekly Church Service of the Year.* London: J. Murray, 1827.

The Helston Case: Twelve letters on the Rubric and Ritual Innovations reprinted from the Standard. London: Hatchard, [c. 1845].

Heron, Henry. *Parochial music corrected: intended for the use of the several charity-schools in London, Westminster, &c., as well as for all congregations: being plain and distinct rules for the more pleasing and correct performance of psalmody, by the children, &c., in their respective parish-churches. With psalms, hymns, and anthems, set to music. . . . To which is added an easy introduction to singing.* London: W. Richardson, 1790.

Heylyn, Peter. *Aërius Redivivus: or the History of the Presbyterians. Containing the Beginnings, Progresse, and Successes of that Active Sect. Their Oppositions to Monarchical and Episcopal Government. Their Innovations in the Church; and their Imbroilments of the Kingdoms and Estates of Christendom in the pursuit of their Designs. From the Year 1536 to the Year 1647.* 2nd ed. London: Printed by R. Battersby for C. Wilkinson, 1672.

————. *Examen Historicum: or A Discovery and Examination of the Mistakes, Falsities and Defects In some Modern Histories. Occasioned By the Partiality and Inadvertencies of their Severall Authours.* 2 vols. London: Printed for H. Seile and R. Roysten, 1659.

Hill, Richard. *Pietas Oxoniensis, or a full and impartial account of the expulsion of six students from St. Edmund Hall By a Master of Arts of the University of Oxford.* N.p.: n.p., 1768.

Hirst, T[homas]. *Familiar Dialogues, In which an attempt is made To Shew the Use and Abuse of Sacred Music, in Divine Worship.* Nottingham: E. Hodson, 1816.

Hodges, Edward. *An Apology for Church Music and Musical Festivals, in Answer to the Animadversions of The Standard and The Record.* London: Rivingtons, 1834.

[Hodson, Septimus]. *Psalms & Hymns selected for Congregational Use.* London: W. Smith, 1801.

———. *Psalms and Hymns, Selected for the use of Tavistock Chapel, Broad Court, Long Acre.* N.p.: n.p., 1788.

[Horne], George. *A Charge intended to have been delivered to the Clergy of Norwich, At the Primary Visitation of George, Lord Bishop of that Diocese.* Norwich: Printed by Yarington and Bacon, 1791.

Horne, Thomas Hartwell. *Historical Notices of Psalmody.* London: C. F. Hodgson, 1847.

———. *A Manual of Parochial Psalmody; Comprising Select Portions from the Old and New Versions of Psalms, Together with Hymns, for the Principal Festivals, Etc. of the Church of England; Revised, and Adapted to the Service of the Church, for Every Sunday, Etc. Throughout the Year.* London: T. Cadell, 1829.

Horne, W. W. *The New Songs of Zion; or, Short Hymns, Collected from the Scriptures of the Old Testament.* Norwich: A. White, [1795].

[Horsley, Samuel]. *An Apology for the Liturgy and Clergy of the Church of England: In Answer to a Pamphlet, entitled Hints, &c.* London: Printed for J. F. and C. Rivington, 1790.

———. *The Charge of Samuel, Lord Bishop of Rochester, to the Clergy of his Diocese, delivered at his second general visitation . . . 1800.* London: n.p., 1800.

Hurn, W. *Psalms and Hymns, The Greater Part Original; and the Selected Compositions altered with a view to Purity of Doctrine and General Usefulness.* Ipswich: J. Raw, 1813.

[Hutchins, John]. *Select Psalms and Hymns, for the use of the Parish Church of St. Botolph without Aldersgate, London.* London: n.p., 1790.

Hymns, for Occasional Use in the Parish Church of Saint Peter, in Nottingham. Nottingham: E. Shorrock and Son, 1824.

The Hymns used at the City of London Lying-in-Hospital, in the City-Road, at the Baptism of Infants, Born There. [London?]: Printed for H. Thorowgood, musical instrument-maker and music printer, [1770?].

An Introduction to Reform Singing: Being An Essay to Sing the Holy Scriptures; Or Repeat them Melodiously in Churches, Instead of Singing Erroneous Rhymes and Human Compositions. London: n.p., [1791?].

J., T. "Observations on the Intellectual Part of Christian Psalmody." *The Christian Observer* 4 (August 1805): 464–468.

James I. *The Psalms of King David.* London: T. Harper, 1637.

James, William. *The Usage of the Church, in Closing the Morning Service with the Sermon, when there is no Communion, Vindicated, as agreeable to the intent of the rubric.* London: F. and J. Rivington, 1845.

Jebb, John. *The Choral Service of the United Church of England and Ireland: Being an Enquiry into The Liturgical System of the Cathedral and Collegiate Foundations of the Anglican Communion.* London: J. W. Parker, 1843.

———. *Dialogue on the Choral Service.* Leeds: T. W. Green, 1842.

Jones, John. *Free and Candid Disquisitions relating to the Church of England, and the Means of advancing Religion therein.* N.p.: n.p., 1749.

Jones, William (of Nayland). *The Diary of the Revd. William Jones, 1777–1821.* Edited by O. F. Christie. London: Brentano, 1929.

————. *The Nature and Excellence of Music. A Sermon Preached at the Opening of a New Organ, in the Parish Church of Nayland in Suffolk; on Sunday, July the 29th, 1787.* London: G. G. J. and J. Robinson, 1787.

————. *Ten Church Tunes for the Organ with Four Anthems in Score.* London: n.p., 1789.

————. *A Treatise on the Art of Music.* Colchester: W. Keymer, 1784.

Joye, George. *Ortulus anime. The garden of the soule: or the englisshe primers (the which a certaine printer lately corrupted & made false to the grete sclaunder of thauthor & greter desayte of as many as boughte and red them) newe corrected and augmented.* Antwerp: n.p., 1530.

Keach, Benjamin. *Spiritual Melody.* N.p.: n.p., 1691.

Keble, John. *The Christian Year: thoughts in verse for the Sundays and Holydays throughout the year.* Oxford: n.p., 1827.

Kempthorne, John. *Select Portions of Psalms, From Various Translations, and Hymns, From Various Authors. The Whole Arranged according to the yearly Seasons of the Church of England; with Attempts at Corrections and Improvements.* London: Printed for J. Hatchard, 1810.

Kennedy, R[ann]. *A Church of England Psalm-Book; or, Portions of the Psalter, adapted, by selections from the New and Old Versions, to the services of the Established Church.* Birmingham: Jabet and Moore, 1821.

————. *Thoughts on the Music and Words of Psalmody, As At Present in Use Among the Members of the Church of England.* London: Longman, Hurst, Rees, Orme, and Brown, 1821.

Kennet, Basil. *An Essay towards a Paraphrase on the Psalms, in English Verse. To which is added a paraphrase on the third chapter of the Revelations [sic].* London: B. Aylmer, 1706.

Kerby, Joseph. *A Selection of Hymns from the best authors.* Wigan: W. Lyon, 1796.

L., R. "Hymns and Hymn-Tunes for Congregational Worship." *Fraser's Magazine* 62 (September 1860):299–318.

Lasco, John à. *Opera.* Edited by A. Kuyper. 2 vols. Amsterdam: n.p., 1866.

Latrobe, J. A. *The Music of the Church Considered in its Various Branches, Congregational and Choral.* London: R. B. Seeley and W. Burnside, 1831.

Lavington, George. *The Enthusiasm of Methodists and Papists Compar'd.* N.p.: n.p., 1749.

Law, [George Henry]. *A Charge Delivered to the Clergy of the Diocese of Chester . . . in July and August, 1820.* London: n.p., 1820.

A letter to the Rev. H. Marsh . . . in confutation of his opinion, that the Dissenters are aiming at the subversions of the Religious Establishment of this country . . . by a Protestant Dissenter and a Layman. London: n.p., 1813.

[Lindsey, T.]. *The Book of Common Prayer Reformed According to the Plan of the Late Dr. Samuel Clarke Together with the Psalter or Psalms of David and a Collection of Hymns for Public Worship.* London: Printed for J. Johnson, 1775.

————. *The Book of Common Prayer Reformed According to the Plan of the Late Dr. Samuel Clarke Together with the Psalter or Psalms of David and a Collection of Hymns for Public Worship.* 3rd ed. London: Printed for J. Johnson, 1785.

————. *The Book of Common Prayer Reformed According to the Plan of the late Dr. Samuel Clarke Together with the Psalter or Psalms of David and a Collection of Hymns for Public Worship.* 4th ed. London: Printed for J. Johnson, 1793.

"Literary and Philosophical Intelligence." *The Christian Observer* 18 (December 1819):810–811.

"Literary and Philosophical Intelligence." *The Christian Observer* 20 (April 1821):258–259.

A Liturgy compiled from The Book of Common Prayer reformed, according to the plan of The Late Dr. Samuel Clarke; together with a Collection of Psalms and Hymns, for Public Worship. Plymouth: M. Haydon and Son, 1791.

M., W. "On the discretionary Use of Psalms and Hymns in Church." *The Christian Observer* 14 (October 1815): 661–662.

Machyn, Henry. *The Diary of Henry Machyn, Citizen and Merchant-Taylor of London, From A.D. 1550 to A.D. 1563.* Edited by John Gough Nichols. London: Camden Society Publications, 1848; reprint edition, New York: AMS, 1968.

Madan, Martin. *A Collection of Psalm and Hymn Tunes, never before Published.* London: n.p., 1769.

————. *A Collection of Psalms and Hymns, Extracted from various Authors.* London: n.p., 1760.

[Maltby, Edward, R. Tillard, and J. S. Banks, eds.]. *Psalms and Hymns, Selected for the Churches of Buckden and Holveach, of Bluntisham cum Earith, and Hemingford Grey, in the Diocese of Lincoln.* London: Printed for T. Cadell and W. Davies, 1815.

————. *Psalms and Hymns, Selected for the Use of Congregations in the United Church of England and Ireland.* 3rd ed. London: Printed for T. Cadell, 1824.

Mant, Richard. *Horae Liturgicae.* London: J. W. Parker, 1845.

————. "On the Use of Psalms and Hymns in the Public Service of the Church." *The Christian Remembrancer* 20 (February 1838):85–88.

————. "On the Use of Psalms and Hymns in the Public Service of the Church." *The Christian Remembrancer* 20 (March 1838):159–164.

————. *Thoughts on the Singing of Unauthorised Hymns, in Publick Worship; Respectfully Submitted to the Consideration of the Archbishops and Bishops of the United Church of England and Ireland.* London: Printed for J. G. and F. Rivington, 1835.

Marbeck, John. *The booke of Common praier noted.* London: n.p., 1550.

————. *The booke of Common praier noted.* London: n.p., 1550; facsimile edn., with extensive introduction by R. A. Leaver. Appleford: S. Courtenay, 1980.

[Marsh, Herbert]. *A Charge, Delivered at the Primary Visitation of Herbert Lord Bishop of Peterborough, In July, 1820. With an Appendix, containing some remarks on the modern custom of Singing in Our Churches Unauthorized Psalms and Hymns.* London: F. C. and J. Rivington, 1820.

————. *A Reply to the Strictures of Isaac Milner, D.D., Dean of Carlisle, etc.* Cambridge: J. Hodson, 1813.

Mason, William. *Essays, Historical and Critical, on English Church Music.* York: W. Blanchard, 1795.

Matlock, John. *Hymns and Spiritual Songs.* London: M. Lewis, 1765.

————. *Hymns and Spiritual Songs.* 2nd edition. London: Hilton, 1774.

————. *A Second Book of Hymns and Spiritual Songs*. London: J. and J. March, 1767.

Merrick, James. *The Psalms, translated or paraphrased in English verse*. Reading: J. Carnan, 1765.

Milbourne, Luke. *Psalmody Recommended in a Sermon Preach'd to the Company of Parish-Clerks, At St. Alban's Woodstreet, November 17. At St. Giles's in the Fields, November 22, 1712*. London: J. Downing, 1713.

————. *The Psalms of David, in English metre; translated from the original*. London: Printed for W. Rogers, etc., 1698.

Miller, Edward. *The History and Antiquities of Doncaster and its Vicinity, with Anecdotes of Eminent Men*. Doncaster: W. Sheardown, [1804].

————. *Thoughts on the Present Performance of Psalmody in the Established Church of England, Addressed to the Clergy*. London: Printed for W. Miller, 1791.

[More, Hannah]. *Florio: A Tale, For Fine Gentlemen and Fine Ladies*. London: T. Cadell, 1786.

Munkhouse, Richard. *A Sermon, Preached in the Church of St. John Baptist, Wakefield*. London: Printed for F. and C. Rivington, 1797.

[Neale, John Mason]. "English Hymnology: its History and Prospects." *The Christian Remembrancer* 18, n.s. (October 1849):302–343.

Newton, Benjamin. *The Church of England's Apology for the Use of Music in her Service. A Sermon Preached in the Cathedral-Church of Glocester [sic], September 10, 1760, at the Annual Meeting of the Three Choirs of Glocester [sic], Worcester, and Hereford; And published at their Joint Request*. Glocester [sic]: R. Raikes, [c. 1760].

[Newton, John]. *Olney Hymns, in Three Books*. London: W. Oliver, 1779.

Noel, Gerald. *A Selection of Psalms and Hymns from the New Version of the Church of England, and others; corrected and revised for Public Worship*. 3rd ed. London: Printed for Hatchard and Son, 1820.

[Novello, Vincent?]. "An Historical Account of Music." *The Christian Remembrancer* 17 (June 1835):345–357.

Nowell, Thomas. *An Answer to a Pamphlet entitled Pietas Oxoniensis*. N.p.: n.p., 1768.

O., S. "On the Singing in our Parochial Churches." *The Christian Observer* 17 (October 1818):646–648.

"On the Duties of Churchwardens, and on Psalmody." *The Christian Remembrancer* 5 (August 1823):498–500.

"On the Use of Psalms and Hymns." *The Christian Remembrancer* 20 (February 1838):85–91.

"On the Use of Psalms and Hymns." *The Christian Remembrancer* 20 (April 1838):233–236.

Parker, William. *The Pleasures of Gratitude and Benevolence improved by Church-Musick*. London: Printed for J. Fletcher, 1753.

Parry, W. *A Selection of Psalms and Hymns*. London: n.p., 1791.

Pastor. "Sternhold's Psalms." *The Christian Observer* 26 (October 1826):600–601.

Phillips, John. *A Specimen of some of David's Psalms in metre, with Remarks upon the late Translators*. N.p.: n.p., 1698.

Philo-Rubric. "Proper Place of the Psalm in the Church Service." *The Christian Observer* 18 (February 1819):86–87.

Plain Considerations on a Return to Rubrical Conformity, chiefly addressed to the Laity: with some suggestions to the Clergy. London: J. Hearne, 1845.

Playford, John. *Psalms & hymns in solemn musick of fovre parts on the common tunes to the Psalmes in metre: used in Parish-chvrches.* London: Printed by W. Godbid, 1671.

———. *The Whole Book of Psalms: with the usual Hymns and Spiritual Songs; together with all the ancient and proper tunes sung in churches, with some of later use. Compos'd in three parts, cantus, medius, & bassus: in a more plain and useful method than hath been formerly published.* London: W. Godbid for the Company of Stationers, 1677.

Porter, William James. *A Selection From the New Version of the Psalms of David, including the 100th Psalm, and Part of the 104th, from the Old Version, For the use of Parish Churches.* Canterbury: J. Saffery, 1807.

Porteus, Beilby. *A Charge Delivered to the Clergy of the Diocese of London, at the Primary Visitation of that Diocese in the year MDCCXC.* London: J. F. and C. Rivington, 1790.

"Psalmody." *Gentleman's Magazine* 51 (August 1781):369–370.

"Psalms and Hymns." *The British Critic, and Quarterly Theological Review* 32 (July 1842):1–33.

Psalms and Hymns for Public or Private Devotion. Sheffield: J. Montgomery, 1802.

Psalms and Hymns for the use of the Congregation of Carlisle Chapel, Kennington-Lane, in the parish of Lambeth. [London?]: W. Perryman, 1797.

Psalms and Hymns, selected for the use of Tavistock Chapel, Broad-Court, Long-Acre. A new edition. N.p.: n.p., 1796.

Psalms, Hymns & Anthems, Used in The Chapel of the Hospital for the Maintenance & Education of Exposed & Deserted Young Children. N.p.: n.p., [177?].

R., L. "On the due Regulation of Instrumental Music in Public Worship." *The Christian Observer* 4 (April 1805):212–214.

[Randolph], John. *A Charge delivered to the Clergy of the Diocese of Bangor.* Bangor: Printed by J. Broster, 1808.

———. *A Charge delivered to the Clergy of the Diocese of Oxford.* Oxford: Oxford University Press, 1802.

———. *A Charge Delivered to the Clergy of the Diocese of Oxford, by John, Lord Bishop of that Diocese at His Triennial Visitation in MDCCCV.* Oxford: W. Hanwell and J. Parker, 1805.

"Review of Pamphlets on Music and Psalmody." *The Christian Observer* 22 (July 1822):420–444.

"Review of Religious Publications." *The Evangelical Magazine* 2, n.s. (Supplement 1824):580.

"Review of Religious Publications." *The Evangelical Magazine* 7, n.s. (February 1829):64–65.

Revise the Liturgy. London: J. Hatchard and Son, 1845.

Richardson, William. *A Collection of Psalms.* York: n.p., 1788.

[Richardson, William?]. *A Collection of Psalms, from the Most Approved Ver-*

sions; in Portions of a Convenient Length for Public Worship. 12th ed. York: C. Peacock, for J. Wolstenholme, 1815.

Richings, B. *A Selection of Psalms and Hymns, from Various Authors, Designed for the Use of Public Worship.* London: Ellerton and Henderson, 1816.

"Right of Clergymen to controul the singing in Church; and the ringing of Church Bells." *The Christian Remembrancer* 4 (June 1822):375–377.

Riley, William. *Parochial Music Corrected. Containing Remarks on the Performance of Psalmody in Country Churches, and on the ridiculous and profane Manner of Singing practised by the Methodists; Reflections on the bad Performance of Psalmody in London, Westminster, &c. with some Hints for the Improvement of it in Public Worship; Observations on the Choice and Qualifications of Parish-Clerks; the Utility of Teaching Charity-Children Psalmody and Hymns; the Use of Organs, and the Performance of Organists.* London: n.p., 1762.

———. *Psalms and Hymns, for the use of The Chapel of the Asylum for Female Orphans.* London: H. Bunce, 1773.

Robinson, Hastings, ed. *The Zurich Letters, Comprising the Correspondence of Several English Bishops and Others, with some of the Helvetian Reformers, During the early part of the Reign of Queen Elizabeth.* Cambridge: Cambridge University Press, 1842.

[Robinson, Thomas]. *A Collection of Psalms and Hymns from Various Authors: Chiefly designed for the use of Public Worship.* 3rd ed. London: T. Bensley, 1791.

[Romaine, William]. *An Essay on Psalmody.* London: n.p., 1775.

[Rous, Francis]. *The Psalms of David, in English meeter.* London: M. Flesher, for the Company of Stationers, 1646.

The Rubric: Its Strict Observance Recommended. London: J. Burns, 1839.

S[andys], G[eorge]. *A Paraphrase upon the Psalmes of David. And upon the Hymnes dispersed throughout the Old and New Testaments.* London: [A. Hebb], 1636.

Scott, Thomas. *A Selection of Psalms and Hymns.* London: W. McDowall, 1804.

———. *A Selection of Psalms and Hymns.* Buckingham: J. Seeley, 1808.

Sedgwick, Daniel. *A Comprehensive Index of Names of Original Authors and Translators of Psalms and Hymns.* [London]: D. Sedgwick, 1860.

Select Hymns and Anthems, on Religious Subjects, Taken from David's Psalms, and other Passages of Holy Scripture; and sung at Tunbridge-Wells Chapel. 6th ed. Tunbridge-Wells: J. Sprange, 1792.

Select Hymns and Spiritual Songs: For the Use of St. Michael's Church, Manchester. Manchester: Printed by Sowler and Russell, 1798.

Select Portions of Dr. Brady's and Mr. Tate's version of The Psalms; together with a few selected from the Old Version. Also a Collection of Hymns and Sanctuses, for the use of St. Ann's Church, Manchester. Manchester: C. Wheeler and Son, 1798.

Select Portions of Psalms, taken from The Old and New Versions, and that of Mr. Merrick: to which are added A Few Hymns from approved Authors: Compiled for the Use of the Congregation of the Holy Trinity Church in Halifax. Halifax: E. Jacobs, 1798.

Select Portions of the Psalms, Both old and new Version: Also. A Collection of

Hymns and Anthems, As they are sung in the Parish Church of Cranbrook. Cranbrook: S. Waters, n.d.

Select Portions of the Psalms, Chiefly from the New Version; with several Hymns, from various authors. In Use at St. Mary's Church, Reading. Reading: R. Snare, 1799.

Select Portions of the Psalms of David, for the Use of Parish Churches. N.p.: n.p., [c. 1780].

Select Portions of the Psalms of David, for the use of Parish Churches: The Words from the Old Version, And the Music from the most approved Compositions. 2nd ed. London: n.p., 1786.

Select Psalms and Hymns, Designed Chiefly for the Use of Public Worship. Shrewsbury: J. and W. Eddowes, 1807.

Select Psalms and Hymns, for Public Worship. Chesterfield: H. Bradley, 1799.

Select Psalms and Hymns For the Use of the Parish-Church and Tabernacle of St. James's Westminster. London: F. Heptinstall, 1697.

Select Psalms and Hymns for the use of the Parish Church of Cardington, in the County of Bedford. London: J. W. Galabin, 1786.

Select Psalms and Hymns, for the use of the Parish Churches in the town of Huntingdon. Huntingdon: A. Jenkinson, 1774.

Select Psalms, from different Versions; to which are added a few Occasional Hymns. Cambridge: J. Archdeacon, 1789.

Select Psalms in Verse, with Critical Remarks, by Bishop Lowth, and others, illustrative of the Beauties of Sacred Poetry. London: Printed for J. Hatchard, 1811.

A Selection of Hymns for Public Worship. London: R. and A. Taylor, 1814.

A Selection of Hymns, for the use of the Parish Church, St. Neots (Hunts). N.p.: J. C. Sharp, 1792.

Selection of Hymns in a Great Variety of Metres, Adapted to the Use of the Established Church. Holt, Norfolk: J. Shalders, 1828.

A Selection of Psalms and Hymns, for the use of Handsworth Church, in Staffordshire. Birmingham: M. M. Chapman, 1826.

Senhouse, Peter. *The right Use and Improvement of sensitive Pleasures, and more particularly of Musick.* London: Printed for J. Palmer, 1728.

Several Select Portions of the Psalms, from Tate and Brady's Version. Collected For the Use of Churches. Newcastle: T. Slack, 1763.

Several Select Portions of the Psalms, from Tate and Brady's Version. Collected For the Use of Churches. A new edition. Newcastle: T. Angus, 1778.

[Sillery, Anthony]. *The Christian Choir, or a system of Christian Psalmody, for Public and Private Worship; Comprising 1. Liturgic [sic] Hymns, in an easy method for Chanting—with Music of Chants and Sanctusses [sic]—some of these original. 2. Selections of Psalms, Anthems, and Hymns, with Arguments and Annotations, practical and devotional. Also, Some account of Psalmody in Public Worship, especially in the Established Church, since the Reformation, with evidence that the Psalms in metre, and Hymns, are in the same position with respect to the laws of the Church.* Dublin: W. Curry Jr., 1835.

[Simeon, Charles]. *A Collection of Psalms and Hymns from Various Authors, chiefly designed for the use of Publick Worship.* Cambridge: J. Archdeacon and J. Burges, [1795].

Simpson, D[avid]. *A Collection of Psalms and Hymns And Spiritual Songs: For the Use of Christians Of Every Denomination.* 2nd ed., with an appendix. Macclesfield: T. Bayley, 1780.

———. *Select Psalms and Hymns.* Macclesfield: n.p., 1776.

———. *Select Psalms and Hymns.* A new edition. Macclesfield: Printed and Sold by E. Bayley, 1795.

Smith, John (of Nantwich). *Select Portions of the Psalms appointed to be Sung in Churches: Taken chiefly from the New Version; with Hymns Collected from various Authors, and intended occasionally to be sung in public Worship.* 2nd ed., with additions. Nantwich: E. Snelson, 1786.

Smyth, Edward. *A Choice Collection of Hymns, Psalms, and Anthems; Principally designed for the Congregation attending Bethesda-Chapel; but calculated for all Denominations of Christians, who desire to worship God in spirit and in truth.* Dublin: B. Dugdale, 1785.

———. *A Choice Collection of Occasional Hymns; Principally designed For the Congregation attending Bethesda Chapel; but calculated for all Denominations of Christians, who desire to worship God in Spirit and in Truth. To which is added, The Form of Prayer, Used in the Chapel.* Dublin: J. Charrurier, 1786.

Sternhold, T[homas]. *Al such Psalmes of Dauid as T. Sternehold late grome of ye kinges Maiesties Robes, didde in his life time draw into English Metre. Newly emprinted.* London: n.p., 1549.

———. *Certayne Psalmes chosen out of the Psalter of Dauid, & drawen into Englishe metre by Thomas Sternhold grome of ye kynges maiesties Roobes.* London: n.p., [1547].

———. *The Whole Booke of Psalms, collected into Englysh metre by T. Sternhold, I. Hopkins & others: conferred with the Ebrue, with apt Notes to synge the[m] withal, Faithfully perused and alowed according to thordre appointed in the Queenes maiesties Iniunctions. Very mete to be vsed of all sortes of people priuately for their solace & comfort: laying apart all vngodly Songes and Ballades which tends only to the norishing of vyce, and corrupting of youth.* London: J. Day, 1562.

———. *The whole booke of Psalmes, collected into Englysh metre by T. Sternhold, I. Hopkins & others: Newly set forth and allowed to be song in all Churches, of all the people together, before & after morning & euenyng prayer: as also before and after the Sermo[n], and moreouer in priuate houses for their godly solace and comfort, laying aparte all vngodly songes and balades, which tend onely to the nourishyng of vice, and corrupting of youth.* London: J. Day, [1566].

Stewart, James H. *A Selection of Psalms & Hymns, Adapted to the Service of the Church of England; Revised for the use of Percy Chapel, Charlotte Street, Fitzroy Square.* London: W. M. Thiselton, 1813.

Strype, John. *Annals of the Reformation and Establishment of Religion and other various occurrences in the Church of England during Queen Elizabeth's Happy Reign together with an Appendix of Original Papers of State, Record, and Letters.* A new edition. 4 vols. New York: B. Franklin, [1966].

[Stubbs, Jonathan]. *A Selection of Psalms and Hymns, for Public and Private Use.* Uttoxeter: R. Richards, 1805.

Sutton, Katherine. *A Christian womans [sic] experiences of the glorious working of Gods [sic] free grace. Published for the edification of others.* Rotterdam: n.p., 1663.

Sutton, T[homas]. *Select Portions of Psalms from the New Version, Hymns and Anthems. Sung at the Parish Church in Sheffield.* Sheffield: Printed for W. Mather, 1807.

———. *Select Portions of Psalms From the New Version, Hymns, and Anthems, Sung At the parish Church, in Sheffield.* 2nd ed. Sheffield: W. Todd, 1816.

T. "On the Neglect of Congregational Singing." *The Christian Observer* 31 (June 1831):338–340.

T., V. "On the Old Tunes and Old Version of the Psalms." *The Christian Remembrancer* 21 (August 1839):486–492.

Tans'ur, William. *A compleat melody: or, The harmony of Sion, the whole is composed in two, three, and four musical parts, according to the most authentick rules for voice or organ.* London: printed by W. Pearson, for J. Hodges, [c. 1735].

[Tate, Nahum]. *An Essay for promoting of Psalmody.* London: n.p., 1710.

———. *An Essay of a New Version of the Psalms of David: Consisting of the first Twenty. Fitted to the Tunes used in Churches.* London: Printed for the Company of Stationers, 1695.

Tate, N[ahum], and N[icholas] Brady. *A New Version of the Psalms of David, Fitted to the Tunes Used in Churches.* London: M. Clark, 1696.

———. *A New Version of the Psalms of David, Fitted to the Tunes Used in Churches.* London: T. Hodgkin, 1699.

———. *A Supplement to the New Version of Psalms.* London: F. Heptinstall, 1700.

Tattersall, William Dechair. *Improved Psalmody. Vol. 1 The Psalms of David, from a Poetrical [sic] Version originally written By the late Reverend James Merrick, A.M. Fellow of Trinity College, Oxford. Divided into Stanzas for the purpose of Public and Private Devotion, With New Music Collected from the most Eminent Composers.* London: T. Skillern, 1794.

———. *A Version of the Psalms . . . by the late Reverend James Merrick, divided into stanzas, and adapted to the purpose of public or private devotion.* London: n.p., [1797?].

———. *A Version of the Psalms; Originally Written by the Late Rev. James Merrick, A. M. Fellow of Trinity College, Oxford; Divided into Stanzas for parochial Use, and Paraphrased in Such Language as will be Intelligible to Every Capacity.* London: Printed for Rivingtons, [1797?].

Thoughts on the Use and Advantages of Music, and Other Amusements. London: Printed for J. Dodsley, 1765.

Todd, Henry John. *Observations upon the Metrical Version of the Psalms, Made by Sternhold, Hopkins, and Others: With a View to Illustrate the Authority with Which this Collection was at First Admitted, and how that Authority has been since regarded, in the Public Service of the Established Church of England: and Thence to Maintain, in This Venerable Service, the Usage of Such Metrical Psalmody Only as is Duly Authorized. With Notices of Other English Metrical Versions of the Psalms.* London: Printed for F. C. and J. Rivington, 1822.

Toplady, Augustus. *Church of England Vindicated from the Charge of Arminianism.* N.p.: n.p., 1768.

―――. *Historic Proof of the Calvinism of the Church of England.* N.p.: n.p., 1774.

―――. *Psalms and Hymns for Public and Private Worship.* London: Printed E. and C. Dilly, 1776.

"Upon the Power of Officiating Ministers to Direct the Manner in which Singing shall be Conducted in Parish Churches." *The Christian Remembrancer* 11 (1829):376–379.

[Venn, John]. *Psalms, Extracted from Various Versions, and adapted to public worship, with an appendix, containing Hymns for the Principal Festivals of the Church of England.* A new edition, revised. Clapham: H. N. Batten, 1824.

―――. *Select Portions of Psalms, Extracted from Various Versions, and Adapted to Public Worship, With an Appendix, Containing Hymns for the Principal Festivals of the Church of England.* 2nd ed. London: March and Teape, 1802.

―――. *Select Portions of Psalms, Extracted from Various Versions, and Adapted to Public Worship, With an Appendix, Containing Hymns for the Principal Festivals of the Church of England.* London: W. Thorne, 1806.

―――. *Select Portions of Psalms, Extracted from various Versions, and Adapted to Public Worship. With an Appendix, Containing Hymns for the Principal Festivals of the Church of England.* 3rd ed. London: H. Teape, 1807.

Vincent, William. *Considerations on Parochial Music.* London: Printed for T. Cadell, 1787.

―――. *Considerations on Parochial Music.* 2nd ed., with additions. London: Printed for T. Cadell, 1790.

W., R. *The excellent use of Psalmody, with a course of Singing Psalms for half a year.* Nottingham: n.p., 1734.

W., W. H. "Inquiry as to Psalms and Hymns." *The Christian Observer* 14 (February 1815):95.

[Wakefield, G.?]. *A Serious Lecture, Delivered at Sheffield; February 28, 1794. Being the Day Appointed for A General Fast; to which are added a Hymn and Resolutions.* 2nd ed. London: n.p., 1794.

Warton, Thomas. *History of English Poetry from the Twelfth to the Close of the Sixteenth Century.* Edited by W. Carew Hazlitt. 4 vols. London: Reeves and Turner, 1871.

Watts, Isaac. *Hymns and Spiritual Songs. In three books . . . With an essay towards the improvement of christian [sic] psalmody, by the use of evangelical hymns in worship, as well as the Psalms of David.* London: J. Lawrence, 1707.

―――. *The Psalms of David Imitated in the Language of the New Testament, And apply'd to the Christian State and Worship.* London: Printed for J. Clark, R. Ford, and R. Cruttenden, 1719.

Wesley, Charles. *Hymns on the Great Festivals and Other Occasions.* London: Printed for M. Cooper, 1746.

Wesley, John. *A Collection of Hymns, for the Use of the People Called Methodists.* London: J. Mason, [1780].

―――. *A Collection of Psalms and Hymns.* Charleston: n.p., 1737.

————. *A collection of tunes, set to music, as they are commonly sung at the Foundery*. London: A. Pearson, 1742.

————. *Hymns and Spiritual Songs, Intended for the Use of Real Christians Of all Denominations*. London: W. Strahan, 1753.

————. *The Letters of the Rev. John Wesley*. 8 vols. Edited by John Telford. London: Epworth, 1931; reprint edition, 1960.

————. *Sacred Melody: or a choice Collection of Psalm and Hymn Tunes*. 2nd ed. London: n.p., 1765.

[Wharton, Robert]. *An Essay on Psalmody, Considered as a Part of the Public Worship*. York: W. Blanchard, 1789.

————. *An Essay on Psalmody, Considered as a Part of the Public Worship*. 2nd ed. York: W. Blanchard, 1791.

Whitefield, George. *A Collection of Hymns for Social Worship, More particularly designed for the Use of the Tabernacle Congregation, in London*. London: W. Strahan, 1753.

Wickham, Robert. *The Rubrics of the Communion Service Examined with a View to Conformity*. London: J. W. Parker, 1845.

Wilkins, David. *Concilia Magnae Britanniae et Hiberniae*. 3 vols. in 4. London: n.p., 1737.

Wise, W[illiam]. *A Selection of Psalms from the New Version, with Select Hymns from Various Authors*. Liverpool: Printed by Robinson and Lang, 1797.

Wither, George. *The Schollers [sic] Pvrgatory*. N.p.: n.p., [1624].

[Wollaston, C. H.]. *A Selection of Psalms, From the New Version, with the Morning and Evening Hymns; For the Use of Parish Churches*. 2nd ed. East Dereham: W. Barker, 1813.

[Woodd, Basil]. *A Collection of Psalms and Hymns, from Various Authors, adapted to the service of the Church of England*. London: C. Watts, 1794.

————. *A Collection of Psalms and Hymns, from various authors, adapted to the service of the Church of England*. London: F. and C. Rivington, 1794.

————. *A New Metrical Version of the Psalms of David; withan Appendix of Select Psalms and Hymns, adapted to The Service of the United Church of England and Ireland; For every Sunday in the Year, Festival Days, Saints' Days, &c*. London: E. Bridgewater, 1821.

————. *The Psalms of David, And other Portions of the Sacred Scriptures, Arranged according to the order of the Church of England, For every Sunday in the Year; also for the Saints' Days, Holy Communion, and other Services*. London: C. Watts, 1794.

————. *The Psalms of David, And other Portions of the Sacred Scriptures, Arranged according to the order of the Church of England, For every Sunday in the Year; also for the Saints' Days, Holy Communion, and other Services*. London: Watts and Bridgewater, [c. 1798].

Woodforde, James. *The Diary of a Country Parson: The Reverend James Woodforde, 1758–1781*. 5 vols. Edited by John Beresford. London: H. Milford, 1924.

[Woodward, Josiah]. *An account of the rise and progress of the religious societies in the City of London, &c*. [2nd ed.] London: n.p., 1698.

Y., W. X. "On the present State of the Methodists." *The Christian Remembrancer* 1 (October 1819):601–604.

Secondary Sources

Abbey, Charles J. *The English Church and its Bishops 1700–1800*. 2 vols. London: Longmans and Green, 1887.

Abbey, C. J., and J. H. Overton. *The English Church in the Eighteenth Century*. 2 vols. London: Longmans and Green, 1878.

Adey, Lionel. *Class and Idol in the English Hymn*. Vancouver: University of British Columbia Press, 1988.

Ahier, Philip. *The Story of the Three Parish Churches of St. Peter the Apostle, Huddersfield*. 3 vols. Huddersfield: Advertiser, 1948.

Altholz, Josef L. *The Religious Press in Britain, 1760–1900*. New York: Greenwood, 1989.

Arnold, Richard. *The English Hymn: Studies in a Genre*. New York: P. Lang, 1995.

Balleine, G. R. *A History of the Evangelical Party in the Church of England*. New edition. London: Church Book Room, 1951.

Bebbington, D. W. *Evangelicalism in Modern Britain: A History from the 1730s to the 1980s*. London: Unwin Hyman, 1989.

Benson, Louis F. "The Development of the English Hymn." *Princeton Theological Review* 10 (1912):39–85.

———. "Dr. Watts' 'Renovation of Psalmody.'" *Princeton Theological Review* 10 (1912):399–436, 606–644; 11 (1913):85–98.

———. *The English Hymn: Its Development and Use in Worship*. G. H. Doran, 1915; reprint edition, Richmond, Va.: John Knox, 1962.

———. "English Hymnody: Its Later Developments." *Princeton Theological Review* 8 (1910):353–388.

———. *The Hymnody of the Christian Church*. New York: G. H. Doran, 1927; reprint edition, Richmond, Va.: John Knox, 1956.

———. "The Hymnody of the Evangelical Revival." *Princeton Theological Review* 12 (1914):60–100.

———. "The Hymnody of the Methodist Revival." *Princeton Theological Review* 11 (1913):420–460.

———. "John Calvin and the Psalmody of the Reformed Churches." *Journal of the Presbyterian Historical Society* 5 (1909):1–21, 55–87, 107–118.

———. "The Liturgical Use of English Hymns." *Princeton Theological Review* 10 (1912):177–211.

———. *Studies of Familiar Hymns, Second Series*. Philadelphia: Westminster, 1923.

Bentley, James. *Ritualism and Politics in Victorian Britain: The Attempt to Legislate for Belief*. Oxford: Oxford University Press, 1978.

Beresford-Hope, A. J. B. *The English Cathedral of the Nineteenth Century*. London: J. Murray, 1861.

Best, G. F. A. "The Evangelicals and the Established Church in the Early Nineteenth Century." *Journal of Theological Studies* n.s., 10 (April 1959):63–78.

———. *Temporal Pillars. Queen Anne's Bounty, the Ecclesiastical Commissioners, and the Church of England*. Cambridge: Cambridge University Press, 1964.

Blankenburg, Walter. "Church Music in Reformed Europe." In *Protestant Church Music: A History*. Edited by Friedrich Blume. New York: W. W. Norton, 1974.

Blume, Friedrich, ed. *Protestant Church Music: A History.* New York: W. W. Norton, 1974.

Bowen, Desmond. *The Idea of the Victorian Church. A Study of the Church of England, 1833–1889.* Montreal: McGill University Press, 1968.

Bowmer, John C. *The Lord's Supper in Methodism, 1791–1960.* London: Epworth, 1961.

Bradley, Ian. *The Call to Seriousness: The Evangelical Impact on the Victorians.* New York: Macmillan Publishing, 1976.

Brightman, F. E. *The English Rite.* 2 vols. London: Rivingtons, 1915.

Brilioth, Yngve. *Three Lectures on Evangelicalism and the Oxford Movement.* London: H. Milford, 1934.

Brown, Ford K. *Fathers of the Victorians.* Cambridge: Cambridge University Press, 1961.

Bumpus, John Skelton. *A History of English Cathedral Music, 1549–1889.* 2 vols. London: T. W. Laurie, [1908].

Bushaway, Bob. *By Rite: Custom, Ceremony and Community in England, 1700–1880.* London: Junction Books, 1982.

Butterworth, Charles C. *The English Primers (1529–1545): Their Publication and Connection with the English Bible and the Reformation in England.* Philadelphia: University of Pennsylvania Press, 1953.

Butterworth, Charles C., and Allan G. Chester. *George Joye 1495?–1553: A Chapter in the History of the English Bible and the English Reformation.* Philadelphia: University of Pennsylvania Press, 1962.

Campbell, Ted A. *The Religion of the Heart: A Study of European Religious Life in the Seventeenth and Eighteenth Centuries.* Columbia: University of South Carolina Press, 1991.

Carpenter, S. C. *Church and People, 1789–1889: A History of the Church of England from William Wilberforce to "Lux Mundi".* London: SPCK, 1933.

————. *Eighteenth Century Church and People.* London: J. Murray, 1959.

Carter, Gerald F. *The Law Regulating the use of Hymns in the Public Services of the Church of England.* London: C. Whittingham, 1908.

Carus, William, ed. *Memoirs of the Life of the Rev. Charles Simeon, M.A., with a Selection from his Writings and Correspondence.* 2nd ed. London: J. Hatchard and Son, 1847.

Chadwick, Owen. *The Victorian Church.* 2 vols. London: A. and C. Black, 1966, 1970.

Clark, G. Kitson. *The Making of Victorian England.* London: Methuen, 1962.

Clarke, W. K. Lowther. *Eighteenth Century Piety.* London: SPCK, 1944.

————. *A Hundred Years of Hymns Ancient and Modern.* London: W. Clowes and Sons, 1960.

Clegg, Herbert. "Evangelicals and Tractarians." *The Historical Magazine of the Protestant Episcopal Church* 35, 2 (June 1966):111–153; 35, 3 (September 1966):237–294; 36, 2 (June 1967):127–178.

Colley, Linda. "Whose Nation?: Class and National Consciousness in Britain 1750–1830." *Past and Present* 113 (November 1986):97–117.

Cornish, F. Warre. *The English Church in the Nineteenth Century.* 2 vols. London: Macmillan, 1910.

Cragg, G. R. "The Churchman." In *Man Versus Society in Eighteenth-Century Britain*. Edited by James L. Clifford. Cambridge: Cambridge University Press, 1968.

Cuming. G. J. *The Durham Book: Being the First Draft of the Revision of the Book of Common Prayer in 1661*. London: Oxford University Press, 1961.

————. *A History of Anglican Liturgy*. London: Macmillan, 1969.

————. *A History of Anglican Liturgy*. 2nd ed. London: Macmillan, 1982.

Curtis, L[ewis] P[erry]. *Anglican Moods of the Eighteenth Century*. Hamden, Conn.: Archon Books, 1966.

Curwen, J. Spencer. "Early Nonconformist Psalmody." *The British Quarterly Review* 71 (January 1880):76–88.

————. *Studies in Worship-Music, Chiefly as Regards Congregational Singing*. London: J. Curwen and Sons, [c. 1880].

Davies, Horton. *Worship and Theology in England*. Vol. 3, *From Watts and Wesley to Maurice, 1690–1850*. Princeton: Princeton University Press, 1961.

Davis, Mary Ann K. "Images of Death in Victorian Hymns." *Cithara* 24, 2 (May 1985):40–48.

Dearing, Trevor. *Wesleyan and Tractarian Worship: An Ecumenical Study*. London: Epworth and SPCK, 1966.

Dearmer, Percy. "Hymn Books and the English Hymnal." *Ecclesia* (October 1913):218.

Demaray, Donald E. *The Innovation of John Newton (1725–1807): Synergism of Word and Music in Eighteenth Century Evangelism*. Lewiston, N.Y.: E. Mellen, 1988.

Dickens, A. G. *The English Reformation*. New York: Schocken Books, 1964.

Dictionary of National Biography. Edited by Leslie Stephen and Sidney Lee. 22 vols. Oxford: Oxford University Press, 1917.

Ditchfield, P[eter] H. *The Parish Clerk*. 2nd ed. London: Methuen, 1907.

Donakowski, Conrad. *A Muse for the Masses: Ritual and Music in an Age of Democratic Revolution, 1770–1870*. Chicago: University of Chicago Press, 1972.

Douglas, Winfred. *Church Music in History and Practice: Studies in the Praise of God*. Revised with additional material by Leonard Ellinwood. New York: C. Scribner, 1962.

Dowden, John. *Further Studies in the Prayer Book*. London: Methuen, 1908.

Drain, Susan. *The Anglican Church in Nineteenth Century Britain: Hymns Ancient and Modern (1860–1875)*. Lewiston, N.Y.: E. Mellen, 1989.

Draper, John W. *William Mason: A Study in Eighteenth-Century Culture*. New York: New York University Press, 1924.

Elbourne, Roger. *Music and Tradition in Early Industrial Lancashire, 1780–1840*. Woodbridge, Engl.: Brewer, 1980.

Elliott-Binns, L. E. *The Early Evangelicals: A Religious and Social Study*. Greenwich: Seabury, 1953.

————. *The Evangelical Movement in the English Church*. Garden City, N.Y.: Doubleday and Doran, 1928.

————. *Religion in the Victorian Era*. [2nd ed.]. London: Lutterworth, 1964.

Ellsworth, L. E. *Charles Lowder and the Ritualist Movement*. London: Darton, Longman, and Todd, 1982.

Fairchild, Hoxie Neale. *Religious Trends in English Poetry.* Vol. 2, *Religious Sentimentalism in the Age of Johnson (1740–1780).* New York: Columbia University Press, 1942.

Fellowes, Edmund H. *English Cathedral Music from Edward VI to Edward VII.* London: Methuen, 1941.

Frere, W. H. *The English Church in the Reigns of Elizabeth and James I.* London: Macmillan, 1904.

Frere, W. H., and W. M. Kennedy, eds. *Visitation Articles and Injunctions of the Period of the Reformation.* 3 vols. London: Alcuin Club, 1910.

Frost, Maurice. *English and Scottish Psalm and Hymn Tunes. 1543–1677.* London: Oxford University Press, 1953.

———. "The Tunes Associated with Hymn Singing in the Lifetime of the Wesleys." *Bulletin of the Hymn Society of Great Britain and Ireland* 4 (Winter 1957/1958):118–126.

Frost, Maurice, ed. *Historical Companion to Hymns Ancient and Modern.* London: W. Clowes and Sons, 1962.

Galpin, F. W. "Notes on the Old Church Bands and Village Choirs of the Past Century." *The Antiquary* 42 (March 1906):101–106.

Gammon, Vic. " 'Babylonian Performances': The Rise and Suppression of Popular Church Music, 1660–1870." In *Popular Culture and Class Conflict, 1590–1914: Explorations in the History of Labour and Leisure,* ed. Eileen Yeo and Stephen Yeo. Sussex: Harvester, 1981.

Gatens, William J. *Victorian Cathedral Music in Theory and Practice.* Cambridge: Cambridge University Press, 1986.

Gilbert, Alan. *Religion and Society in Industrial England: Church, Chapel and Social Change, 1740–1914.* London: Longmans, 1976.

Gillman, F. J. *The Evolution of the English Hymn: An Historical Survey of the Origins and Development of the Hymns of the Christian Church.* New York: Macmillan, 1927.

Glover, Raymond F., ed. *The Hymnal 1982 Companion.* 3 vols. New York: Church Hymnal Corporation, 1990–1994.

Gould, George, ed. *Documents relating to the Settlement of the Church of England by the Act of Uniformity of 1662.* London: W. Kent, 1862.

Gray, [Almyra]. *Papers and Diaries of a York Family, 1764–1839.* London: Sheldon, 1927.

Gray, Donald. *The Influence of Tractarian Principles on Parish Worship, 1839–1849.* London: Alcuin Club, 1984.

———. "The Revision of Canon Law and Its Application to Liturgical Revision in the Recent History of the Church of England." *The Jurist* 48, 2 (1988):638–652.

Grisbrooke, W. Jardine. *Anglican Liturgies of the Seventeenth and Eighteenth Centuries.* London: SPCK, 1958.

Harlan, Lowell B. "Theology of Eighteenth Century English Hymns." *Historical Magazine of the Protestant Episcopal Church* 48 (June 1979):167–193.

Harper, John. *The Forms and Orders of Western Liturgy: From the Tenth to the Eighteenth Century.* Oxford: Clarendon, 1991.

Hart, A[rthur] Tindal. *The Eighteenth Century Country Parson*. Shrewsbury: Wilding and Son, 1955.

Hildebrandt, Franz, and Oliver A. Beckerlegge, eds. *A Collection of Hymns for the use of the People called Methodists*. Vol. 7, *The Works of John Wesley*. Nashville: Abingdon, 1983.

Hobsbawm, E[ric] J. *Labouring Men: Studies in the History of Labour*. London: Weidenfeld and Nicolson, 1964.

Hole, Robert. *Pulpits, politics and public order in England, 1760–1832*. Cambridge: Cambridge University Press, 1989.

Hope, A. J. B. Beresford. *Worship in the Church of England*. London: J. Murray, 1874.

Hunter, David. "English Country Psalmodists and Their Publications, 1700–1760." *Journal of the Royal Musical Association* 115, 2 (1990):220–239.

Hutchings, Arthur. *Church Music in the Nineteenth Century*. New York: Oxford University Press, 1967.

Huttar, C. A. "English Metrical Paraphrases of the Psalms, 1500–1640." Ph.D. diss., Northwestern University, 1956.

Hylson-Smith, Kenneth. *Evangelicals in the Church of England, 1734–1984*. Edinburgh: T. and T. Clark, 1989.

Ingles, Faith. "The Role of Wesleyan Hymnody in the Development of Congregational Song." D.M.A. dissertation, Combs College of Music, 1986.

Jasper, R. C. D. *The Development of the Anglican Liturgy 1662–1980*. London: SPCK, 1989.

———. *Prayer Book Revision in England 1800–1900*. London: SPCK, 1954.

Johnson, Dale A. "Is This the Lord's Song?: Pedagogy and Polemic in Modern English Hymns." *The Historical Magazine of the Protestant Episcopal Church*. 48, 2 (June 1979):195–218.

Julian, John. *A Dictionary of Hymnology: Setting Forth the Origin and History of Christian Hymns of All Ages and Nations*. Revised edition, with new supplement. London: J. Murray, 1907.

———. *Modern Hymnody and Hymns: A Sermon Preached in Christ Church, Scarborough on Sunday, September 6, 1903*. London: SPCK, 1909.

Kent, John. *The Unacceptable Face: The Modern Church in the Eyes of the Historian*. London: SCM, 1987.

Koenigsberger, H. G. "Music and Religion in Modern European History." In *The Diversity of History: Essays in Honour of Sir Herbert Butterfield*, ed. J. H. Elliott and H. G. Koenigsberger. Ithaca, N.Y.: Cornell University Press, 1970.

Kollar, René. "The Opposition to Ritualism in Victorian England." *Irish Theological Quarterly* 51 (1985):63–74.

Leaver, Robin A. "British Hymnody from the Sixteenth through the Eighteenth Centuries." In *The Hymnal 1982 Companion*, ed. Raymond F. Glover. 3 vols. New York: The Church Hymnal Corporation, 1990–1994.

———. "English Metrical Psalmody." In *The Hymnal 1982 Companion*, edited by Raymond F. Glover. 3 vols. New York: The Church Hymnal Corporation, 1990–1994.

———. *"Goostly psalmes and spirituall songes": English and Dutch Metrical Psalms from Coverdale to Utenhove, 1535–1566.* Oxford: Clarendon, 1991.

———. "Isaac Watts's Hermeneutical Principles and the Decline of English Metrical Psalmody." *Churchman* 92 (1978):56–60.

———. *The Liturgy and Music: A Study of the Use of the Hymn in Two Liturgical Traditions.* Bramcote, Nottingham: Grove Books, 1976.

———. "A Newly-discovered Fragment of Coverdale's Goostly psalmes." *Jahrbuch für Liturgik und Hymnologie* 26 (1982):136–150.

———. "Theological Dimensions of Mission Hymnody: The Counterpoint of Cult and Culture." *Worship* 62, 4 (July 1988):316–331.

Leaver, Robin A., ed. *Bibliotheca Hymnologica (1890).* London: C. Higham, 1981.

———. *The Liturgy of the Frankfurt Exiles 1555.* Bramcote, Nottingham: Grove Books, 1984.

Legg, J[ohn] Wickham. *English Church Life: From the Restoration to the Tractarian Movement, Considered in Some of its Neglected or Forgotten Features.* London: Longmans and Green, 1914.

le Huray, Peter. *Music and the Reformation in England 1549–1660.* New York: Oxford University Press, 1967.

Lightwood, James T. *Methodist Music in the Eighteenth Century.* London: Epworth, 1927.

Long, Kenneth R. *The Music of the English Church.* New York: St. Martin's, 1971.

MacArthur, Donald. "Old Village Church Music." *The Musical Times* 64 (April 1923):264–266.

MacDermott, K. H. *The Old Church Gallery Minstrels.* London: SPCK, 1948.

———. *Sussex Church Music in the Past: An account of the old Singers and Minstrels, the Bands, Psalmodies and Hymn-books of Sussex Churches from the end of the 17th Century to the latter half of the 19th Century.* Chichester: Moore and Wingham, 1922.

McLeod, Hugh. *Religion and the People of Western Europe 1789–1970.* Oxford: Oxford University Press, 1981.

Manning, Bernard Lord. *The Hymns of Wesley and Watts.* London: Epworth, 1943.

Marshall, M. F., and J. Todd. *English Congregational Hymns in the Eighteenth Century.* Lexington: University Press of Kentucky, 1982.

Mather, F. C. "Georgian Churchmanship Reconsidered: Some Variations in Anglican Public Worship 1714–1830." *Journal of Ecclesiastical History* 36 (April 1985):255–283.

Morris, J. N. *Religion and Urban Change, Croydon: 1840–1914.* Woodbridge, Engl.: Boydell, 1992.

Nicholson, Sydney H. *Quires and Places Where They Sing.* London: G. Bell and Sons, 1932.

Norman, E. R. *Church and Society in England 1770–1970.* Oxford: Clarendon, 1976.

Obelkevich, Jim. "Music and Religion in the Nineteenth Century." In *Disciplines of Faith,* edited by Jim Obelkevich, Lyndal Roper, and Raphael Samuel. London: Routledge and Kegan Paul, 1987.

Odom, W. *Memorials of Sheffield: Its Cathedral and Parish Churches.* Sheffield: J. W. Northend, 1922.

Overton, John H. *The English Church in the Nineteenth Century 1800–1833.* London: Longmans, 1894.

Overton, John H., and Frederic Relton. *The English Church from the Accession of George I to the End of the Eighteenth Century, 1714–1800.* London: Macmillan, 1906.

[Paget], Francis. *The Recommendations of the Royal Commission on Ecclesiastical Discipline.* London: Longmans and Green, 1906.

Parks, Edna D. *Early English Hymns: An Index.* Metuchen, N.J.: Scarecrow, 1972.

———. *The Hymns and Hymn Tunes Found in the English Metrical Psalters.* New York: Coleman Ross, 1966.

Payne, E. A. "The Theology of Isaac Watts as Illustrated in His Hymns." *Bulletin of the Hymn Society of Great Britain and Ireland* 45 (October 1948):49–58.

Peaston, Alexander Elliott. *The Prayer Book Reform Movement in the Eighteenth Century.* Oxford: B. Blackwell, 1940.

Phillips, C. Henry. *The Singing Church: An Outline History of the Music Sung by Choir and People.* New edition. London: Faber, 1968.

Plumb, J. H. *England in the Eighteenth Century.* Harmondsworth: Penguin, 1950.

Porter, Roy. *English Society in the Eighteenth Century.* Harmondsworth: Penguin, 1982.

Prichard, Robert W. *A History of the Episcopal Church.* Harrisburg, Pa.: Morehouse, 1991.

Rainbow, Bernarr. *English Psalmody Prefaces: Popular Methods of Teaching, 1562–1835.* Kilkenny, Ire.: Boethius, [c. 1982].

Rattenbury, J. E. *The Eucharistic Hymns of John and Charles Wesley.* London: Epworth, 1948.

———. *The Evangelical Doctrines of Charles Wesley's Hymns.* 3rd edition. London: Epworth, 1954.

Raynor, Henry. *Music and Society Since 1815.* New York: Taplinger, 1978.

Report of the Royal Commission on Ecclesiastical Discipline. 5 vols. in 3. London: Printed for H. M. Stationery Office by Wyman and Sons, 1906.

Reynolds, J[ohn] S[tewart]. *The Evangelicals at Oxford, 1735–1871.* Appleford, Engl.: Marcham Manor, 1975.

Rodes, Robert E. Jr. *Law and Modernization in the Church of England: Charles II to the Welfare State.* Notre Dame: University of Notre Dame Press, 1991.

Routley, Erik. *The Music of Christian Hymns.* Chicago: G.I.A. Publications, 1981.

———. *The Musical Wesleys.* New York: Oxford University Press, 1968.

Rowell, Geoffrey. *The Vision Glorious: Themes and Personalities of the Catholic Revival in Anglicanism.* Oxford: Oxford University Press, 1983.

Rupp, Gordon. *Religion in England 1688–1791.* Oxford: Clarendon, 1986.

[Seymour, A. C. H.]. *The Life and Times of Selina, Countess of Huntingdon.* 2 vols. London: W. E. Painter, 1844.

Shaw, Watkins. "Church Music in England from the Reformation to the Present Day." In *Protestant Church Music,* edited by Friedrich Blume. New York: W. W. Norton, 1974.

Smith, G. Gregory, ed. *Elizabethan Critical Essays.* 2 vols. London: H. Milford, 1904.

Smith, Hallett. "English Metrical Psalms in the Sixteenth Century and their Literary Significance." *Huntington Library Quarterly* 9 (1946):249–271.

Smith, S. E. Boyd. "The Effective Countess: Lady Huntingdon and the 1780 edition of *A Select Collection of Hymns*." *The Hymn* 44, 3 (July 1993):26–32.

Soloway, Richard Allen. "Episcopal Perspectives and Religious Revivalism in England 1784–1851." *Historical Magazine of the Protestant Episcopal Church* 40 (March 1971):27–61.

―――. *Prelates and People: Ecclesiastical Social Thought in England 1783–1852*. London: R. Routledge and K. Paul, 1969.

Stainer, Sir John. "On the Musical Introductions Found in Certain Metrical Psalters." *Proceedings of the Royal Musical Association* 27 (November 1900):1–50.

Stephenson, A. M. G. "Archbishop Vernon Harcourt." *Studies in Church History* 4 (1967):143–154.

Stock, Eugene. *The English Church in the Nineteenth Century*. London: Longmans and Green, 1910.

Sykes, Norman. *Church and State in England in the Eighteenth Century*. Cambridge: Cambridge University Press, 1934.

[T., W. G.]. *Some of the Rubricks of the Book of Common Prayer Regarded in the Light of Tradition*. London: Rivingtons, 1887.

Tamke, Susan. "Hymns for Children: Cultural Imperialism in Victorian England." *Victorian Newsletter* 49 (1976):18–22.

―――. *Make a Joyful Noise unto the Lord: Hymns as a Reflection of Victorian Social Attitudes*. Athens: Ohio University Press, 1978.

Temperley, Nicholas. "John Playford and the Metrical Psalms." *Journal of the American Musicological Society* 25 (1972):331–378.

―――. *Jonathan Gray and Church Music in York, 1770–1840*. York: Borthwick Papers, 1977.

―――. *The Music of the English Parish Church*. 2 vols. Cambridge: Cambridge University Press, 1979.

―――. "The Tunes of Congregational Song in Britain from the Reformation to 1750." In *The Hymnal 1982 Companion*, edited by Raymond F. Glover. 3 vols. New York: The Church Hymnal Corporation, 1990–1994.

Thompson, E. P. "The Moral Economy of the English Crowd in the Eighteenth Century." *Past and Present* 50 (February 1971):76–136.

―――. "Patrician Society, Plebeian Culture." *Journal of Social History* 7 (Summer 1974):382–405.

Till, B. D. "The Administrative System of the Ecclesiastical Courts in the Diocese and Province of York, Part III: 1660–1883." Thesis, University of York: Borthwicke Institute of Historical Research, 1963.

Venn, John, FRS, FSA. *Annals of a Clerical Family: Being Some Account of the Family and Descendants of William Venn, Vicar of Otterton, Devon, 1600–1621*. London: Macmillan, 1904.

Vidler, Alec. *The Church in an Age of Revolution: 1789 to the Present Day*. Harmondsworth: Penguin, 1972.

Virgin, Peter. *The Church in an Age of Negligence: Ecclesiastical Structure and Problems of Church Reform 1700–1840*. Cambridge: J. Clarke, 1989.

Voll, Dieter. *Catholic Evangelicalism: The Acceptance of Evangelical Traditions by the Oxford Movement during the Second Half of the Nineteenth Century.* Translated by Veronica Ruffer. London: Faith, 1963.

Walsh, J. D. "The Beginnings of the Evangelical Revival." In *Essays in Modern English Church History in Memory of Norman Sykes,* edited by G. V. Bennett and J. D. Walsh. New York: Oxford University Press, 1966.

Ward, W. R. "Power and Piety: The Origins of Religious Revival in the Early Eighteenth Century." *Bulletin of The John Rylands University Library* 63 (Autumn 1980): 231–252.

———. *Religion and Society in England 1790–1850.* New York: Schocken, 1972.

Ward, W. Reginald, and Richard P. Heitzenrater, eds. *The Works of John Wesley,* vol. 18. Nashville: Abingdon, 1988.

Watson, J. R. *The English Hymn: A Critical and Historical Study.* Oxford: Clarendon, 1997.

Whitley, William Thomas. *A History of British Baptists.* 2nd edition, revised. London: Kingsgate, 1932.

Whitney, Arthur P. *The Basis of Opposition to Methodism in England in the Eighteenth Century.* New York: New York University Press, 1951.

Wibberley, Brian. *Music and Religion: A Historical and Philosophical Survey.* London: Epworth, 1934.

[Willis], Anthony Armstrong. *The Church of England, the Methodists and Society, 1700–1850.* London: University of London Press, 1973.

Wilson, Stephen. "Religious and Social Attitudes in 'Hymns Ancient and Modern' (1889)." *Social Compass* 22 (1975):211–236.

Wilson-Dickson, Andrew. *The Story of Christian Music: From Gregorian Chant to Black Gospel, an Authoritative Illustrated Guide to All the Major Traditions of Music for Worship.* Oxford: Lion, 1992.

Yates, Nigel. *Buildings, Faith, and Worship: The Liturgical Arrangement of Anglican Churches 1600–1900.* Oxford: Clarendon, 1991.

———. *The Oxford Movement and Anglican Ritualism.* London: Historical Association, 1983.

Young, Percy M. *A History of British Music.* New York: W. W. Norton, 1967.

Index

149

About the Author

Thomas McCart received a Ph.D. in Church History (Modern European) from Vanderbilt University (1994). A student of hymnody for more than thirty years, he has lectured extensively and is currently rector of St. Mark's Episcopal Church, Upland, California. As a consultant to the Standing Commission on Church Music, he contributed to the development of the Episcopal *Hymnal 1982* and is also a contributor to its three-volume *Companion*.